Introduction to Data Science for Social and Policy Research

Real-world data sets are messy and complicated. Written for students in social science and public management, this authoritative but approachable guide describes all the tools needed to collect data and prepare it for analysis. Offering detailed, step-by-step instructions, it covers collection of many different types of data including web files, APIs, and maps; data cleaning; data formatting; the integration of different sources into a comprehensive data set; and storage using third-party tools to facilitate access and shareability (from Google Docs to GitHub).

Assuming no prior knowledge of R and Python, the author introduces programming concepts gradually, using real data sets that provide the reader with practical, functional experience.

JOSE MANUEL MAGALLANES REYES is an associate professor of political science and public policy at Pontificia Universidad Católica del Perú, senior data science fellow at the eScience Institute, and visiting professor at the Evans School of Public Policy and Governance at the University of Washington, Seattle. His research focuses on social complexity, applying computational thinking to governance issues to inform public policy. Over the past 15 years he has served in government and has been involved in several initiatives in Peru's public sector to make better use of data for policy, political research, and decision making.

Introduction to Data Science for Social and Policy Research

Collecting and Organizing Data with R and Python

JOSÉ MANUEL MAGALLANES REYES

*University of Washington and Pontificia
Universidad Católica del Perú*

CAMBRIDGE
UNIVERSITY PRESS

CAMBRIDGE
UNIVERSITY PRESS

University Printing House, Cambridge CB2 8BS, United Kingdom

One Liberty Plaza, 20th Floor, New York, NY 10006, USA

477 Williamstown Road, Port Melbourne, VIC 3207, Australia

4843/24, 2nd Floor, Ansari Road, Daryaganj, Delhi - 110002, India

79 Anson Road, #06-04/06, Singapore 079906

Cambridge University Press is part of the University of Cambridge.

It furthers the University's mission by disseminating knowledge in the pursuit of education, learning, and research at the highest international levels of excellence.

www.cambridge.org
Information on this title: www.cambridge.org/9781107117419
DOI: 10.1017/9781316338599

First published 2017

Printed in the United Kingdom by Clays, St Ives plc

A catalogue record for this publication is available from the British Library.

Library of Congress Cataloging-in-Publication Data
Names: Magallanes Reyes, Jose Manuel, author.
Title: Introducing data science to social and policy analysts :
from collecting to organizing data with R and Python / Jose Manuel
Magallanes Reyes, Pontificia Universidad Católica del Perú.
Description: Cambridge, United Kingdom ; New York, NY :
Cambridge University Press, 2017. | Includes bibliographical references and index.
Identifiers: LCCN 2017020965 | ISBN 9781107117419 (alk. paper)
Subjects: LCSH: Policy sciences – Statistical methods. |
Policy sciences – Data processing. | Python (Computer program language) |
R (Computer program language)
Classification: LCC H97.M336 2017 | DDC 300.72/7 – dc23
LC record available at https://lccn.loc.gov/2017020965

ISBN 978-1-107-11741-9 Hardback
ISBN 978-1-107-54025-5 Paperback

Contents

Illustrations

Tables

PART ONE

GETTING STARTED

1

Introduction

This book is based on class notes used to teach undergraduate and graduate students in political science and public policy how to prepare their data to conduct further analysis and provide recommendations to inform decision making. At both levels of education, I found students with different backgrounds in quantitative tools. That required me to develop a teaching approach to address the needs of students new to data analysis, so you should expect detailed explanations in this book.

My courses address different skills: from collecting, organizing, modeling, and analyzing the data, to visualizing and publishing it. This book focuses on data organization and collection and all their related procedures. This stage is arguably the most time-consuming and has been my main concern over the years. In general, books for quantitative analysis devote most of their pages to teaching quantitative concepts while sharing data that has already been well organized into a table readable by most software (Stata, SPSS, SAS, etc), or into a simple comma-separated values (CSV) file to be used by any software. However, every scholar (student, researcher, or professor) or professional will need to prepare a particular data set for his or her current needs. It is then that they may experience a hard time. The literature lacks material on preparing data sets for students in the social sciences, so it has been my goal to provide those competences in basic data organization.

When I embarked on teaching this stage to students, I discovered there is no simple, right, or unique way of doing it. In this book, I simply share my way of teaching it, not how it should necessarily be done. This is a potential challenge or weakness of this book because I do not present a formal paradigm for data organization. Nevertheless, I share strategies that have proven to be helpful for students who lack a quantitative or computational background.

My target audience might be familiar with particular software, but may never have used it to collect or clean data or to automate those processes. There is

3

no function in an SPSS/Stata/Excel window menu that says either *collecting* or *cleaning* the data. Collecting, cleaning, and formatting data require the flexibility that programming languages provide, which motivated me to teach some coding skills to my students.[1]

1.1 Road Map for the Reader

The use of data has become so pervasive that there is now a field of *data science*. It seems that it is not enough that we already have qualitative disciplines rich in empirical data collection techniques (anthropology, sociology, psychology, history, etc.) and quantitative fields that have dealt with data modeling (statistics, operations research, economics, and so on); now, we feel the need to create a science of data. Rather than being a completely new field, data science is emerging from ad-hoc interdisciplinary combinations that nevertheless use a common tool: the computer (hardware and software).

Advances in computing technology have not simply led to "cool" personal gadgets but also, most importantly, to a different strategy for doing science by means of algorithmic thinking. An algorithm is a finite set of instructions to process some input and effectively reach an output; algorithms enable you not only to create computer programs but also to design a teaching lesson, devise a strategy, establish organizational norms, and so on. Because algorithmic thinking is so closely related to design,[2] it is a key approach to understanding institutions and designing policies. Although I recognize it may be too early for most people to make the connection between binary codes and policy making, I am consciously in favor of calling your attention to this relationship.

This book will neither make a case for data science nor turn you into a data scientist, but it will teach you the first steps to becoming a user of tools to effectively deal with data. And, in my experience, that instruction has been enough to motivate policy scholars to become computational policy analysts.

There are several stages for doing data science, starting with deciding what to study and ending by proposing what actions to take. As you see, the process is no different from a traditional research design where research questions will

---

[1] If you do not want to learn R or Python while doing the tasks of this book, you may want to take a look at some programs that offer cleaning and formatting capabilities like *Wrangler* (http://idl.cs.washington.edu/papers/wrangler), *OpenRefine* (http://openrefine.org), or *Trifacta* (https://www.trifacta.com).

[2] You can detect my closeness and empathy to Simon (1996) in these lines.

drive much of the project. However, the source of the question is not mainly theoretical as in a dissertation, but is also intuitive, as in any decision-making situation. Once you have identified what matters for your research, you will first get the data, which will be analyzed and interpreted into findings and then shared and stored. This book deals with the first and third steps: getting the data you need, cleaning and formatting it, and sharing and storing, all with the goal of increasing its usefulness.

But, what is the meaning of "getting the data you need'? This simple road map should give you a better idea:

1. **Relevant sources have been *identified* and confirmed to be *trustworthy*.** To realize your research goals, you must know what data you need and where you can get it. Most of the time, you also need to know if the source is trustworthy: Do you believe those police reports? Would people be likely to answer this census question honestly? Is this a good proxy for this unobserved social feature? Would this variable be a good instrument for your posterior regression analysis? A mistake here may cause your data to work poorly in the next stages. Knowledge and experience with your subject is more helpful than computer knowledge at this stage.

2. **Data sources have been obtained.** This is the data collection stage. If you requested a survey, you would get a file with the results; if the data you need is in a web repository, you can download it; you may even need to get the data from websites or Twitter messages. Most of the time, you are collecting data from different sources, and this will take a while because some data, by its nature, has some legal constraints and/or technical limitations. You may even wonder how to get and use the data in an ethical manner. Although you may want to be as exhaustive as possible, remember that you need to finish the research in your lifetime. Two key consideration here are the unit of analysis and the time frame. The data collected should share the same units of analysis; that is, if you need information at the city level, you may welcome data at the neighborhood level, but you do not want data at the state level or country level (too aggregated). Similarly make sure that the data is for the same period of time; that is, you do not want one variable from the year 2000 and another from the year 2010; if you are collecting one variable for different years, you will want other variables for those same years. Respect your research goals, and work hard at this stage to keep your data collection coherent.

3. **The values of the data obtained have been cleaned.** Do not expect that all the files you obtained are ready to be compared, integrated, or analyzed. At these later stages the computer needs to read each value you see as you do.

Imagine a spreadsheet with symbols in each cell that may not be correctly interpreted by other software (i.e. ≈, $, €, etc.), or cells with missing values typed in strange ways (n/a, for instance); a cell can have footnotes that inform you of something important, but will add an irrelevant value to your data. The problem you have in one file may be different from the one you have in another one. You will be surprised by the different kinds of dirtiness you will encounter. This a very time-consuming stage; just be patient and do your best.

4. **The values have been** *formatted*. Your value is now well read by your computer, and it is syntactically valid so far. But now comes a problem of semantics, which again needs your intervention. You may need to tell the computer that the number being read is not an integer but a date or a category, and you need to be careful to apply the right kind of function to those values. At this time, it is even necessary to organize the clean data source into another data structure, particularly if you are planing to analyze longitudinal or relational (network) data. Some people may still call this organizational stage "cleaning"; however, formatting, in this book, is considered a different process than cleaning.

5. **The multiples sources of data have been** *integrated and saved*. The last stage combines all your data sources and stores them. You cannot expect that all the variables you need will come from the same source, so you need to find a mechanism to merge all your files. Even though each file is clean and well formatted, you may still find some issues when trying to combine them into one. Once you know they can be well combined, you can safely store what you have, so that the next steps in data science work smoothly.

If you have been used to receiving files ready for analysis and have worked with only one kind of data (censuses, surveys) in your organization, these steps may not be familiar to you. If you need to get and analyze data from different sources, this book will be helpful by sharing the tools you need to do this work; it will give you the flexibility of writing code to automate these processes.

1.2 Main Tools

This book introduces readers to *programming languages*. Readers should not expect to become programmers; instead, they should expect to learn the bright side of programming to make their job easier. There are hundreds of programming languages. From the set of programming languages, I offer you two very popular high-level languages: Python and R.

Why R or Python?

I chose these languages not because they are necessarily the best ones, but because their use is spreading beyond the computer science domain. That has not happened before with JAVA or C, and as powerful as those languages are, policy analysts may find no reason to learn them to carry out their customary tasks. But, as data becomes available in huge amounts and varying complexity, many analysts are feeling the need for a more flexible way to deal with data organization, analysis, and visualization. This book will use R and Python to deal with the organization stage, showing you how some coding can put more power in your hands.

Python and R are also attractive because they are well documented, with lots of applications in different areas of knowledge and active communities in the web sharing code and examples; and, of course, you can use R and Python free of charge. Some other details follow:

- **R** is a high-level programming language. That is, its creators have tried to abstract it, so that some commands are in English. In contrast, low-level languages *talk* to the computer in a language closer to what a computer understands (but far from direct human understanding). Because it is free of charge and open source, R has allowed many scholars not only to carry out data analysis but also to contribute to R itself by adding very specific functionalities, so that R now has support for almost any kind of quantitative technique. It has been said that R poses a slow learning curve at the beginning, but I find this statement to be quite inaccurate. Working with R is very easy. However, that depends in the coding style the user develops. This book emphasizes a good coding style and habits to make R usable.
- **Python** is an all-purpose programming language with many more features for computational work than R has, but for the goals of this book, these differences are not spelled out in the book. I can only say that you cannot build sophisticated information systems with R, but certainly can with Python. Python, as well as R, has a very active community of users and developers, and you can practically write a question about Python in your browser and find an answer. I would suggest reading this book first, before posing any questions, because the repliers are often advanced experts using jargon that a novice user may not understand.

Both R and Python have something in common that you will soon realize: They both need to install and use external programs called *packages / modules / libraries* (I will use these terms interchangeably). These packages are very useful when you need to carry out complicated tasks with a large amount of code, because it is likely that someone has created a package that does what you need. You do not need to know every package available, but progressively you will become familiar with ones that will save you lots of coding time. As for speed, regular users may not find a difference between Python and R. If you find that computing results is taking too much time, writing a better code can increase the speed, but advanced programming techniques require more preparation, and the code may turn out to be more difficult to read. This book will not turn you into an advanced programmer, but into an effective user of both languages to deal with situations similar to the examples presented here. Your code may be very good, so take into consideration that other factors also affect speed, such as the size and contents of the file, your hardware (laptop, tablet, etc.), your internet provider, your operating system version, the memory available, and so on. For the examples in the book, speed will not be an issue.

I will show you to use Python and R in particular environments:

- **Anaconda**
- **RStudio**

These two programs will make the use of Python and R easier. Anaconda is a free Python distribution that includes the most popular Python packages needed in this book for data analysis: It is almost ready to be used without much downloading. Nevertheless, Anaconda has a simple way to add packages not already included, and I will highlight that when needed. RStudio is an environment that makes the R experience easier and more versatile. However, it does not include R, so you will need to install R first. RStudio is also free.

Both RStudio and Anaconda offer business options, which are not free. These options are needed to deploy large-scale applications. Not everything is free in the data analytics business, but the free versions are enough for all applications you need for academic work.

1.3 Additional Tools

In the world of data science, programming languages are used in combination with lots of other tools to organize the workflow, improve performance, allow for collaboration, and so on. In this book, I will talk about some additional tools for file management. I do not want this to be a burden and you can feel free to not use them; however, I recommend paying attention to the sections where I describe them, in case you believe they are worth learning to help your work.

These are:

- **Google Drive**
- **Dropbox**
- **Github**

All are free. However, you may need to purchase space if you want more than what is offered freely. Google Drive will give you 15 Gigabytes (Gb);[3] Dropbox gives you 2 Gb;[4] and GitHub has no established limit for an account.[5]

Both Google Drive and Dropbox are used very widely. They offer an easy way to create a folder in your computer to store your files and have them available anywhere. I will guide you how to set them up. GitHub is not as common among social scientists as the others, but it will be helpful to become familiar with it. GitHub is very convenient to use when you are programming (developing software) because it is conceived for *version control*.[6]

1.4 The Rest of the Book

In the next chapter, I will guide you to get your computer ready for Python, R, and the associated tools. The installation chapter is very important, so please follow the directions before going on.

Part Two deals with data collection and cleaning, including reading different formats and collecting data from online sites. Because data from different sources may not be ready to be used immediately, the data cleaning process is essential but very time consuming. The chapters in this part seek to make you a more efficient data collector and cleaner. Even if you think that you will only be working with well-formatted data, I recommend paying close attention to these chapters in case you ever need to do data collection and cleaning. In my early years of teaching I always used Excel to do cleaning, and in fact, I still do so for small data sets. Most people in social and policy sciences may also use it for the same purpose. I will show how R and Python can help us in these tasks and be as least as efficient as Excel or any other program in doing these.

Part Three deals with data organization. After reading these chapters, you will be able to make the data ready for modeling, analysis, and visualization (not covered in the book). There are several issues to deal with when preparing your data, particularly deciding if your data will go through posterior

---

[3] This includes the space for your email account

[4] Free space can increase up to 16 Gb if you invite friends to become Dropbox users, because you get 500 Megabytes (Mb) for each referral.

[5] Please read these restrictions: https://help.github.com/articles/what-is-my-disk-quota/.

[6] This concept is further developed here: http://oss-watch.ac.uk/resources/versioncontrol.

cross-sectional or longitudinal techniques. I will cover these issues including the format for networks and maps.

1.5 For the Reader

In this book, each section depends on something previously presented. It is not a long book, so I would recommend you read it from beginning to end. Of course, if you know most of the material covered, you are most welcome to visit the chapter or section you believe you need, while skipping previous material. I tried to include references to previous sections as needed.

This book has been written for students, professors, and professionals in the social and policy sciences at all levels. It can be used for self-learning and to complement any quantitative analysis course.

I will request that you collect some data using some links, but in case those links are not working when you read this book I will maintain a Dropbox with a copy of those files. I hope you have fun while learning.

1.6 Acknowledgments

I am very grateful to Cambridge University Press for giving me the opportunity to share my work. I am also very grateful to the reviewers who took the time to comment on and suggest improvements for my initial drafts.

This book was made possible by the research appointment I was granted by the eScience Institute at the University of Washington (UW) and my teaching experience while a Visiting Professor at the UW's Evans School of Public Policy and Governance. I have to express my particular gratitude to Ed Lazowska, Bill Howe, Magdalena Balazinska, Tyler McCormick, Bernease Herman, Valentina Staneve, Anthony Arendt, Micaela Parker, and Sarah Stone from the eScience Institute; and to Sandra Archibald, Craig Thomas, Mark Long, and Greg Traxler from the Evans School. They were very supportive during my stay at UW and helped me finish this book in different ways. I am also thankful to the graduate students at the Evans School, whose feedback about my teaching helped me better organize these contents. I also very grateful to my learning, researching, and teaching experience I had at George Mason University. My interactions with Claudio Cioffi-Revilla, Robert Axtell, William Kennedy, Qing Tian, and Andrew Crooks were critical to fine-tuning my exploration of computational social science. During my stay as a Visiting Scholar at Duke University's Social Science Research Institute, I was able to make the final revisions to this work. I am very thankful to Scott De Marchi for that opportunity and to the EITM class of 2016 for sharing some relevant ideas on what a book like this should contain.

I also express my deepest thanks to my home institution, the Department of Social Sciences of the Pontificia Universidad Católica del Perú, which has made every effort to support my stay in the United States. I particularly appreciate the support of Alejandro Diez, Alan Fairlie, Aldo Panfichi, Edmundo Beteta, Francisco Durand, Jorge Aragon, Ismael Muñoz, Carlos Alza, David Sulmont, Eduardo Dargent, Sinesio Lopez, and Catalina Romero. I would also like to express special thanks to my former teaching assistants who were always there to support and improve my work, especially Jose Luis Incio, Noam Lopez, Maria Paula Brito, Samuel Sanchez, Kely Alfaro, Fernando Contreras, Jorge Abanto, Marylia Cruz, Jorge Vela, Luis Mas, Alejandra Ocaña, Mariana Ramirez, Valerie Tarazona, Rodolfo Benites, Silvana Rebaza, Yamile Guibert, Manuel Figueroa, Rafael Arias, Roberto Diaz, Rosa Arevalo, Veronica Hurtado, Juan Carlos Gonzales, Paolo Rivas, Mariale Campos, Maria Alejandra Guzman, Angela Bravo, Andrea Moncada, Jeniffer Perez, Daniela Lopez, Lorena Levano, Sakimi Leon, and Mariela Mosqueira.

And of course, my eternal thanks to my partners in all my adventures, Diana, my wife, and our son, Rafael.

2

Setting up the Tools

It is time to start working. Here, I share with you the ways in which Python and R, and their associated tools, should be installed on your computer. For most of this book, and for this chapter in particular, you need to be connected to the Internet. If you are a Windows, Linux, or Mac OS X user, each installation requires the usual steps for your system, which in general requires that you accept every option; however, I give you some suggestions when necessary.

2.1 Installing R

To download R, you need to visit https://cran.r-project.org/. That webpage clearly indicates the options for Windows, Mac, or Linux users. Windows and Mac users need to visit the appropriate link and get the file you need, checking if the version offered is the right one for your operating system. As Linux users may expect, after they go to the Linux link, R will ask you to choose among the *Debian, redhat, suse,* or *ubuntu* options.

After you download the file from R, you need to install it. This is simply done by clicking the file you downloaded to your computer. Just run it and keep all the default settings.[1] The Linux versions have particular instructions to run in the terminal once the right file is chosen. You do not need to run R now (if you opened it, just close it). We will run R always from RStudio.

Installing RStudio. To get RStudio, just go visit the downloads website.[2]

---

[1] If your Mac does not want to install it when you click the file, just use the secondary menu ("right-click" menu) and select open; as you are installing it you may need to write your password; as always, if your Mac asks you to drag a file into the Application folder, do it. If using Windows, it is better if you execute all the installations in this chapter using the "right-click" option "Run As Administrator." You can download R in any folder, but R will be installed in the appropriate folders, so please keep the defaults given.

[2] https://www.rstudio.com/products/rstudio/download/

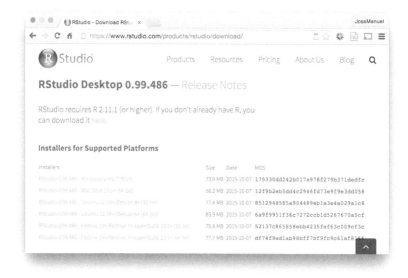

Figure 2.1 The RStudio download site (you may find different versions by the time you read this book, just use the latest).

Once in that webpage, you will find links to the different *desktop* versions available (as opposed to the *server* versions, which you do not need). The webpage with the installers looks like Figure 2.1. Download the version you need according to your machine, install it, and accept all the default options. Now, when you start RStudio, you will see a *graphical user interface* (GUI), composed of a set of windows as shown in Figure 2.2.

The RStudio GUI has four windows. You may have a different set of windows in RStudio, so Figure 2.2 should be only a reference. The four windows are as follows:

- *Source* in the lower left, where you will write the commands for R. You will interact a lot with this window because all your writing will be here. If this window is missing, go to the top menu bar and select *FILE*, then *NEW FILE*, and finally *FILE SCRIPT*.
- *Console* in the upper left, where you will see the numeric result of the computations. You will be looking at this window most of the time.
- *Environment & History* in the upper right, where you will see the information related to the data you are working with, including the variables you have created. This window is for your reference but is not very important.
- *File, Packages, & Plots* in the lower right. This is a very important window. From here, you can tell RStudio where to find the files you are working on,

Figure 2.2 The RStudio GUI. All our R work will be here.

install packages, and see the plots resulting from your commands (in the *Console* you only see text results); you can also use the Help function to request information on how a package works (we will see this later).

This configuration of the GUI windows can easily be altered. Select TOOLS from the top menu bar in RStudio, and choose *Global Options . . . .* A window like the one in Figure 2.3 will appear. You can alter the location of each window and its contents. It may not be useful to have the *plots* in a tab near *files*, so you can decide to put the plots tab next to *environment*. I do not have any preferences about location. I can only say that sometimes I like to move the tabs and windows a little just for fun or to add some variety.

Because we are going to use RStudio intensively, please make sure it is easily reachable via shortcuts on your desktop (Windows / Linux) or it is in the dock (Mac OS X).

2.2 Installing Python

You only need to download Anaconda to have Python. In fact, some Mac-/Linux-based machines have basic Python pre-installed, but I will not pay

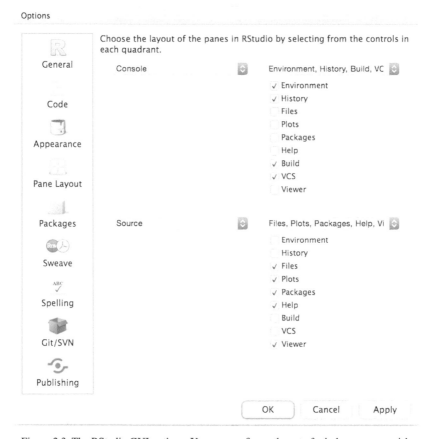

Figure 2.3 The RStudio GUI options. You can configure the set of windows as you wish.

attention to that installed version (and neither should you). Our Python programs will be developed using Anaconda.

Anaconda is here: https://www.continuum.io/downloads. There, you will get to a website similar to the one you see in Figure 2.4.

You will see different icons on the page, which are links to get the installer file according to the operating system you use (Windows/OS X/Linux).[3] When you visit those links, make sure to select the **Python version 3.5** (or the latest available), as well as the **Graphical Installer**. Once you download the installer, execute it. I recommend not installing it *as administrator* when you are in Windows. In all cases, Anaconda asks if it should be the default Python version.

---

[3] The design of this website may be different from what is shown here; however, the options for each operating systems should always be easily found.

Figure 2.4 The Anaconda download page.

Please allow that (it is not the default otherwise). If you are using a Mac, I rec-ommend you put the Anaconda Navigator icon (see Figure 3.1b) in the dock; if you are in Windows or Linux, you should have a shortcut on the desktop.

2.2.1 Creating an "Environment" in Anaconda

Although you should download the latest Python version, you should use **Python 2.7** for the book's examples. I use it here because Python 2.7 is standard.

To have Python 2.7 work, you need to create an **environment**. Simply speak-ing, it is a folder where your projects will work with a particular Python version without interfering with other projects that may need a different version. If you click the Anaconda navigator icon, you will see something like Figure 2.5.

You will see that some applications (apps) invite you to **launch** them, which means they are installed (others invite you to *install* them). You need to do nothing now, because those are apps that will offer you a way to create Python programs, but in version 3.5, not in 2.7. So to create an environment for version 2.7, do the following, as shown in Figure 2.6:

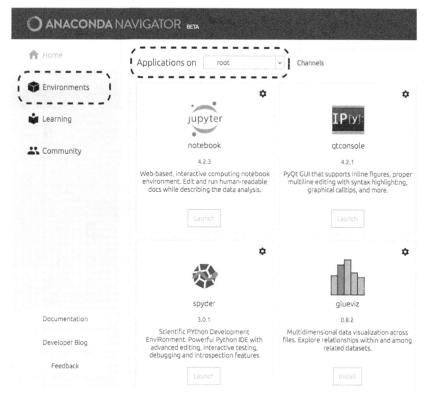

Figure 2.5 Anaconda Navigator home. This is the root environment.

1. Select Environments from the options to the right (this is the option in the dotted oval in Figure 2.5).
2. Click on Create, an option at the bottom of the window.
3. Select the version (2.7) in the window that will pop up after the previous step.
4. Give a name to this new environment.

The steps above are shown in Figure 2.6.

I named my environment "BookCambridge." Remember that Anaconda lets you share an environment, so choose a descriptive name.[4]

The root environment is ready for Python 3.5; the one created is ready for Python 2.7. The examples in this book need packages that work for the 2.7 version, so you need to install the ones available and see what packages are

---

[4] I will not go into further detail about sharing environments, but you can learn more in the link http://conda.pydata.org/docs/using/envs.html.

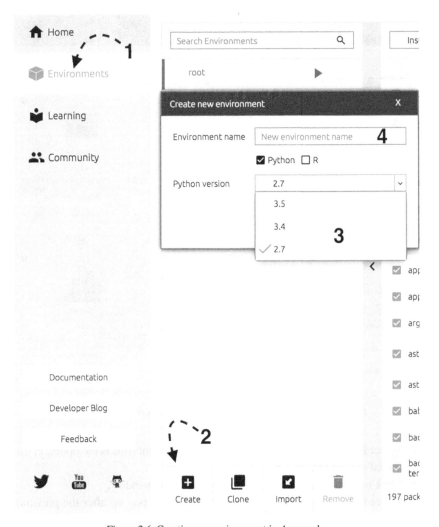

Figure 2.6 Creating an environment in Anaconda.

INSTALLED or NOT INSTALLED. Figure 2.7 shows you where to look for those packages.

Please, check and install these packages if they are not installed (the versions I used in this book are shown for your reference):

- pandas (version 0.18.1)
- beautifulsoup4 (version 4.5.1)
- matplotlib (version 1.5.3)

Figure 2.7 Finding out the packages available in an environment.

- numpy (version 1.11.1)
- networkx (version 1.11)
- xlrd (version 1.0.0)

Follow these steps if they are NOT installed in your environment:

1. Make sure you are in the list of packages "not installed."
2. Update the list of packages.
3. Check the box near the name of the package not installed. You can check several.
4. After you check one box, the option **Apply** will show at the bottom; click that after selecting all the packages you need. You can use the option `Clear` to unselect all boxes checked.

All these steps are shown in Figure 2.8.

You will need your **terminal** or *console* to install packages not available in that list. The terminal is a window similar to the one in Figure 2.9.

You have terminals for Windows and Linux. In Windows, the terminal is also called the `Command Prompt`. If you do not know where to find it, search for a YouTube video on "how to start the terminal" or "how to start the command prompt" in your operating system, because its location varies according to the operating system version. It is critical that you know where it is, because you need to install packages *in the environment* for this book. Each package needed has a simple command to install it, and you can install even the ones in the Anaconda list from the terminal. However, you first MUST run one of these commands, according to your operating system:

- Linux, OS X: `source activate` **MYenvironment**
- Windows: `activate` **MYenvironment**

You need to change the word **MYenvironment** to the actual name of the environment you have created for this book. If you simply install packages in a

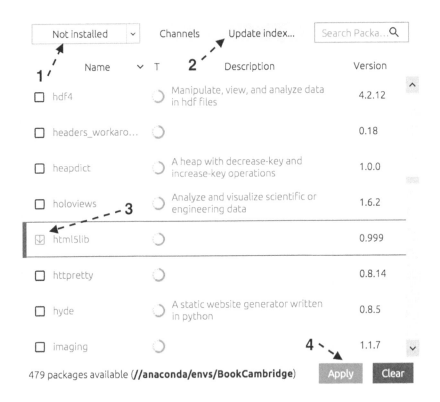

Figure 2.8 Installing a package in Anaconda. You will see something similar when you need to install a package.

Figure 2.9 The Mac terminal (customized for black background).

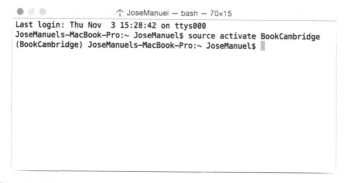

Figure 2.10 Environment activated in the terminal (I changed the color of the background to white in this case).

window like the one shown in Figure 2.9, the package will be installed in the root, and NOT in your environment. For example, you can see in Figure 2.10 that my machine is ready to install packages in my environment.

A final step in this section is to tell Anaconda other places to look for packages. This is done by modifying the *channel* it uses to search for packages. A reliable channel is **conga-forge**, and to include it, we simply follow these steps, as shown in Figure 2.11:

1. Click on **Channels** on the page "Environments in Anaconda."
2. After clicking, select **Add**.

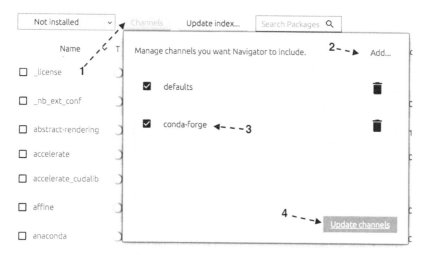

Figure 2.11 Adding a channel to Anaconda.

3. You will be asked for the name of the channel: write **conda-forge**, and press ENTER in your keyboard.
4. Click on **Update channels**. A new channel is available for Anaconda (**not only for your environment**).

These above are shown in Figure 2.11.

In the next chapter, I will show you how to install packages not available in Anaconda.

2.3 Setting up Additional Tools

If you use Gmail, you already have access to **Google Drive**. You should download Google Drive to your computer.[5] Installing Google Drive in your computer will create a **Google Drive folder** that allows you to have access to those data directly from your computer, while Google saves your file updates to Google Drive in the Google server (in the "cloud") automatically. If you do not have a Gmail account, it is time for you to create one.[6]

If you do not want to create a Gmail account, you may consider signing up for **Dropbox**.[7] You will only need an email to create your account, so use your personal one. While you create your account, Dropbox will ask to be installed in your computer; please install it.[8] This will create a **Dropbox folder** where you can save data, which will be synchronized with your Dropbox (in the "cloud"). In this sense, Dropbox and Google Drive work identically.[9] I strongly recommend installing Dropbox now, because I use it in most of my examples of the book.

To create your **GitHub** account simply visit https://github.com/. If you have used Git before with the command line, you are welcome to keep using it. However, I recommend using the desktop version because it will make life easier for the novice user. After creating your GitHub account, GitHub will give you the option to install the desktop version. If you do not see it, just visit: https://desktop.github.com/. Installing the desktop version will not create a system of folders like Dropbox or Google Drive. It is just a program to help

---

[5] https://www.google.com/drive/download/
[6] Some organizations use Gmail for their email; if you have that kind of email there is no need for an additional Gmail account.
[7] Just visit https://www.dropbox.com to sign up.
[8] You can also use this link to install it on your computer: https://www.dropbox.com/install.
[9] Notice that the space Google Drive gives you is shared with the space your Gmail account is using.

with management of your files. I will give some examples later on how to benefit from using this tool.

So far, you have only created accounts and installed apps. I hope this was not a big deal.[10] In the following chapters, I will guide you on how to use these services. I will also give you the option of not using them at all: It is up to you to decide if you work or not with them. As mentioned before, Google Drive or Dropbox provides the same capabilities for our needs, so that you may need to use only one. GitHub is different, as you will understand from the examples.

---

[10] I recommend going to YouTube and watching a video on how to install these services, if you would like visual directions.

3

Basics of R and Python

In this chapter, you will become familiar with the R and Python languages. Here, R and Python will be used in parallel, but the rest of the book may not always follow that pattern; there may be a situation in which R would seem simpler to use than Python or a situation in which Python would seem like the wiser alternative. However, I need to be clear here: the choice of R or Python for a particular task does not mean that the task cannot be done in the option not chosen. It simply means that it would be harder, less elegant, or too confusing to use the other language, or it might require the use of techniques and concepts not covered in this book.

3.1 First Contact with R and Python

You will need first to locate the RStudio and Anaconda environments in your computer. The icons are shown in Figure 3.1.

3.1.1 Becoming Familiar with R

Let's start running RStudio first, as shown in Figure 3.2. In this case, I decided to change the position of the RStudio of the windows, so the **source** is to the left and the **console** is to the right (the other windows are not shown). The console is showing only the first message you see when you start RStudio. In your case, the source window should be empty, but mine is not. Please write the code[1] as it is shown in Figure 3.2. Keep reading after you finish typing the code.

---

[1] Yes, you actually need to type. There is no windows menu to use.

24

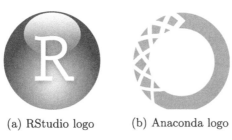

(a) RStudio logo   (b) Anaconda logo

Figure 3.1 Finding the icons to run Python and R.

Let's use the numbers that RStudio offers in the source window to review the code you have typed:

- Lines 1 and 15 are very special in RStudio. They create a **code section**, several lines of code that run together. It is a good practice to organize your code in sections: you need to structure your work to improve it progressively and facilitate debugging. A section starts with the symbol #; then you write the name of the section, and finally you add at least four dashes,[2] so that the section is recognized as such. You can quickly visit the sections you create using the drop-down list you find in the bottom corner to the left of the source window and selecting the label of the section you want. In Figure 3.2 you can see that the label "Calculator" appears in that area, close to a pound symbol.
- Lines 3 and 7 are comments. R does not care what you write after a #. You should always add as many comments as needed as a reminder of what you were implementing in code. In this case, I only remind myself what that code represents: that I have an "input" area and a "process" area.
- Lines 4, 5, and 8–13 show different things:
  - The use of the = sign,[3] which does not mean "equals to," but represents how my *objects*[4] to the left (x, y, addition, etc.) receive a value; it also stores it temporarily (if you turn off the computer, the value this variable received will get lost). Line 4 tells us that the object (variable) x has the value 27, and line 10 indicates what the variable division will receive when the operation to the right is performed.

---

[2] You can add more, but if R finds less than four dashes, the section will not be recognized.

[3] In this case, the character= can be replaced by the characters <-, symbols you may find in many R codes. You can also find the combination –> that serves a similar purpose, but does the assignment in the opposite direction; that is, x=7 is the same as x<–7 or 7–>x

[4] These objects are simply a way to store a value; you need to define if that object is a variable or constant.

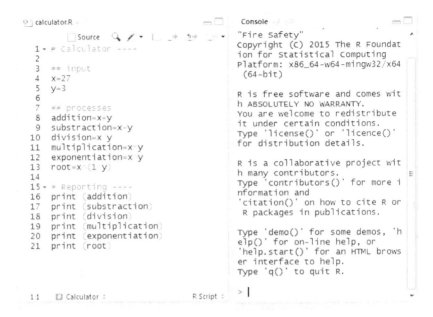

```
calculator.R

        Source
 1 ▾ # Calculator ----
 2
 3   ## input
 4   x=27
 5   y=3
 6
 7   ## processes
 8   addition=x+y
 9   substraction=x-y
10   division=x y
11   multiplication=x y
12   exponentiation=x y
13   root=x (1 y)
14
15 ▾ # Reporting ----
16   print (addition)
17   print (substraction)
18   print (division)
19   print (multiplication)
20   print (exponentiation)
21   print (root)

1:1    Calculator          R Script
```

```
Console

"Fire Safety"
Copyright (C) 2015 The R Foundat
ion for Statistical Computing
Platform: x86_64-w64-mingw32/x64
  (64-bit)

R is free software and comes wit
h ABSOLUTELY NO WARRANTY.
You are welcome to redistribute
it under certain conditions.
Type 'license()' or 'licence()'
for distribution details.

R is a collaborative project wit
h many contributors.
Type 'contributors()' for more i
nformation and
'citation()' on how to cite R or
 R packages in publications.

Type 'demo()' for some demos, 'h
elp()' for on-line help, or
'help.start()' for an HTML brows
er interface to help.
Type 'q()' to quit R.

> |
```

Figure 3.2 R as a calculator.

- The use of arithmetic operators. From line 8 to 13, an arithmetic operation is carried out on the right side of the = sign. I use an explicit name for the variable that will receive the result of the operation. I recommend using explicit names for variables instead of acronyms or mnemonics, when possible.
- Line 13 shows an important use of parentheses. This should remind us that computers will translate a formula following their own internal rules. To avoid further problems, always use parentheses to avoid a bad code interpretation. In this line, if you omit the parentheses, R will raise x to 1, and the result will be divided by y.
- Lines 16–21 show the use of the command **print**, which tells us the current value stored in a variable. The print command requires the use of parentheses and is very valuable in debugging the code. You can include a print command in parts of the code to verify that the code is computing what it is supposed to, especially during intermediate computations.

It is now time to run our first R code. To run all the code in a section, put the mouse cursor anywhere in that section and, on your keyboard, press:

- CONTROL ALT T if you are in Windows or Linux.
- COMMAND OPTION T if you are in Mac OS X.

Figure 3.3 Results of running the calculator.

The code is organized in two sections. let Run the first section; that is, give values to x and y, and do arithmetic operations with both, while storing each result in a variable. Then, run the second section, so that you can see what the results are. If you do not remember the combination of keys to run the code, go to the Menu Bar in RStudio and select *Code*, then select *Run Region*, and then select *Run Code Section*. The results are shown in Figure 3.3.

3.1.2 Becoming Familiar with Python

Find and *click* on the Anaconda Navigator icon (see Figure 3.1b on page 25), and a window similar to the one in Figure 3.4 will appear.

You must be in the ennvironment created (see Chapter 2). You may see some updates and installations available. We will use **Jupyter notebook**[5]

---

[5] Previously known as the IPython notebook.

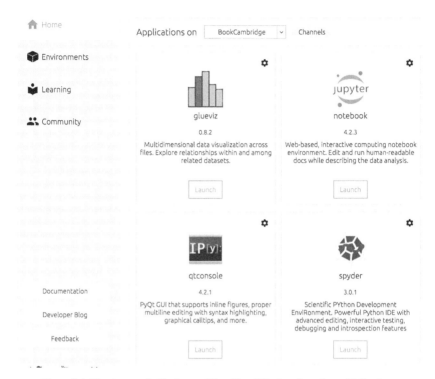

Figure 3.4 The Anaconda Navigator. We will call Python from here. Notice I am in my *environment*.

and **Spyder**, so please update those. Do not install or update anything else in the Navigator. When Jupyter and Spyder have been updated, please launch **Spyder**. When **Spyder** is ready (it may take a while), you will see a screen similar to Figure 3.5, but without my code. The code will accomplish the same tasks as did the R code we saw earlier but I highlight some differences later. In Figure 3.5, the code is on the left (as it was in RStudio), and the results are shown on the window on the bottom right. You can alter the layout using the option *View* on the top menu bar.

Here is what the code does (you may find the text easier to read in Figure 3.6):

- Lines 1 to 8 are not needed, but are recommended:
  - Line 1 will appear automatically in **Spyder** (and other standard Python versions). It is giving Python some instructions, telling Python your source file is saved as utf-8; that is how the interpreter reads the characters in the file.

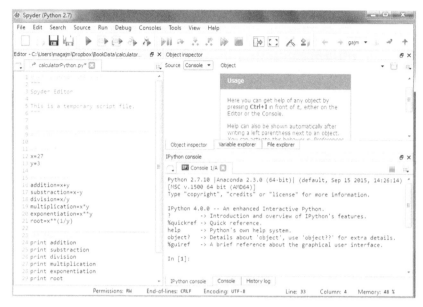

Figure 3.5 The calculator in Python. This example is similar to the one we just saw in RStudio.

– Lines 2 to 6 use triple quotations to explain what the code does. You want to modify this later to explain your codes.

• Lines 9 and 23 create a **code cell** (similar to the *code section* in RStudio), where all those lines of code can be executed together. Remember code in cells improves readability and makes debugging easier. **Spyder** signals a section with the symbols #%%; optionally, you should write a name for the cell. Nothing else is needed.[6] To run all the code in a cell you can use the option **Run** located in the upper menu bar, selecting *Run cell and advance*; another way to run the code is simply to press the icon:

• Lines 11 and 15 are comments. Python does not care what you write after a #. You should use comments to remind yourself in plain English the logic

---

[6] There is no drop-down list in **Spyder**, as there is in RStudio, to see the code cells.

Figure 3.6 First interaction with Python. There is a mistake here.

behind the code; doing so allows external readers to understand how you are implementing your ideas.

- Lines 12, 13, and 16–21 work the same as the example in R:
  - The = sign represents how the variable to the left (x, y, addition, etc.) receives a value and stores it.
  - Arithmetic operators are used in lines 16–21. Notice that lines 20 and 21 do not use ∧ for exponentiation, but use ** instead.
  - Line 21 shows again the important use of parentheses.
- Lines 24–29 show the use of the command print in Python. Unlike in R, this command does not require parentheses, but you can use it optionally

in **Spyder** (Python 3 requires parentheses). As mentioned before, print is extremely valuable in debugging your code.

When you understand these steps, it is time to run the code. The result is shown in Figure 3.6. There, you may notice two things:

- Python reads the code in a cell and then produces all the results. In R, the results were displayed as a line was read in a section.
- All the results are *almost* the same. There is something wrong with the last result: the result should be **3**, not **1**.

In this first contact with Python you have already found an unexpected error, especially if you are an R user. The problem here is that

- x and y (lines 12 and 13) receive *integers*, so Python will perform arithmetic with integers.
- Using integer values may cause unexpected results in division and root computing, which may return real numbers (integers do not have decimals). For example, in our case Python is truncating $1/y$ (0.333..) to 0 (the integer part). Then, $x**1/y$ equals 1.
- To make Python work as expected, assign 27.0 to x and 3.0 to y (*floats* instead of integers).

Some Python packages will make life easier in terms of receiving an unexpected truncated value, but I wanted to share this issue so you can see a very important difference between R and Python.[7]

From what we have just seen, R and Python handle data types differently. Each has a particular advantage, so it is important to know how each works. The most important difference concerns the use of numbers. You should always know what data type you have; to find out the data type of *x*, simply write

- type(x) in Python, and
- class(x) in R[8]

Knowing the data type may become unnecessary as you become familiar with the languages, but I often use it in my examples. For now, it is more important to focus on and learn about data structures, functions, and the control of execution in both R and Python.

---

[7] If you are using Python 3.5, you will not encounter this situation (it will behave as in R).
[8] You also have typeof() in R.

3.2 Introducing Data Structures

You are reading this book because you work with data, but data in a computer is organized and saved in a particular fashion, which is called **data structure**. The study of data structures is not common among social and policy scientists. But if you have used data files, you have dealt with data structures. In particular, if you are familiar with spreadsheets, you are dealing with data organized in a table or **frame** (or matrix), which is a data structure (but not a simple one).

Data structures are very important in programming. In general, a data structure serves as a repository of data and informs how the data is being organized. Both Python and R have native data structures that allow for the creation of more complex ones. In this section, I review the common data structures you will deal with and show you how to use them. Because my emphasis here is on these structures and the particular functions they use, my data will be very simple (you will actually type in the data, which you will not have to do in the following chapters).

3.2.1 Simple Structures

In Figure 3.7, you see the basic structures Python offers: the **list**, the **tuple**, and the **dictionary**.[9]

- **Lists** can store different kinds of data: text, real (float) or integer numbers, other lists or structures, and so on). You create a list within square brackets "[ ]" or using the command list(). As you see in line 9, the list has the name "numbersInList,"[10] and it is storing five values: four numbers and one character; keep in mind that to represent a character or set of characters (string) in Python and R, you need to use simple (' ') or double (" ") quotations.[11] In a spreadsheet, a list can be a column of values, and in that situation,

---

[9] I am omitting, on purpose, the structure known as a **set**, which is a structure similar to a list, but that does not admit duplicates.

[10] Notice that the name of the list uses a combination of lowercase and "CamelCase" style. I may be overriding some conventions in my examples for the sake of clarity; however, if you are planing on becoming an advanced user, it will be important to review the conventions Python recommends for writing names. Please visit https://www.python.org/dev/peps/pep-0008 and go to **naming conventions**.

[11] If you write a string without using quotation marks, it means that you are using the name of an assigned value (i.e., USA=51). If that is your intention, there is no problem. However, if that is not your intention two bad things will happen: in one case, R or Python will use that variable name if previously assigned, and your list may include an unwanted value; in another case, you will get an error message because Python and R do not understand why you want as an element in the list a variable that you have not previously created. This same situations apply to the other data structures I teach in this book.

```
 1# -*- coding: utf-8 -*-
 2"""
 3Showing Basic Data Structures
 4@author: JoseManuel
 5"""
 6#%% LIST
 7## Lists are alterable collections of items
 8## that need not be homogeneous.
 9numbersInList=[1,2,3,4,'5']
10numbersInList
11
12#%% TUPLE
13## Tuples cannot be altered,
14## should be used to represent
15## collections of items
16## that are constant during a program
17numbersInTuple=(1,2,3,4,'5')
18numbersInTuple
19
20#%% DICTIONARIES (dicts)
21## dicts are alterable but
22## are presented as items
23## consisting of key and value:
24numbersInDictionary={'first':1, 'second':2, 'third':'3'}
25numbersInDictionary
```

Figure 3.7 Creating basic structures: the list, the tuple, and the dictionary.

you expect that the list will have the same kind of values; if a list is to represent a spreadsheet row, you can expect the list to have different kinds of values.

- A **tuple** can store the same kind of elements a list does, but the main difference is that you cannot modify a tuple, also known as an **immutable sequence**, once it is created.[12] In contrast, a list, a mutable container, can be modified at will. You create a tuple within parentheses "( )" or using the command tuple().[13] As you see, in line 17, the tuple I created stores the same values as the list in line 9. In a spreadsheet a tuple could be a row or column, depending, as in the case of lists, whether the tuple contains heterogeneous or homogeneous kinds of values, respectively.
- A **dictionary**, or **dict**, is a more complex but very useful structure. As you see in line 24, this dict has three items, and each has two components: a *key* and the *actual* value I want to store. You create a dict within curly

---

[12] It should not be that hard to think about values that cannot be modified, such as Social Security numbers.

[13] In fact, you can create a tuple if you just write the values: aTuple=1,2,3,4.

```
In [1]: numbersInList=[1,2,3,4,'5']
   ...: numbersInList
   ...:
   ...:
Out[1]: [1, 2, 3, 4, '5']

In [2]: numbersInTuple=(1,2,3,4,'5')
   ...: numbersInTuple
   ...:
   ...:
Out[2]: (1, 2, 3, 4, '5')

In [3]: numbersInDictionary={'first':1, 'second':2, 'third':'3'}
   ...: numbersInDictionary
   ...:
   ...:
Out[3]: {'first': 1, 'second': 2, 'third': '3'}
```

Figure 3.8 Results for basic structures.

braces { } or with the command dict(). Notice that a dict is precisely the kind of structure you want for heterogeneous values and to make explicit what each value represents. It is hard to think of a dict as a column in a spreadsheet, but a row is a better analogy: Imagine you have a spreadsheet of every county (or province) in your state (or region) with information on population counts, land area, and the capital city; then a row in a spreadsheet could be transformed into a dictionary. However, although this information in a list can be written as [200001, 550,'City Linda'], the dict will represent it as {'population':200001, 'area':550, 'capital':'City Linda'}.

All the code shown in Figure 3.7 has been organized in three cells. Please notice that I have changed the heading comments (lines 2 to 5) and added some comments in each cell. The results of running each cell are shown in Figure 3.8. As you see, the results appear after the message "**Out**" followed by a sequential number in brackets. There are no error messages after running the code. Python has accepted these values in every structure without any complaint and without any changes or coercion.[14]

Now, let's go to RStudio and see what R offers for data structures. Let's look at Figure 3.9 first.

As before, I have organized the code into sections, so that you can run a whole section from RStudio. After running the code, you see two of the most important and commonly used structures in R: the list and the vector[15]:

---

[14] Coercion, intuitively, is a feature of a program that serves to automatically convert the class of a value to a different one (i.e., from integer to real), because the program considers it to be the correct one.

[15] The standard R does not offer tuples and dictionaries.

```
 1 ▾ # LISTS ----
 2
 3   ## First Case
 4   numbersInListI=list(1,2,"3")
 5   numbersInListI
 6
 7   ## Second Case
 8   numbersInListII=list('first'=1,'second'=2,'third'="3")
 9   numbersInListII
10
11
12 ▾ # VECTORS ----
13   ## First Case
14   numbersInVectorI=c(1,2,"3")
15   numbersInVectorI
16
17   ## Second Case
18   numbersInVectorII=c('first'=1,'second'=2,'third'="3")
19   numbersInVectorII
```

Figure 3.9 Code for lists and vectors in R.

- The section LISTS shows you two ways of creating lists in R. The first one is very similar to how you create Python lists; the second one creates a list in a way similar to creating dicts in Python, but the resulting list will not work as a Python dict.
- The section VECTORS also shows two ways of creating vectors in R. In both cases, the vector coerces the numbers into characters. When we deal with vectors (or matrices by extension) some coercion may take place because those structures require that all their values belong to the same class.[16]

Notice that no special characters are needed in R to create lists or vectors (in Python we needed three different pairs of characters).

Figure 3.10 shows that a list in R is very similar to a list in Python (it accepts any value). Notice that the values are printed vertically for both lists. However, coercion took place in both vectors. This can be useful, as when R gives a real value when doing arithmetic with integers (see page 27), but may cause problems if your numeric values have a "dirty" value.

- From this code (notice I use ";" to write several commands together),

```
aVector=c(1,2,3) ; mean(aVector)
```

---

[16] Standard Python software offers neither vectors nor matrices, but some packages do empower Python with those capabilities.

```
Console
> numbersInListI=list(1,2,"3")
> numbersInListI
[[1]]
[1] 1

[[2]]
[1] 2

[[3]]
[1] "3"

> numbersInListII=list('first'=1,'second'=2,'third'="3")
> numbersInListII
$first
[1] 1

$second
[1] 2

$third
[1] "3"

> numbersInVectorI=c(1,2,"3")
> numbersInVectorI
[1] "1" "2" "3"
> numbersInVectorII=c('first'=1,'second'=2,'third'="3")
> numbersInVectorII
 first second  third
   "1"    "2"    "3"
```

Figure 3.10 Lists and vectors in R.

you get:

```
[1] 2
```

- But from this one,

```
anotherVector=c(1,2,"3") ; mean(anotherVector)
```

you get

```
[1] NA
```

3.2.2 The Data Frame

You may have not discussed lists, tuples, dicts, or vectors before. Most social and policy scientists are used to working with data in tables that are visible when one opens a file in, for instance, MS Excel, SPSS, or STATA; in these programs there is a value in each cell, rows represent the units of analysis, and columns represent the variables. This structure, in its simplest version, is known

```
 1 ▾ # DataFrame ----
 2
 3   #Case1
 4   x=c('a','b','c','d')
 5   x1=c(20,32,53,56) ; x2=c('male','female','male','male')
 6   aDataFrame1=data.frame(cases=x, ageOfCases=x1,sexOfCases=x2)
 7   #Case2
 8   cases=c('a','b','c','d')
 9   ageOfCases=c(20,32,53,56) ; sexOfCases=c('male','female','male','male')
10   aDataFrame2=data.frame(ageOfCases,sexOfCases,row.names = cases)
11   #Case3
12   a=list(ageOfCases=20,sexOfCases='male'); b=list(ageOfCases=32,sexOfCases='female')
13   c=list(ageOfCases=53,sexOfCases='male'); d=list(ageOfCases=56,sexOfCases='male')
14   aDataFrame3=data.frame(rbind(a,b,c,d))
15
16 ▾ # Show Results ----
17   aDataFrame1
18   aDataFrame2
19   aDataFrame3
```

Figure 3.11 Creating data frames in R. Three ways of creating a data frame, using vectors and lists, are shown here.

in R and Python as a **data frame**, which is easily created by using less complex structures, as shown in Figure 3.11.

Figure 3.11 shows three data frames. In the first two examples, vectors create the columns of the data frame. This makes sense, because a variable should reflect a particular scale for the unit of analysis.[17] In the third example, I use lists to represent each row entry. Using lists here is the right thing to do, because each row can have many variables and each variable can belong to a different scale. Let's now go step by step:

- The Case1 code creates three vectors. One vector holds the name or ID of the row. Their names are not informative of their data contents. The command **data.frame** binds all the three vectors as columns and gives a explicit name to each one.
- The Case2 code creates three vectors. One vector holds the name or ID of the row. Their names inform what the contents are about. The command data.frame binds the vectors as columns, and those names are the column names in the data frame (notice the use of the option row.names.).
- The Case3 code creates four lists. Each list holds the information of a row entry. Each list element associates each value to a variable. The command data.frame binds all the lists as rows, with the help of the command rbind.

---

[17] Variables are recorded in a particular scale. Common scales are nominal, ordinal, interval, and ratio (presented in Stevens (1946)). For more information on typologies of measurement scales see also Chrisman (1998); Mosteller and Tukey (1977); and Velleman and Wilkinson (1993).

```
> # Show Results ----
> aDataFrame1
  cases ageOfCases sexOfCases
1   a         20        male
2   b         32      female
3   c         53        male
4   d         56        male
> aDataFrame2
  ageOfCases sexOfCases
a        20        male
b        32      female
c        53        male
d        56        male
> aDataFrame3
  ageOfCases sexOfCases
a        20        male
b        32      female
c        53        male
d        56        male
```

Figure 3.12 Differences among data frames in R.

In Figure 3.11, there are two code sections: one that creates the data frames, and another that displays them. You need to run the first section first. After you run the second section you will see something similar to Figure 3.12.

In the first case in Figure 3.12, R did not know the names of the rows, so it simply added the sequential numbers you see in the leftmost column (row names have no column titles in R[18]). This will happen in most cases, and it may be the format you need. However, if you need R to use particular row names, you can use the second example (using the `row.names` option) or the third one if your data is in lists.

Data frames are not present in native Python. However, I will create one with the help of a package named **pandas** (which you installed in the previous chapter). The data frame created by pandas is comparable to the one in R.

The code shown in Figure 3.13 follows a similar approach to build the data frames as I used in R, but with some interesting differences:

- The first cell does the set up (lines 7–23). First, I needed to call pandas, using the command `import`. Now Python has more powers! Then, in line 13, I entered the data, row by row. Each row is a tuple (Did you notice the parentheses?). Then, I organized the data frame components: the variable names

---

[18] Python does not have a title for the column of row names in a data frame; it also calls row names "indexes."

```
 1 # -*- coding: utf-8 -*-
 2 """
 3 Using Data Frames in Python with
 4 the help of the pandas package
 5 @author: JoseManuel
 6 """
 7 #%% Setting Up
 8
 9 # Calling pandas
10 import pandas
11
12 #Data
13 a=(20,'male'); b=(32,'female'); c=(53,'male'); d=(56,'male')
14
15 #Organizing
16
17 variablesNames=['ageOfCases','sexOfCases']
18 ids=['a', 'b','c','d']
19 ## this is list of tuples
20 valuesList=[a,b,c,d]
21 ## this is dict of lists
22 valuesDict = {'ageOfCases' : [20,32,53,56],
23               'sexOfCases' : ['male','female','male','male']}
24
25 #%% Creating Data Frames
26
27 #Case1: no row names using values in list
28 aDataFrame1 = pandas.DataFrame(valuesList, columns=variablesNames)
29 #Case2: with row names using values in list
30 aDataFrame2 = pandas.DataFrame(valuesList, columns=variablesNames,index=ids)
31 #Case3: no row names using values in dict
32 aDataFrame3 = pandas.DataFrame(valuesDict)
33 #Case4: with row names using values in dict
34 aDataFrame4 = pandas.DataFrame(valuesDict,index=ids)
35
36 #%% Displaying Case 1
37 aDataFrame1
38
39 #%% Displaying Case 2
40 aDataFrame2
41
42 #%% Displaying Case 3
43 aDataFrame3
44
45 #%% Displaying Case 4
46 aDataFrame4
```

Figure 3.13 Creating data frames in Python. Notice the margin line that Spyder
displays to the right, which displays the recommended limit of your code.

(line 17) and the name of each row (line 18). In lines 19 to 23, I created
composite data structures that will serve the same purpose:

– In line 20, I created a list of tuples, where each tuple represents the rows
  defined in line 13.
– In lines 22 and 23, I created a dict of lists. Notice that I had to rewrite
  the data in line 13 in a different format. The key of the list represents the
  variable names.
• The second cell (lines 25–34) created the data frame by writing the command
  pandas.DataFrame; this means you are using the function DataFrame()
  from pandas. I created four data frames with the same data:

```
In [3]: aDataFrame1
   ...:
   ...:
Out[3]:
   ageOfCases sexOfCases
0          20       male
1          32     female
2          53       male
3          56       male

In [4]: aDataFrame2
   ...:
   ...:
Out[4]:
   ageOfCases sexOfCases
a          20       male
b          32     female
c          53       male
d          56       male

In [5]: aDataFrame3
   ...:
   ...:
Out[5]:
   ageOfCases sexOfCases
0          20       male
1          32     female
2          53       male
3          56       male

In [6]: aDataFrame4
   ...:
   ...:
Out[6]:
   ageOfCases sexOfCases
a          20       male
b          32     female
c          53       male
d          56       male
```

Figure 3.14 Displaying the data frames in Python.

- The aDataFrame1 uses the list of tuples as data and informs Python that the columns have as names the values in variablesNames.
- The aDataFrame2 uses the list of tuples as data and informs Python that the columns have as names the values in variablesNames, and that the index column (rows names) must use the values in ids.
- The aDataFrame3 uses the dict of lists as data and gives no more information to Python.[19]
- The *aDataFrame4* uses the dict of lists as data and informs Python that the rows have as names the values in *ids*.
- The next four cells display, Cases 1–4, each data frame created.

The results are displayed in Figure 3.14. In the first and third data frames, you see a default index column with sequential numbers as in R (remember that "index columns" in Python are "row names" in R). Here you see again that

---

[19] Creating data frame with dictionaries is very easy. However, it may be difficult to control the order of the columns. I will show how to keep the order you want using *Ordered Dictionaries* on page 124.

Python always starts counting from **zero**. The default was applied following lines 28 and 30 in Figure 3.13. The second and fourth data frames show you a customized index column, because you do not see numbers but rather the names you provided when creating those data frames. For me, it seems easier to create data frames using a dict of lists; in this case, the key of the list is immediately interpreted by Python as the column name. This is very similar to R, which can use the name of the object containing the values of the columns as the column name (see particularly Case2 in Figure 3.11 on page 37). Data frames are more complex than lists or similar data structures, but they are the key structure for all of the examples in the next chapters.

Before moving on, I recommend that you review and play again and again with the code, and explore alternatives I have not shown. For example,

- If I erase one value in x2 (so there are only three values where we had four before):

```
x=c('a','b','c','d');
x1=c(20,32,53,56); x2=c('male','female','male')
aDataFrame1=data.frame(cases=x,
                       ageOfCases=x1,sexOfCases=x2)
```

- I will get this message:
Error in data.frame(cases = x, ageOfCases = x1, sexOfCases = x2) : arguments imply differing number of rows: 4, 3

This is a mistake that is easy to make and occurs when you forget to write a value or you write a different character instead of the right one. Python will also give an error if we eliminate a value in the tuples or in the lists in lines 13, 22, or 23 in the code in Figure 3.13. But now take a look at the code in Figure 3.15.

I again eliminated a value in d (no "male" value), but now I am using lists for the rows (not tuples as in Figure 3.13). The execution of the code (on the right) shows that Python is not giving an error, but instead, has added the value **None**, which is quite clever (using tuples in rows gives an error if this value or any other is missing).

3.2.3 Basic Manipulation of Data Structures

One chooses a particular data structure because of the operations available in that structure. Before moving on, let's create a folder for your codes with two subfolders inside: one for Python and one for R.

First, let me create some data to use in the next subsections.

```
 1 # -*- coding: utf-8 -*-
 2 """                                                    ...:
 3 Using Data Frames in Python with                       ...:
 4 the help of the pandas package                         ...:
 5 @author: JoseManuel                                    ...:
 6 """                                                    ...:
 7 #%% Setting Up                                          ...:
 8 # Calling pandas                                        ...:
 9 import pandas                                           ...:
10 #Data                                                   ...:
11 a=[20,'male']; b=[32,'female']                          ...:
12 c=[53,'male']; d=[56]                                   ...:
13 #Organizing                                             ...:
14 variablesNames=['ageOfCases','sexOfCases']              ...:
15 ids=['a', 'b','c','d']                                  ...:
16 ## this is list of lists                                ...:
17 valuesList=[a,b,c,d]                                    ...:
18 #%% creating Data frame                                 ...:
19 aDataFrameXtra = pandas.DataFrame(valuesList,           ...:
20                          columns=variablesNames)        ...:
21 #%% Displaying Case 1                                   ...:
22 aDataFrameXtra                               Out[9]:
23                                                 ageOfCases sexOfCases
24                                              0         20       male
25                                              1         32     female
26                                              2         53       male
27                                              3         56       None
```

Figure 3.15 Python data frame and incomplete values.

Data to Be Manipulated

Figure 3.16 shows the code that creates the data structures in R.

- I am creating a data frame with data generated randomly.[20] I include the instruction set.seed() in line 11. If I do not include that line (or write a different value than 123), everything will work, but your data frame will have values different from mine.
- Line 13 activates an R package using the command library(). This is similar to import in Python. However, before this activation, you need to **install** that library. You can do that in RStudio by simply selecting the *packages* tab from the *Files, Plots, and Packages* window; selecting *install*; and typing the name of the package you want to install[21] (as I show in Figure 3.17). Installation must only be done once, but activation is required every time you run the code. Please install the package now.
- In line 15, I use the function randomNames to get 30 first names (no last names) randomly in the console window. For example, if you want to see other options and examples for this command, simply type ?randomNames in the *console* window. This function saved me time and space.
- Lines 18 and 20 generate random numbers. You want to use sample() when you need integers, and runif() when you want floats (values that can have decimal values).

---

[20] You may never need to create data randomly. I am creating it here because I have not showed you yet how to use a file, which will be explained later.

[21] Or just type: **install.packages("randomNames")** in the *console* window before the activation.

```
 1 ▾ #Data ----
 2   ##List
 3   aList = list(name='John', age= '20' , male = T)
 4   aListOfChars=list('d','a','b','c')
 5   ##Vector
 6   aVector = c(10,20,30,"50")
 7   vectorA=c(1,2,3); vectorB=c(9,10,11)
 8   vectorWithDuplicates=c(1,2,3,4,4,5,6,6,6,6,8)
 9   ##Data Frame
10   ## Set the seed to allow replicability
11   set.seed(123)
12   ## Install this library first!
13   library(randomNames)
14   ## Now generate randomly 30 names:
15   names=randomNames(30, which.names="first")
16   ## Now generate randomly 30 age values from 25 to 50, inclusive.
17   ## Values can repeat.
18   ages=sample(25:50,30,replace=T)
19   ## Now create randomly 30 height values from 5 to 7 feet.
20   heights=runif(30,5,7)
21   ## Now create the Data Frame:
22   aDataFrame=data.frame(ages,heights,row.names = names)
```

Figure 3.16 Creating data to be manipulated in R.

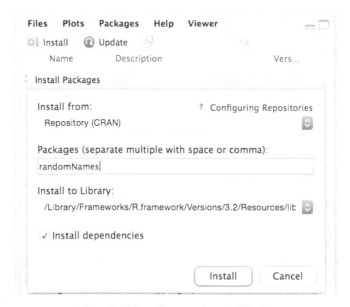

Figure 3.17 Installing a package in RStudio.

```
 1 # -*- coding: utf-8 -*-
 2 """
 3 File name: ManipulationData
 4 @author: JoseManuel
 5 my own modules: ManipulationData
 6 packages: see below
 7 """
 8 #%%
 9 #Packages
10 import random
11 import pandas
12 import names
13 import numpy
14
15 ##Dictionary
16 aDictPy = {'name':'John', 'age': '20' , 'male' : True}
17 aDictOfCharsPy={'fourth':'d','first':'a','second':'b','third':'c'}
18
19 ##List
20 aListPy = [10,20,30,"50"]
21 aListPyA=[1,2,3]; aListPyB=[9,10,11]
22 aListPyWithDuplicates=[1,2,3,4,4,5,6,6,6,6,8]
23
24 ##Tuple
25 aTuplePy = 10,20,30,"50"
26 aTuplePyA=(1,2,3)
27 aTuplePyB=(9,10,11)
28 aTupleWithDuplicates=1,2,3,4,4,5,6,6,6,6,8
29
30 ##Data Frame
31 ## Set the seed to allow replicability
32 random.seed(321)
33 numpy.random.seed(321)
34 ## Now generate randomly 30 names:
35 names=[names.get_first_name() for quantity in range(30)]
36 data={
37 ## 30 random age values from 25 to 50 (with replacement)
38 'ages' : numpy.random.randint(25, 51, 30),
39 ## 30 random height values from 5 to 7 feet.
40 'heights':numpy.random.uniform(low=5, high=7, size=30)
41 }
42 ## Now create the Data Frame:
43 aDataFrame1=pandas.DataFrame(data,index = names)
```

Figure 3.18 Creating data to be manipulated in Python.

- Line 22 creates the data frame. You should now save this code in the R code folder created.

In Python, I will create lists, tuples, dictionaries, and a data frame using the code shown in Figure 3.18. Please save the code before continuing. Save it with the name **ManipulationData**[22] (Spyder will add the **.py** by default).

The code only has two parts. The first one has information about the code, and the second one creates the structures. Notice that I used several packages.

---

[22] Notice, and respect, the *CamelCase* style of writing, when I use it.

```
●  ◉  ●                    ⌃ JoseManuel — bash — 77×17
Last login: Thu Nov  3 15:29:03 on ttys000
JoseManuels-MacBook-Pro:~ JoseManuel$ source activate BookCambridge
(BookCambridge) JoseManuels-MacBook-Pro:~ JoseManuel$ pip install names
Collecting names
  Downloading names-0.3.0.tar.gz (789kB)
    100% |████████████████████████████████| 798kB 468kB/s
Building wheels for collected packages: names
  Running setup.py bdist_wheel for names ... done
  Stored in directory: /Users/JoseManuel/Library/Caches/pip/wheels/c0/2b/1d/6
aae7258144c1cf2dd6afb990e09ffbbe17790bf0193adb3d8
Successfully built names
Installing collected packages: names
Successfully installed names-0.3.0
You are using pip version 8.1.2, however version 9.0.0 is available.
You should consider upgrading via the 'pip install --upgrade pip' command.
(BookCambridge) JoseManuels-MacBook-Pro:~ JoseManuel$ ▎
```

Figure 3.19 Installing a new package in Anaconda. I am installing it in my environment for the book. You must install it in yours before running the code in Figure 3.18.

Three of them are already available in Anaconda, but one of them, **names**, is not, so you will need to install that package. In Section 2.2.1 you learned that packages can be installed from the Navigator, but if the package you need is not available, you need to use the terminal (Mac) or a similar command prompt for Windows/Linux, as described earlier. In fact, you can install any package from the terminal. in Anaconda another way to install the package is to use the command, **conda install xxx**, where xxx is the name of the package.

That command will not work for the package names. However, the website of this package instructs users to type the command **pip install names**,[23] and that is the process shown in Figure 3.19.

Now let's review the code in Figure 3.18:

- Lines 9 to 13 show the packages we will need in the code. You already knew the **pandas** package, but now I am using three different ones. The names (boldface) package we just installed will be useful to generate names, as we did in R. I only use it in line 35. The **numpy** package is used to create random values, as I do in line 38 and 40. Because I want you to see the same values I create randomly, I will also use the packages **random** and **numpy**, to produce the same random data every time we run this code.
- From lines 15 to 28, I create the simplest data structures.

---

[23] You should have pip installed on your computer, if you do not have it just follow these instructions: https://pip.pypa.io/en/latest/installing/; or watch this video (for Windows) https://www.youtube.com/watch?v=AVCcFyYynQY. There are many videos for Mac or Linux, but just make sure to request an installation for your Mac OS or Linux version.

- From line 32, I start the creation of the data frame. Line 32 and 33 set the seeds with `random.seed` and `numpy.random.seed`. Notice I am setting the seed two times. That is because numpy functions need their own seed. The command in line 33 has an effect on lines 38 and 40. The command in line 32, in contrast has no effect on those lines, but only has an effect on line 35.
- Line 35 creates a list of names using a **list comprehension** (more details on page 50) approach. For that, we only need to write the commands between the brackets. The function **get_first_name**() creates a name, and the **for** tells the times that function is going to be executed.
- Line 38 uses `numpy.random.randint` to obtain random integers, and line 40 uses `numpy.random.uniform` to get random floats. Line 40 uses the parameter names (`low`, `high`, `size`), which I omitted on line 38, although I could have used them. Notice that in this case the *path* to a function: numpy refers to the main library, `random` refers to a sub library in numpy, and `uniform` refers to a function in that sub library. Instead of line 13, I could simply write:

```
from numpy.random import seed, randint, uniform
```

Then you can use those function names on lines 33, 38, and 40. This is similar to what you do in R, where it is uncommon to write the path to a function. However, keep in mind that when R activates a package and finds that some of its functions have the same name as others that are currently active, the oldest ones will be *masked*; that is, they will not be called when you call them. In that situation, you need to write a path relating the package and the function using two colons : : so that you can call the specific function you want, even though it is masked.

Basic Operations for Lists and Vectors in R

Now allow me to use different **operations** with the list and vectors. Please type the following commands to confirm I am getting what I want:

1. **Slicing**:

```
## I want to see the ages in the list:
aList$age
## I want to see the names and sex in the list:
aList[c('name','male')]
## I want to see the second element in the vector:
aVector[2]
## I want to see the last element in the vector:
tail(aVector,1)
## I want to see all elements, but the second and third:
aVector[-c(2,3)] #inverse selection!
```

2. **Copying**:

```
## I want a copy of a list
aListCopy=aList
## I want a copy of a vector
aVectorCopy=aVector
```

You need to make a copy because you will make changes later and do not want to lose your original data.

3. **Deleting**:

```
## I want to delete the 2nd element of the list
aListCopy = aListCopy[-c(2)]
## I want to delete element sex in the list
aListCopy['male']=NULL
## I want to delete the last element in the vector
aVectorCopy=head(aVector,-1)
## I want no duplicates in my vector
vectorWithNODuplicates=unique(vectorWithDuplicates)
```

After you run the deletion command, you will have a different list; that is what makes this operation different from the slicing operation. Notice I am using copies of the reduced list or vector, so that the original values are actually unaltered and I can keep applying these operations to the original data.

4. **Replacing**:

```
## I want to replace the '20'' string for number>
aList$age=as.numeric(aList$age)
## I want to replace the current age for 30
aList$age=30
## I want to replace all the string values
## for the same values in numeric form
aVector=as.numeric(aVector)
```

5. **Inserting**:

```
## I want to add the city in the list
aList$city="Seattle"
## I want to add the number 40 in the vector
aVector= append(aVector, 40)
## I want to insert the values of one vector to another:
## Try this first: vectorA + vectorB
vectorA=c(vectorA,vectorB)
```

Notice that append inserts the value at the end. You may need to sort the vector if you need it (see below). Also, pay attention to how I insert one vector at the end of another simple concatenating (c() command).

6. **Sorting**:

```
##I want to sort my vector data:
sort(aVector)
##I want to sort my vector in descending order
##and saved it as another vector:
aSortedVector=sort(aVector,decreasing=T) # or TRUE.
## I want to sort a list... BUT
### I need to make it into a vector, and then sort it!
sort(unlist(aListOfChars))
### Now I want to turn it into a list again!!
newestListOfChars=as.list(sort(unlist(aListOfChars)))
```

In R, sorting is a natural operation for vectors, but not lists, because lists may contain different classes of data.

7. **Other important operations**:

```
## I want to know the size of my list and my vector
length(aList)
length(aVector)
## I want to know max and minimun value in my vector
max(aVector)
min(aVector)
## I want to know max and minimun value in my list...
max(unlist(aListOfChars))
```

Basic Operations for Lists, Dicts, and Tuples in Python

There are many operations that manipulate those structures, but I have chosen the ones that can be implemented easily. Now, let's try similar operations to the ones I used in R. You should save each chunk of code in a file. Each file has to be in the same folder as the *ManipulationData.py* file:

1. **Slicing**. Please save this code as *ManipulationSlicing*. We are using our *ManipulationData* file, which is called in the first line. If both files are not in the same folder, this will not work. Notice that I am giving Manipulation-Data a shorter name (nickname) data, which I use in the path to its elements in the code.[24]

```
import ManipulationData as data

#%% I want to see the ages in the dict:
data.aDictPy['age']
#%% I want to see the names and sex in the dict:
data.aDictPy['age'],data.aDictPy['male'] #you get a tuple!
#%% I want to see second element in the list:
data.aListPy[1] #first element in Python has index '0'!
#%% I want to see second element in the tuple:
```

---

[24] You could write from ManipulationData import *, which means to use everything available in that file (or module), and then you will directly use every element without the nickname; however, the use of the "*" is considered a bad practice. Please try this, and you will see Spyder showing a warning at that line, but the code will run without problems.

```
data.aTuplePy[1] #first element in Python has index '0'!
#%% I want to see last element in the list:
data.aListPy[-1]
#%% I want to see last element in the tuple:
data.aTuplePy[-1]
#%% I want to see all elements, but the second and fourth,
## in the list:
out=[1,3]
# data.aListPy is  [10, 20, 30, '50']
[val for idx, val in enumerate(data.aListPy) if idx not in out]
```

As I mentioned before, the first element in a structure in R always has index **1**, while in Python it is **0**. Indexes are used very frequently in R and Python for many important operations; it is important to keep this difference in mind when you define lowest and highest values for indexes in some operations. Notice in the code above the use of **enumerate**. This function will return **two** values for each element in data.aListPy: the second value is simply the values in the list, and the first value is the position of that element in the list. The list comprehension I am using has an **if**, which will filter out the positions (idx) that are in the list **out** (**not** and **in** are important Python logical operators).

2. **Copying and Deleting.** Please save this code as *ManipulationCopying-Deleting*. I have organized the code in to three sections. The first one is the importing section, where I am showing a way to import external elements by calling each element needed from the imported file. I do it in two lines to respect the width limit mentioned before; I also import the function deepcopy from the package copy. In the second part, I am making copies of my data, so that I can apply deletions to those copies, because, unlike slicing, a deletion will change the data structure. It is important to avoid *shallow* copies in Python, because the changes in those copies still will affect the original.[25] Because tuples cannot be modified, I create a list with the tuple's values. The third section is about deleting, which I will do on copies. The command del works for dicts and lists. You can optionally use the command pop for lists, which by default deletes the last element in the list.[26] Also, keep in mind that it is not safe to speak of first or last elements in dictionaries, because their elements are not reachable via indexes but via keys.

```
#%% PART I: IMPORTS
from ManipulationData import aDictPy, aListPy
from ManipulationData import aTuplePy,aListPyWithDuplicates
from copy import deepcopy
```

---

[25] Making deep copies is playing it safe; you do it because you want a copy of data to play with, without changing the original. The R copies of lists and vectors always give deep copies.

[26] If you give pop() a valid index, this function will eliminate that position in the list.

```
#%% PART II: COPYING
# I want a copy of a dict
aDictPyCopy=deepcopy(aDictPy)
aDictPyCopy
#%% I want a copy of a list
aListPyCopy=deepcopy(aListPy)
# SHALLOW: aListPyCopy=aListPy
# SHALLOW: aListPyCopy=list(aListPy)
aListPyCopy
#%% I want a copy of a tuple
aTuplePyCopy=list(aTuplePy)
aTuplePyCopy #this will work, but will not be used!

#%% PART III: DELETING
#I want to delete element sex in the Dict
del aDictPyCopy['male']
aDictPyCopy
#%% I want to delete the 2nd element of the list
del aListPyCopy[1]  #first element in Python has index '0'!
aListPyCopy
#%% I want to delete the last element in the list
aListPyCopy.pop() #then see aListPyCopy !
aListPyCopy
#%% I want to delete the last element in the tuple
### SORRY, that is not possible!

#%% I want no duplicates in my list
# (it is a kind of deletion)
aListPyWithNoDuplicates=list(set(aListPyWithDuplicates))
aListPyWithNoDuplicates
```

I also use the command **set** to reduce a list to its unique values. Notice that **set** is another data structure that only holds nonrepeated values, so I intentionally convert the list to a set, and then to a list again.

3. **Replacing**. Please save this code as *ManipulationReplacing*. Here, in the first line, I am also importing a list and a dict created in the Manipulation-Data module.

```
from ManipulationData import aDictPy,aListPy
#%% I want to replace the '20' string for number 20 in age
aDictPy['age']=int(aDictPy['age'])
aDictPy
#%% I want to replace the current age for 30
aDictPy['age']=30
aDictPy
#%% I want to replace all the string values in the list
## for the same values in numeric form

## USING LIST COMPREHENSION
aListPy=[int(value) for value in aListPy]
aListPy
#%% An alternative without LIST COMPREHENSION:
aNewListPy=['1','3','5']
aNewListPy=map(int,aNewListPy)
aNewListPy
```

In this last code, I use again a **list comprehension**, a feature present in Python (not in R), to turn all the characters into integers. Let me give you more details on this feature. Because you write the instructions inside brackets, it is necessary for the result to be a list. List comprehension is fairly simple to read: int(xx) for xx in YY means simply *turn into an integer every xx in YY*. The last code section does the same thing using the command map(), which can be read as *apply the function "int" to "aNewLisPy."* Both are equivalent, but list comprehensions are more *pythonic*, while using map represents a coding style that can be found in R too.

4. **Inserting and Sorting**. Please save this code as *ManipulationInserting-Sorting*. I start by doing precise imports. You should run all these codes in the order I show. In this case, I am calling two structures in Manipulation-Replacing whose original values, in ManipulationData, were replaced. These two structures have not yet been manipulated. Notice the use of extend and append.

```
from ManipulationReplacing import aDictPy,aListPy
from ManipulationData import aListPyA, aListPyB


#%% I want to add the city in the dict
aDictPy['city']="Seattle"
aDictPy
#%% I want to add the number 40 in the list
aListPy.append(40)
aListPy
#%% I want to insert the values of one list to another:
aListPyAB=aListPyA + aListPyB
aListPyAB #new list created
#%% Other option:
aListPyC=[3,6,9]; aListPyD=[2,4,6]
aListPyC.extend(aListPyD)
aListPyC #no new list created
#%% Be careful with this
aListPyE=[3,6,9]; aListPyF=[2,4,6]
aListPyE.append(aListPyB)
aListPyE #aListPyB becomes AN element of aListPyA.

#%% I want to sort my list data:
aListPy=sorted(aListPy)
aListPy
#%% sorting a tuple is possible, but sorting will
#turn the tuple into a list.
#%% I want to sort my vector in descending order
##and save it as another vector:
aListPySorted=sorted(aListPy,reverse=True)
aListPySorted
```

5. **Other Important Functions**. Please save this code as *ManipulationOther*. Notice the module I am importing.

```
from ManipulationReplacing import aListPy

#%% I want to know the size of my list
len(aListPy)
#%% I want to know the max value in my list
```

```
max(aListPy)
#%% I want to know the minimun value in my list
min(aListPy)
#%% I want to sum the values (I know this list is clean)
sum(aListPy)
```

All these basic commands are very important. They give you enough power to do many basic operations on the data. However, for R and Python to be good choices for you, you need to know how to work with data frames.

Basic Data Frame Manipulation

Let's take a look a our data frame using R[27]:

```
## What are the dimension of my data frame?
dim(aDataFrame)
```

```
[1] 30  2
```

```
## How many cases?
nrow(aDataFrame)
```

```
[1] 30
```

```
## How many variables?
ncol(aDataFrame)
```

```
[1] 2
```

```
## variable names?
names(aDataFrame)
```

```
[1] "ages"    "heights"
```

```
## show me the top cases?
head(aDataFrame) # use: tail(aDataFrame) for bottom cases
```

```
         ages  heights
Anthony   28  6.295787
Lauren    41  5.639641
Travis    33  5.615440
Britnnie  42  5.439535
Scarlett  33  5.738978
Thomas    29  6.968438
```

---

[27] If you created the data frame following my code, we should have the same data, so you will see the same results.

These operations are easily understood. Notice that the row names are not considered variables, so they are not counted as another dimension. Another important basic operation for data frames is **str**():

```
## what are its components?
str(aDataFrame)
```

```
'data.frame':   30 obs. of  2 variables:
 $ ages   : int  28 41 33 42 33 29 45 27 37 38 ...
 $ heights: num  6.3 5.64 5.62 5.44 5.74 ...
```

The operations **str**() and **class**() should be used frequently. For instance, sometimes I need to access the data frame column, and other times I need to access the data frame column element. Please see the difference here:

```
#This is a data frame (a part)
class(aDataFrame[1])
```

```
[1] "data.frame"
```

```
#This is a vector
class(aDataFrame[,1])
```

```
[1] "integer"
```

When you have a data frame, you will want to use `str()` to determine how clean your data is; that is, if every column has the kind of values you expect. If `str` informs you that age is a character, then you know there is something wrong:

```
# changing one value
aDataFrame$ages[1]='38'  # or: aDataFrame[1,1]='38'
# here you do not see the difference!
head(aDataFrame)
```

```
          ages  heights
Anthony     38  6.295787
Lauren      41  5.639641
Travis      33  5.615440
Britnnie    42  5.439535
Scarlett    33  5.738978
Thomas      29  6.968438
```

```
# here you do!
str(aDataFrame)
```

```
'data.frame':   30 obs. of  2 variables:
 $ ages   : chr  "38" "41" "33" "42" ...
 $ heights: num  6.3 5.64 5.62 5.44 5.74 ...
```

So, this operation will not work[28]:

```
sum(aDataFrame$ages)
```

Then, it is necessary to do some *cleaning* (converting that column to the right kind of values) again:

```
aDataFrame$ages=as.numeric(aDataFrame$ages)
sum(aDataFrame$ages)
```

```
[1] 1148
```

Let's turn to Python to show how to get similar results. Please run these cells and see the results for yourself:

```python
from ManipulationData import aDataFrame1

#%% What are the dimensions of my data frame?
aDataFrame1.shape

#%% How many cases?
nrows,ncols=aDataFrame1.shape # pythonic 'unpacking'
nrows

#%% How many variables?
ncols

#%% Variable names?
list(aDataFrame1)

#%% What are its components?
aDataFrame1.info()

#%% Show me the top cases?
aDataFrame1.head()

#%% Show me the bottom cases?
aDataFrame1.tail()
```

I have also made changes to one of the numeric values in the code below to show you how basic cleaning works in Python:

---

[28] You will get **Error in sum(aDataFrame$ages) : invalid "type" (character) of argument.**

```
from ManipulationData import aDataFrame1

#%% replacing a number by a string:
aDataFrame1.iloc[0,0]='45'

#%% seeing the new structure:
aDataFrame1.info()

#%% this will not work:
sum(aDataFrame1['ages'])

#%% have all values changed to strings?
type(aDataFrame1.iloc[0,0])

#%% have all values changed to strings?
type(aDataFrame1.iloc[2,0])

#%% defensive cleaning:
agesFloat=[float(value) for value in aDataFrame1['ages']]
aDataFrame1['ages']=agesFloat
# These work the same (all are pandas "series"):
## aDataFrame1.ages=agesFloat
## aDataFrame1.iloc[0::,0]=agesFloat

# NOT THIS ONE: aDataFrame1[[0]] is "dataframe"
## aDataFrame1[[0]]=agesFloat

#%% Now this works:
sum(aDataFrame1['ages'])
```

The command `info()` in Python will work in the same way as `str()` in R, but it also provides extra information on the amount of memory the data frame is using. Notice that after I changed the number by a string, pandas informs you that now you have a column of type *object*, not string. As you see, I used the command `type` to show you that only the first value (the one I changed) is a string, while the others are still numbers (float); that is, Python allows you to have a column (also known as *series*) with different types of values (in R everything will become one kind of value). Then, I decide to perform a *defensive cleaning* to make sure every value becomes a number. I also share different ways to access the data in a pandas frame. When you have a `series` or a `data frame`, notice that some operations work in either or both, and you will see that in most examples in the book.

In addition to becoming familiar with these basic features, you will have to learn how to manipulate the contents of a data frame with accuracy. In this book, you will see many examples of data frame manipulation in particular situations. Let me give you a first look at the art of manipulating data frames. Here are two data frames with information about the 10 most visited cities for 2015 and 2013[29]:

---

[29] According to MasterCard's *Global Destination Cities Index*, which can be found at http://newsroom.mastercard.com/digital-press-kits/.

```
          City in2015  region
1       Bangkok  18.24    Asia
2         Dubai  14.26    Asia
3     Hong Kong   8.66    Asia
4      Istanbul  12.56  Europe
5  Kuala Lumpur  11.12    Asia
6        London  18.82  Europe
7      New York  12.27 America
8         Paris  16.06  Europe
9         Seoul  10.35    Asia
10    Singapore  11.88    Asia
```

```
          City in2013  region
1       Bangkok  15.98    Asia
2     Barcelona   8.41  Europe
3         Dubai   9.89    Asia
4     Hong Kong   8.72    Asia
5      Istanbul  10.37  Europe
6  Kuala Lumpur   9.20    Asia
7        London  15.96  Europe
8      New York  11.52 America
9         Paris  13.92  Europe
10    Singapore  11.75    Asia
```

Please write the code to create those data frames, and give the data for 2013 as c13, and c15 for the 2015 data in R and Python. After that, try the following operations:

- **Sorting**: You know how to sort a list, but sorting a data frame is different: you need to indicate which column is to be used to sort and whether the sorting should be in ascending or descending order:

```
# Notice use of brackets and comma at the end!
c15[order(c15$in2015,decreasing = T),]
```

```
          City in2015  region
6        London  18.82  Europe
1       Bangkok  18.24    Asia
8         Paris  16.06  Europe
2         Dubai  14.26    Asia
4      Istanbul  12.56  Europe
7      New York  12.27 America
10    Singapore  11.88    Asia
5  Kuala Lumpur  11.12    Asia
9         Seoul  10.35    Asia
3     Hong Kong   8.66    Asia
```

The above code in R shows that sorting of data frames is done with the command order(), which uses a Boolean argument decreasing; if you do not use the argument, the sorting will be ascending by default. Notice that the data frame is outside the brackets and the order is inside. Another important detail is the "," before the closing bracket. You could also use multiple columns, if you wanted to have multiple sorting:

```
c15[order(c15$region,-c15$in2015),]
          City  in2015    region
7      New York  12.27   America
1       Bangkok  18.24      Asia
2         Dubai  14.26      Asia
10    Singapore  11.88      Asia
5  Kuala Lumpur  11.12      Asia
9         Seoul  10.35      Asia
3     Hong Kong   8.66      Asia
6        London  18.82    Europe
8         Paris  16.06    Europe
4       Istanbul  12.56    Europe
```

The command above did not set decreasing, but used the "-" instead. It instructs R to sort the data frame by region (ascending) and then to sort the cities in each region by the number of visitors (descending). The same outcome in Python can be achieved with this code:

```
toSort=["region", "in2015"]
Order=[True, False]
c15.sort_values(by=toSort, ascending=Order,inplace=False)
```

Notice that in Python, I begin by declaring in a variable toSort which columns will be sorted (order matters), using sort_values. Notice the parameter by needs that list of column names (saved in toSort), and for each variable, the parameter ascending expects that you confirm if each column should be sorted in ascending order (True) or not (False). I create a variable Order that has a list of *logical* values that provide that information to this function. The function sort_values has another parameter, inplace, which is very common in other pandas functions, because it makes the changes immediately in the data frame.[30] Therefore in this case, you will see how the data frame will look after sorting, but the data frame will not be altered. I use some of these values later, so please do not use the examples below if you have not run this code before.

- **Slicing/dicing**: Slicing/dicing are needed to get subsets of data frames. Those operations include simple index selections (positions) or selection based on some criteria, which opens up huge possibilities to query a data frame. To slice/dice, keep in mind this basic pattern for both Python and R:

  * aDataFrame[*rows,columns*]

  However, each package has variations for particular situations. Let's see how to query our data frames:

---

[30] If you set it to False, the original data frame is not changed and you just see the result of the operation.

1. Show me all cities and their regions for 2013 using R:

```
c13[,c("City","region")] ## all rows!
```
```
         City  region
1      Bangkok    Asia
2    Barcelona  Europe
3        Dubai    Asia
4    Hong Kong    Asia
5     Istanbul  Europe
6 Kuala Lumpur    Asia
7       London  Europe
8     New York America
9        Paris  Europe
10   Singapore    Asia
```

Notice the use of c() to request a set of values; this command is very versatile because it allows indexing even when positions are not contiguous or for inverse selection (as shown on page 46).[31] It is important here to verify what information is generated by the query; in general we want to know whether we are getting a data frame or something else:

```
is.data.frame(c13[,c("City","region")])
```
```
[1] TRUE
```
```
#YES, it is:
```

If you know the positions, you can also request:

```
c13[,c(1,3)]
```
```
         City  region
1      Bangkok    Asia
2    Barcelona  Europe
3        Dubai    Asia
4    Hong Kong    Asia
5     Istanbul  Europe
6 Kuala Lumpur    Asia
7       London  Europe
8     New York America
9        Paris  Europe
10   Singapore    Asia
```

And you still have a data frame. But, let's see those query outputs:

```
is.data.frame(c13[,c(1)])
```
```
[1] FALSE
```
```
# OR:
# is.data.frame(c13[,c("City")])
# is.data.frame(c13$City)
```

---

[31] In fact, for data frames, the functionality of c() in R is not found in Python pandas.

You get FALSE because they are vectors. In these cases, you do not even need to use c() because you have one value. But take a look a this code:

```
is.data.frame(c13[c(1)])
```
```
[1] TRUE
```
```
# OR:
# is.data.frame(c13[c("City")])
```

As you see, the simple presence or absence of the "," can give you a different structure (keep this in mind when you see the example on the commands tapply, sapply, and so on, on page 201).

The Python code to replicate the above result is as follows:

```
# subsetting and getting a data frame
c13[[0,2]]
# ".loc" is used to select index labels (rows or columns)
c13.loc[:,['City','region']]
# ".iloc" is used to select positions (rows or columns)
c13.iloc[:,[0,2]]
# This gives you column values as a series
c13.iloc[:,0]
# This gives you column values as a data frame
c13.iloc[[0]]

# Extra examples of sequences (good and bad)
# c13.iloc[:,0:2] # good!
# c13.iloc[:,[0:2]] # bad!
# c13.loc[:,[0:2]] # bad!
# c13[[0:2]] # bad!
```

We are using pandas iloc and loc to access data frames. Please run this code, line by line, to understand the differences:

```
x=c13.copy() # new data frame
x.drop(6,axis=0,inplace=True) # altering it
x.iloc[6,:] # 7th position - it works!
#%% This will not work:
x.loc[6,:] # label 6 in index - it doesn't work!
```

First, I use copy to make a deep copy of a pandas data frame (c13).[32] Then, I delete the seventh row. Notice, the use of the inplace argument, which is an alternative to x=x.drop(6, axis=0).[33] You are using **iloc** because you want the row in the seventh position, which is New York. But if you try to use **loc**, you will get an error, because it is requesting the row whose index label is 6, and that value is not there (I deleted it).

---

[32] So, x=c13 does not create a new data frame.
[33] The use of axis=0 is optional when deleting rows, but you must set it to "1," if you want to delete columns (I return to this later).

2. What was the most visited city in 2015 (in R)?

```
c15[c15$in2015==max(c15$in2015),]$City
```
```
[1] "London"
```
```
#OR:
# c15[which.max(c15$in2015),]$City
```

Here you got the concrete answer, but by omitting $City, you receive the whole row.

Now let's look at the Python version:

```
#What is the most visited city in 2015?
c15[c15["in2015"]==max(c15["in2015"])]["City"]
#c15[c15.in2015==max(c15.in2015)].City
```

Did you see that in Python we did not need to use the comma?

3. What was the least visited city in Europe in 2013 in R?

```
c13[c13$region=='Europe' & c13$in2013==min(c13$in2013),]$City
```
```
[1] "Barcelona"
```
```
# OR:
# c13[c13[3]=='Europe' & c13[2]==min(c13[2]),]$City
```

In the following code, I show an alternative way to answer the same question by making your data set the default for R with the combination of attach and detach; in that way you will not need to write the name of the data frame next to the variables all the time.

```
# ALTERNATIVE:
# attach(c13)
# c13[region=='Europe' & in2013==min(in2013),]$City
# detach(c13)
```

I would recommend doing this only if you work with one data set. When you have multiple data sets, you may have similar names in different data frames, so you want to be sure to which data frame the variables belong. I do not use "attach" in any of my examples.

Let me show you the Python version:

```
#%%#What is the least visited city in Europe in 2013:
criteria1="Europe" ; criteria2=min(c13.in2013)
c13[(c13.region==criteria1)&(c13.in2013==criteria2)].City
```

4. Give me the information of the top three most visited cities in Asia in 2015 in R:

```
# direct way:
head( c15[order(-c15$in2015),]
      [c15[order(-c15$in2015),]$region=="Asia",],3)
```

```
        City in2015 region
1    Bangkok  18.24   Asia
2      Dubai  14.26   Asia
10 Singapore  11.88   Asia
```

Some of you may like the code above, but it is safer to build code in steps so you are sure where to make changes in case you are not getting a correct result. A step-by-step approach could be as follows:

```
# ordering
temp1=c15[order(-c15$in2015), ]
# dicing
temp2=temp1[temp1$region=="Asia",]
# slicing top
answer=head(temp2,3)
answer
```

```
        City in2015 region
1    Bangkok  18.24   Asia
2      Dubai  14.26   Asia
10 Singapore  11.88   Asia
```

```
# rownames(temp2)=NULL to reset row names
```

The answer is correct, but of course, as you can see, the indexes are not sequential, because they are "inherited" from the original data frame ("c15"), so answer[3,] is the same as writing answer["10",]. I add a comment to the last line, which gives the optional command to reset the label of the indexes using NULL; sometimes this command is useful. The most important thing to notice is that in all of the previous queries in R, I **did not** "save" my results, but just showed them. The code above also shows the use of intermediate objects to save intermediate results (temp1, etc.). Remember that = or <- assigns a result to the object to the left. This assignment can create a new object (or replace it, if you use a previous object). Notice that you can use ": " to slice a sequence of values, but keep in mind the flexibility of using c() to slice. More on that in the next examples. Now let me use Python to answer the same question:

```
#%% top 3 most visited cities in Asia in 2015:
temp1=c15.sort_values(by=['in2015'],ascending=[False])
temp2=temp1[temp1["region"]=="Asia"]
answer=temp2.iloc[[0,1,2],] # NOT: temp2.loc[[0,1,2],]
#or
answer=temp2.iloc[:3,] # NOT answer=temp2.loc[:3,]
answer
# reset the index with:
# answer.reset_index(drop=True)
```

Notice that following sort_values I am giving just a list of one element to the parameter by; this is the only column by which I want the data frame to be sorted. The parameter ascending also receives a list of one element. There will be a different implementation in the next example of Python code.

5. Give me the most and least visited city in Asia in 2013 (in R):

```
# Ordering:
temp=c13[order(-c13$in2013),]
# Dicing:
temp=temp[temp$region=="Asia",]
# Slicing
answerA=temp[c(1,nrow(temp)),]    #smart way to get last row!
answerA
```

	City	in2013	region
1	Bangkok	15.98	Asia
4	Hong Kong	8.72	Asia

Notice this time I use only one temp variable because I am rewriting its contents several times.[34] Notice the "smart" way to get the first and the last city; this is very important if you do not know what the last position is.

Here is the Python code for this question:

```
#%% The most and least visited city in Asia in 2013
# Ordering:
temp=c13.sort_values(by="in2013", ascending=False)
# Dicing:
temp=temp[temp.region=="Asia"]
# Slicing
answerA=temp.iloc[[0,len(temp)-1],]  # smart way for last
answer
```

Now, see that the parameters by and ascending in sort_values have no lists. So when there is just one element, you can simply avoid using lists.

6. Give me the cities in between the most and least visited in Asia in 2013 (in R):

```
# Ordering:
temp=c13[order(-c13$in2013),]
# Dicing:
temp=temp[temp$region=="Asia",]
# Slicing (either works!)
answerB=temp[2:(nrow(temp)-1),]   #direct selection
answerB=temp[-c(1,nrow(temp)),]   #inverse selection
answerB
```

	City	in2013	region
10	Singapore	11.75	Asia

---

[34] I should also be using less memory, which is irrelevant in this case, because it is a simple operation, but could be important in other cases.

```
| 3          Dubai    9.89    Asia
| 6   Kuala Lumpur    9.20    Asia
```

As you see, this is another example of inverse selection.

The Python code for this question shows you two ways of answering it too:

```
#%% Cities between the most and least visited in Asia in 2013:
# Ordering:
temp=c13.sort_values(by="in2013", ascending=False)
# Dicing:
temp=temp[temp.region=="Asia"]
# Slicing
answerB=temp.iloc[1:-1,] # direct selection
answerB=temp[~temp.index.isin(answerA.index)] #inverse selection.
answerB
```

Notice that iloc has the value -1. You can use that value to get the last element. Also notice the inverse selection, which is done is using answerA, the output of the previous exercise in the function isin. What this line says is "not to select the indexes in temp that are in the indexes of answerA." As you see, using .index can provide the indexes of that data frame in pandas.

7. Give me the top two most and two least visited cities in Asia in 2015 (in R):

```
# Ordering:
temp=c15[order(-c15$in2015),]
# Dicing:
temp=temp[temp$region=="Asia",]
# Slicing
answer=rbind(head(temp,2), tail(temp,2))
answer
```

```
       City  in2015  region
1   Bangkok   18.24    Asia
2     Dubai   14.26    Asia
9     Seoul   10.35    Asia
| 3 Hong Kong   8.66    Asia
```

This example shows again the use of the basic functions head() and tail() and how they can be connected with rbind() (order matters!).

I use a similar approach in Python:

```
#%%The top 2 most and least visited cities in Asia in 2015:
temp=c15.sort_values(by="in2015", ascending=False)
temp=temp[temp.region=="Asia"]
answer=temp.iloc[:2,].append(temp.iloc[-2:,])
answer
```

Here I have appended (added) a data frame to another one, like we did before with lists. The most interesting here is the [-2:,] slice, which is how you can easily get the last two elements. In general Python slices have the form:

[start:end:increment]

The increment by default is one, so `[-2:,]` represents the indexes `-2` and `-1` (the last two).

- *Merging*: This operation is used when there are two data frames. The order of writing the data frames matters, becauase the first one written is **x** and the second **y** in R; or **right** and **left** in Python, respectively. Merging can be done if the data frames share at least one column (the "key"[35]). The titles of the columns do not need to be the same; what matters is that contents are the same.[36]

  The code in R for merging is:

```
merge(c13,c15)
```
```
            City    region  in2013  in2015
1        Bangkok      Asia   15.98   18.24
2          Dubai      Asia    9.89   14.26
3      Hong Kong      Asia    8.72    8.66
4       Istanbul    Europe   10.37   12.56
5  Kuala Lumpur      Asia    9.20   11.12
6         London    Europe   15.96   18.82
7       New York   America   11.52   12.27
8          Paris    Europe   13.92   16.06
9      Singapore      Asia   11.75   11.88
```

The above code shows you only the common rows and columns (the default). Notice R detects the common columns, which are two in this case: "city" and "region" are (present in both data frames.

The alternative in Python is:

```
#%% Merging
from pandas import merge

merge(c13,c15,how="inner")
```

I do not need to add the parameter how, because even without it Python does what R did. However, this parameter gives this merge more flexibility.

The following code in R shows all the common columns, as well as all the rows of the second data frame (y). Notice the missing value (NA) in the column of the first data frame where a city from the second data frame is not present.

---

[35] This is not related to the key concept in dictionaries.
[36] If they are not exactly the same – that is, if one column has more rows – different results can be obtained, as shown later in this section.

```
merge(c13,c15,all.y=T)
```

```
        City   region in2013 in2015
1       Bangkok    Asia  15.98  18.24
2        Dubai     Asia   9.89  14.26
3    Hong Kong     Asia   8.72   8.66
4     Istanbul   Europe  10.37  12.56
5 Kuala Lumpur    Asia   9.20  11.12
6       London   Europe  15.96  18.82
7     New York  America  11.52  12.27
8        Paris   Europe  13.92  16.06
9        Seoul    Asia     NA  10.35
10   Singapore    Asia  11.75  11.88
```

The alternative in Python is:

```
merge(c13,c15,how="right")
```

Next, I show in R all the common columns and also all the rows of the first data frame (x) (notice the missing values):

```
merge(c13,c15,all.x=T)
```

```
         City   region in2013 in2015
1       Bangkok    Asia  15.98  18.24
2     Barcelona  Europe   8.41     NA
3        Dubai     Asia   9.89  14.26
4    Hong Kong     Asia   8.72   8.66
5     Istanbul   Europe  10.37  12.56
6  Kuala Lumpur   Asia   9.20  11.12
7       London   Europe  15.96  18.82
8     New York  America  11.52  12.27
9        Paris   Europe  13.92  16.06
10   Singapore    Asia  11.75  11.88
```

The Python code for that is

```
merge(c13,c15,how="left")
```

The following code shows all the common columns, as well as all the rows of the data frames that do not match values in both data frames (notice the missing values):

```
merge(c13,c15,all.x=T,all.y=T)
```

```
         City   region in2013 in2015
1       Bangkok    Asia  15.98  18.24
2     Barcelona  Europe   8.41     NA
3        Dubai     Asia   9.89  14.26
4    Hong Kong     Asia   8.72   8.66
5     Istanbul   Europe  10.37  12.56
6  Kuala Lumpur   Asia   9.20  11.12
7       London   Europe  15.96  18.82
8     New York  America  11.52  12.27
9        Paris   Europe  13.92  16.06
```

```
| 10        Seoul      Asia        NA   10.35
| 11        Singapore  Asia     11.75   11.88
```

In Python, here is the code:

```
merge(c13,c15,how="outer")
```

Be careful with the next code, which does not allow R to identify the common columns. In that case, notice that the region is duplicated with altered names (one for each data frame):

```
merge(c13,c15,by="City",all.x=T,all.y=T)
```

```
|               City  in2013  region.x  in2015  region.y
| 1          Bangkok   15.98      Asia   18.24      Asia
| 2         Barcelona   8.41    Europe      NA     <NA>
| 3            Dubai    9.89      Asia   14.26      Asia
| 4        Hong Kong    8.72      Asia    8.66      Asia
| 5          Istanbul  10.37    Europe   12.56    Europe
| 6     Kuala Lumpur    9.20      Asia   11.12      Asia
| 7           London   15.96    Europe   18.82    Europe
| 8         New York   11.52   America   12.27   America
| 9            Paris   13.92    Europe   16.06    Europe
| 10           Seoul      NA     <NA>   10.35      Asia
| 11       Singapore   11.75      Asia   11.88      Asia
```

In Python, the code is as follows:

```
merge(c13,c15,on="City",how="outer")
```

- *Applying functions*: Make sure to apply a function to the right type of value and structure. In the next examples I use a shorter version of the merging of both files:

```
|               City   region  in2013  in2015
| 1            Dubai     Asia    9.89   14.26
| 2        Hong Kong     Asia    8.72    8.66
| 3          Istanbul  Europe   10.37   12.56
| 4     Kuala Lumpur     Asia    9.20   11.12
| 5           London   Europe   15.96   18.82
| 6         New York  America   11.52   12.27
```

In this example, I first use a code in R where I apply a function to a dimension of the data frame; in this case the number "2" means *vertically*. So, by summing the two columns (third and fourth) with the number of visitors, you will get two results, one for each column (you will need to set na.rm (remove missing values) as true, otherwise the function sum() will try to add NA to the other values, and you will get an NA as result). The parameter of the function is optional na.rm in some cases (but not in this one, if you want the sum of the non-missing values):

```
#'apply' works like this:
#apply(dataframe, dimension, function, function parameter)

apply(c13c15[c(3,4)], 2,sum, na.rm = T)
```
```
in2013 in2015
65.66  77.69
```

You can get the same results with this code in Python:

```
#%%APPLYING functions:
#Use axis=0 to apply a method vertically
c13c15[[1,3]].apply(sum,axis=0)
# ALTERNATIVE!
# c13c15[[1,3]].sum(axis=0)
```

Next, I request in R the same operation but applied *horizontally*. This will produce an additional column with the sum of both years for every city.

```
apply(c13c15[c(3,4)], 1,sum, na.rm = T)
```

The Python version is:

```
#Use axis=1 to apply a method horizontally
c13c15[[1,3]].apply(sum,axis=1)
```

In fact, you can use the R code above to create a new column, named "sum1315" in this case:

```
c13c15$sum1315=apply(c13c15[c(3,4)], 1,sum, na.rm = T)
c13c15
```
```
            City  region in2013 in2015 sum1315
1          Dubai    Asia   9.89  14.26   24.15
2      Hong Kong    Asia   8.72   8.66   17.38
3       Istanbul  Europe  10.37  12.56   22.93
4   Kuala Lumpur    Asia   9.20  11.12   20.32
5         London  Europe  15.96  18.82   34.78
6       New York America  11.52  12.27   23.79
```

You can get the same in Python like this:

```
c13c15["sum1315"]=c13c15[[1,3]].apply(sum,axis=1)
#this works too:
#c13c15["sum1315"]=c13c15[[1,3]].sum(axis=1)
```

Pay close attention to the next two examples, in which the data frame has a new column. The R command **lapply**() maps a function to the columns of the data frame, so you do not need to write a dimension. The code below works as **apply** with dimension 2, as expected:

```
#lapply(dataframe,function,function parameter)
lapply(c13c15[c(3,4)], sum, na.rm = T)
```

```
$in2013
[1] 65.66

$in2015
[1] 77.69
```

However, it does not work when you want to map a function that cannot give a total result. For example, `toupper`, which transforms a string to its uppercase version in R, cannot produce a simple result for a column, Instead of giving an error, it will be applied to each value:

```
lapply(c13c15[c(1,2)], toupper)
```

So, if you want to change the look of those strings in the data frame, you can write this in R as follows:

```
c13c15[c(1,2)]=lapply(c13c15[c(1,2)], toupper)
c13c15
```

```
          City  region in2013 in2015 sum1315
1        DUBAI    ASIA   9.89  14.26   24.15
2   HONG KONG    ASIA   8.72   8.66   17.38
3     ISTANBUL  EUROPE  10.37  12.56   22.93
4 KUALA LUMPUR    ASIA   9.20  11.12   20.32
5       LONDON  EUROPE  15.96  18.82   34.78
6     NEW YORK AMERICA  11.52  12.27   23.79
```

If you replace `lapply` for `sapply` in R, you will get the same result but in a different data structure. When you use `lapply` you get a list, whereas `sapply` will give you vectors. In the code above, you will see no difference, because either result will replace the columns requested, but keep in mind the difference.

You should also be careful in this situation with Python. It is easy to get a result, but problems arise when you do not get results the way you need them (in the right structure) or when a function that works for one structure does not work for another. For example, these codes are very similar, and they are applied to the same data frame, but the slicing can give you either a series or a data frame:

```
#%% same result but not the same structure:
#type(c13c15.iloc[:,0])       # series
#type(c13c15.City)            # series
#type(c13c15['City'])         # series
#type(c13c15.iloc[:,[0,2]])   # data frame
#type(c13c15[[0]])            # data frame
#type(c13c15[['City']])       # data frame
```

Then, when applying uppercase as we did in R, we need to be careful if we want to use the str.upper function in Python. This function works with series, but this code will NOT work in Python:

```
c13c15[['City']].apply(str.upper)
```

But this code will (with a little problem!):

```
c13c15['City'].apply(str.upper)
```

The problem is that from what we have just seen, we cannot convert the two columns at once as we did in R, because two columns (i.e., a series) will make a data frame, which an str.upper will break. Fortunately, pandas has the function applymap() that will apply the function to a data frame, element by element, like this in Python:

```
#%% works for a data frame, what we need!
c13c15[[0,2]].applymap(str.upper)

#%% so altering both columns
c13c15[[0,2]]=c13c15[[0,2]].applymap(str.upper)
```

As you see, Python and R are very powerful and versatile. I will use most of these features in the examples of the book, and some new properties and functions will be explained as needed.

3.3 Functions and Control of Execution

Both R and Python let you create your own functions and allow for lots of flexibility when programming with control of execution. A **function** does not need to be a particular mathematical representation; it also can be a procedure you will be using many times, and so it will be convenient to create a function for that. Functions also help increase the readability of the code. **Control of execution** is a key concept in programming, so learning how it works is the first step in becoming an effective user of R and/or Python.

3.3.1 Controlling the Execution

We are going to quickly review three important concepts here:

- Conditional execution: This is used when a section of your code can be executed only if a particular condition is met.

- Loops: They are used when you need to repeat a section of your code several times, while making sure you know how many times those repetitions occur (making sure they do not repeat indefinitely).
- Error handling. This allows your code to anticipate possible errors during the execution and to instruct what to do in those situations. It is a complex conditional execution, but worth treating separately.

Conditional execution using **if**: This is a key command to *teach* code how to make decisions. A basic example in R is:

```
#Is the age of the tenth case an even number?
if (aDataFrame$ages[10]%% 2 == 0) #clause between parentheses
  { # code affected by if between braces
  print ('it is even')
}
```

```
| [1] "it is even"
```

The operator % % tells you the remainder of a division; in this case I want to know if aDataFrame$ages[10] divided by 2 has 0 as the remainder, so I can determine if it is an even or an odd number. Notice the use of == to make that comparison. The if clause needs to be between parentheses.

Conditional execution using **if - else**: Very often, **if** is used in combination with **else**. Let's see how it works in R:

```
#Is the age of the fifth case an even number?
if (aDataFrame$ages[5]%% 2 == 0)
{print ('it is even')
}else {print ('it is odd')} #else next to "}"
```

```
| [1] "it is odd"
```

Notice again that R needs to use *curly braces* to indicate the commands that are under the influence of **if** or **else**. In addition, **else** needs to be next to the closing curly brace of its **if**. We can say that the **if - else** is the general structure, and that the if alone is a simple case of that.

Let's see how we can code this in Python:

```
from ManipulationData import aDataFrame1

#%% Is the age of the FIFTH case an even number?
if aDataFrame1['ages'][4]%2 == 0: # no parentheses, but colon!
    #no curly braces, but 4 spaces (one tabulation)
    print 'it is even'
else: # no parentheses, but colon!
    #no curly braces, but 4 spaces (one tabulation)
    print 'it is odd'
```

Because we created the data frame with seeded random values you should have the value 33 in the fifth position; your message should say you got an odd. Notice also that the arithmetic symbol for modulo is % in Python. One important new detail is the use of *four spaces* or tabulation to tell Python what set of commands are under the effect of another instruction. Also notice that the consitional clause does not use parentheses, but only ends with a colon.

LOOPING via **for**: You need to become an expert in the use of this command. It allows you to visit each of the values in our structures to perform a particular action many times. Using for requires that we organize our thoughts. For example, if you want to find out **how many** people are **older than 30** years old in a list, you need to take the following into account:

- The computer is not going to guess your reasoning, so you need to be explicit. If you want to request **how many**, then it means the computer needs to keep count of some events. Make sure the computer is counting those events.
- But the computer cannot be counting forever, so you need to tell the computer when it should stop.
- The computer is in a loop doing something. Make sure the computer is visiting the elements of the data structure (list, data frame) that you need. Sometimes it needs to visit all the elements, and sometimes not.

This is a possible solution in R:

```
# position of the last case:
lastCase=nrow(aDataFrame)
# current situation of the counter:
count = 0
# position starts in 1 and ends in lastCase:
for (position in 1:lastCase)
    # checking if the value of age in THAT position
    # meets condition:
    { if (aDataFrame$ages[position]>30)
        # if condition is met,
        #we add 1 to the current counter value:
        count=count + 1
        # if the condition is not met,
        # we go back to for and get new position.
        # All these commands between curly braces
        #are under control of FOR.
}
# After ''position'' has reached the value in 'lastCase'
# the For loop is abandoned.
count #result:
```

A Python version could be as follows:

```
from ManipulationData import aDataFrame1
#%% Counting
# Position of the last case:
lastCase=len(aDataFrame1)
count = 0

for position in range(lastCase): # colon
    # indentation
    if aDataFrame1['ages'][position]>30:
        # indentation
        count+=1 #incrementing counter in 1
count #result:
```

Notice again that Python requires indentation instead of curly braces.[37] Also, I have used an alternative way to increase the counter (count+=1). Python could also increase the counter the way I did it in R, but the reverse is not true. The use of range in the for clause is very important: The range(X) will give a sequence of discrete values from 0 up to X - 1. Because indexes in Python start in 0, this command makes sure every index is visited.

The for loop is used for more than counting. We can make a program in R to find the height of the oldest in the data frame:

```
# last value ''for'' will visit:
lastCase=nrow(aDataFrame)
# age of the oldest:
maxAge=max(aDataFrame$ages)
for (position in 1:lastCase){
    if (aDataFrame$ages[position]==maxAge){
        # 'position' is changing in the 'for'
        # when we find a 'position' that match the 'maxAge'
        # we assign that value to 'positionOfOldest'
        positionOfOldest=position # this is not the answer!
        break
        # if we found the position, 'break'
        # forces abandoning the 'for'.
    }
}
# this is the height we wanted to find:
heightOfOldest=aDataFrame$heights[positionOfOldest]
# this is the answer:
heightOfOldest
```

```
[1] 6.474155
```

Of course, this last program has a mistake: it assumes there is only one oldest person, when in fact there could be many people at that same age. An improved version could be

---

[37] Graphical interfaces such as Spyder may take care of indentation for basic coding. If there are many nested indentations, you need to be aware of the indentation of particular pieces of code.

```
# last value 'for' will visit:
lastCase=nrow(aDataFrame)
# age of the oldest:
maxAge=max(aDataFrame$ages)
#initializing the vector that will hold the positions
maxAgePositions=vector()
for (position in 1:lastCase){
  if (aDataFrame$ages[position]==maxAge){
    # saving every position that met criteria:
    maxAgePositions= append(maxAgePositions, position)
  }
}
# now, showing the heights of the oldest people:
aDataFrame[maxAgePositions,'heights']
```

```
[1] 6.474155 5.623404 5.367699 5.153382
```

As you see, there were four people who were at the oldest age in the group (the data frame).[38]

The next code in Python also finds cases; in this example I want to find the heights of the youngest people in the data frame:

```
from ManipulationData import aDataFrame1

#%% finding the heights of youngest people in the data frame:
numberOfCases,numberOfVariables=aDataFrame1.shape #unpacking
minAge=min(aDataFrame1['ages'])
minAgePositions=[]

for position in range(numberOfCases):
    if aDataFrame1['ages'][position]==minAge:
        # saving every position that met criteria:
        minAgePositions.append(position)

#%% now, showing the answers:
for position in minAgePositions:
    print aDataFrame1['heights'][position]

#%% now, showing the answers:
for position in minAgePositions:
    print aDataFrame1.iloc[position]
```

In the previous example, I used len() to get the number of rows. Now I use unpacking, a feature not present in R. You can use this if you know beforehand how many elements a structure, a tuple in this case, has. This tuple has two values, so I write to the left of = two variables, numberOfCases, numberOfVariables, to receive the values returned by shape (number of rows and number of columns, in that order).

---

[38] I could also have done this using some combination of R commands designed to make **subsets** of rows from a data frame, but that will come later.

Error Handling.

There are situations in programming when you know you are likely to get errors while running your code, and you want your code to have an adequate response when those appear. Then you need to catch that error and not expect good luck to take care of it. Let me create in R the following difficult situation (see Figure 3.20).

```
> sqrt(100)
[1] 10
> sqrt(-100)
[1] NaN
Warning message:
In sqrt(-100) : NaNs produced
> sqrt('-100')
Error in sqrt("-100") : non-numeric argument to mathematical function
```

Figure 3.20 Some difficult situations in R: Errors and warnings.

Before, when we encountered a situation like the one shown, we just made changes and kept coding. Now the task is different: You want to be sure you catch the error and, as I show here, send an alert (I give more detail on this later). Here is an example to give you a better idea:

```
value=100
tryCatch(
  #part 1: what to do if no problem
  print(sqrt(value)),
  #part 2: what to do if input not right for function
  warning = function(w) {print("Wrong number!")},
  #part 3: what to do if input not understood
  error = function(e) {print("Not even a number!!")}
)
```

```
[1] 10
```

The command **tryCatch** is a powerful one. It has three parts, as the comments show. Whether a *warning* or an *error* is generated depend on the function or command you are using. The difference may sometimes not be very clear. In this case, the square root function sends a warning if you want to input a negative number and an error if it is a text. We know that from Figure 3.20, because the messages you get say so. So let's input a negative value using tryCatch:

```
value=-100
tryCatch(
  print(sqrt(value)),
  warning = function(w) {print("Wrong number!")},
```

```
error = function(e) {print("Not even a number!!")}
)
```

| [1] "Wrong number!"

As we expected, the message in part 2 was sent. Let's input a text now:

```
value="100"
tryCatch(
  print(sqrt(value)),
  warning = function(w) {print("Wrong number!")},
  error = function(e) {print("Not even a number!!")}
  )
```

| [1] "Not even a number!!"

You see we are *catching the errors* the function sqrt is producing, which gives us more power to control our programs. Notice that I am declaring "warning" and "error" as a **function** in R. You will be introduced to functions in the next section, but for now, it is only necessary to understand that if possible errors or warnings are predetermined, the complete code will run swiftly, without aborting. That is, aborting is expected if we do not plan to catch errors.

Python is also very versatile in error handling, but it differs from R in some aspects:

- Python does NOT issue a warning when runing your code. If something wrong is detected it will give an **error**.
- Python informs what **kind** of error has happened. This is extremely important when figuring out how to deal with the error.
- Python does not catch errors via functions, as R does.

Let me replicate the example in Figure 3.20, this time using Python. Please go directly to the console in Spyder, and type the code I show in Figure 3.21.

The first command you need to type to replicate the previous R example is **import math**; Python cannot take the square root without it. Then you want call sqrt from math. I pay attention to the messages you get when you input the negative and the string values. Again, keep in mind that these messages depend on how the person who coded that function wants to let you know you made a particular mistake. When Python gets that message it simply displays it.

You need to keep in mind the errors you got in Figure 3.21. Python is informing that, when you entered a negative, that value is not in the range of the function; it also is telling you that when you entered a string, the function rejected it because it was not a float. Python, in this case, sends messages that are

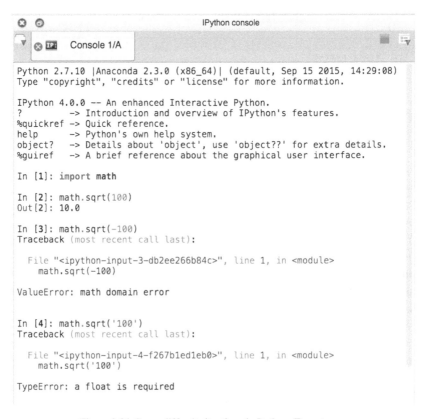

Figure 3.21 Some difficult situations in Python: Error types.

more informative and easier to understand than in R (in Figure 3.20, R is not telling why the negative was rejected). Python gives you a better understanding of what is going on. For example, the sqrt function accepts values of type float, and because the negative is a float it is not a type error, it is a **ValueError**. The value "100" is not a float, so you get a **TypeError**. In addition, Python gives some more information than just the error type. Now, let's catch those errors.

- First let's look at the case that has no problems. Please run this code:

```
#%% Case 1: no problem
from math import sqrt # notice this!
value=100

#part 1: what to do if no problem
try:
    print sqrt(value)
```

```
#part 2: what to do according to error
except ValueError:
    print "Wrong number!"
except TypeError:
    print "Not even a number!!"
```

As shown above, the handling of errors has two main parts: one with **try** and another with **except**. The `try` part will be evaluated if no error occurs. When an error occurs, the `except` part will become active. The type of error will determine what will happen.

- Now write and run this second cell. You will see that the error is handled as expected.

```
#%% Case 2: negative as input
from math import sqrt
value=-100
try:
    print sqrt(value)
except ValueError:
    print "Wrong number!"
except TypeError:
    print "Not even a number!!"
```

- Please write and run this third cell. You will see that the error is handled as expected.

```
#%% Case 3: string for input
from math import sqrt
value='-100'
try:
    print sqrt(value)
except ValueError:
    print "Wrong number!"
except TypeError:
    print "Not even a number!!"
```

Controlling the execution of your code will allow you to write smart code that can tackle many of your problems. However, your basic preparation for the next section of the book is not complete until you know how to write functions, which is coming next.

3.3.2 Building Functions

As mentioned before, when you learn and get used to including functions in your code, it becomes more readable. Building functions also saves time: As you become an experienced user of R or Python, you will be able to abstract some repetitive task and turn it into a function. By combining the basics of control of execution and functions, you will be ready to get the best of Python and R.

Writing a function is very easy in R and Python. If you need a function to convert Fahrenheit into Celsius, I can offer you the following in R:

```
converterToCelsius=function(valueInFarenheit){ #input
   #transformation
   resultInCelsius= (valueInFarenheit-32)*5/9
   #output
   return (resultInCelsius)}
```

You start with the name of the function **converterToCelsius**, and you code it by using the command **function**. A function consists of three parts: *input, transformation*, and *output*. In the code above, the input is `valueInFarenheit`,[39] the transformation consists of a one-line arithmetic operation (you can have several lines):

(valueInFarenheit-32)*5/9,

and the variable `resultInCelsius` is used by the command **return** to give you the output (notice that the output is inside the parentheses). Now R has a new function available (`converterToCelsius`). To use it simply type,

```
converterToCelsius(100) # so 100 is 'valueInFarenheit'
```

```
[1] 37.77778
```

It works the same in Python, but with a different structure:

```
#%% functionBasic 1
def converterToCelsius(valueInFarenheit): #input

    #transformation
    resultInCelsius= (float(valueInFarenheit)-32)*5/9
    #output
    return resultInCelsius

#%%
converterToCelsius(100)
```

In this case, you create a function with the command **def**, which has in parentheses the input values that can be used; after that a colon is needed. The transformation begins in the first indented line. The **return** command is at the same level of the first indented line. Notice that I needed to make sure the input value is treated as a float during the transformation process.

---

[39] The more familiar name for an input is *argument*.

Python also has the **lambda** style function, which could be useful for simple functions (one-line functions):

```
#%%Lambda for converter
toCelsius=lambda f: (float(f)-32)*5/9
# So it works like this
toCelsius(10)
```

Lambda functions are practical as long as they remain simple. If you need more than one line, you should go with the standard way to build a function. However, lambda can handle more complex situations by using some extra commands:

- **map**:

```
#%% map

#function:
toCelsius=lambda f: (float(f)-32)*5/9
# MAP to applies function to each element
FS = [12, 28, 29, 32, 67, 44, 48, 52, 37]

# you can expect the SAME AMOUNT of elements
map(toCelsius, FS)
```

- **filter**:

```
#%% filter

# function:
veryCold=lambda temp: temp < 40
# FILTER uses logical (boolean) functions
# to keep the elements that are TRUE for the function
FS = [12, 28, 29, 32, 67, 44, 48, 52, 37]

# you can expect LESS elements
filter(veryCold, FS)
```

- **reduce**:

```
#%% reduce

#function:
greatestVal=lambda t1,t2: t1 if (t1>t2) else t2

# REDUCE applies function to pairs of elements
# from left to right
FS = [12, 28, 29, 32, 67, 44, 48, 52, 37]

# you can expect ONE element
reduce(greatestVal, FS)
```

The commands to create functions are very versatile in R and Python. This versatility is shown in the following codes:

1. In R:

```
aCalcb=function(val1,val2=2){

    #tranformation
    inputValues=paste(val1,',',val2) #paste to concatenate
    a=val1+val2
    s=val1-val2
    m=val1*val2
    ##'ifelse' is a one line conditional
    d=ifelse(val2!=0,val1/val2,'undefined')

    #return (no 'return' command, then last line is returned)
    ##all the output are organized into data frame
    data.frame(sum=a,sub=s,mul=m,div=d,row.names=inputValues)
}
```

This function will take two inputs and give you as output their addition, subtraction, multiplication, and, possibly, their division results. You may never need to use this function; but, it is a simple one that is an example of the satility that functions should have:

• This function uses more than one input.
• The function has default inputs (val2=2). So, if you give the function only one input (val1), the function always assumes val2 is 2; but if you give two inputs, you will change the value of val2.
• The function makes many transformations to val1 and val2 producing several outputs. You can use the data.frame command to return all the outputs.
• The command *return* was not used. Without this command, R will return by default to the last line of code. If we omitted the last line in this case, the function would perform all the arithmetic operations, but only the division result would be returned (the other results are lost).

I also introduced paste to concatenate values, because I want to report the inputs I have as the row name. I also used a new conditional: **ifelse**, which allows me to get a conditional structure in one line. This should be used in very simple conditionals. Then, we can run this command:

```
results=aCalcb(10,-10)
```

And see the results this way:

```
results
           sum  sub   mul  div
10 , -10    0    20  -100  -1
```

Or a specific result in this way:

```
results$div
```
```
[1] -1
```

2. In Python:

```
#%% functionBasic 2
def aCalcb (val1,val2=2):
    #Calling DataFrame from pandas and giving it a nickname
    from pandas import DataFrame as df
    #concatenating needs number coercion into string
    inputValues=[str(val1) +','+ str(val2)]
    a=val1+val2
    s=val1-val2
    m=val1*val2
    #The 'if...else' one-line conditional in Python
    d= val1/val2 if val2!=0 else 'undefined'
    #all the output are organized into a dictionary
    sol={'add':a,'sub':s,'mul':m,'div':d}
    #input and output organized into a tuple
    return df(sol,index=inputValues)
```

The cell shown above does the same thing as the last code section in R. However, some remarks are important:

- The function starts by calling just one command from pandas, which avoids loading other functions from pandas if they are not needed. I give this command, DataFrame, a nickname, df. When I do this, I no longer need to write **pandas.DataFrame**, only **df**.
- For my results to be recovered as they were in R (where I used a data frame), I need to use a dictionary here.
- The **return** command cannot be omitted.

The followimg chapters, use everything that you learned in this chapter. However, I also introduce more commands and techniques where needed. Please keep in mind that there may be many alternative ways to do things when using R and Python. However, as you may have noticed, I am trying to be as explicit as possible. If my options are (i) to code in very few lines, while losing readability or (ii) to code using many more lines than in the previous case, while gaining readability, I will always choose the second option for sure.

PART TWO

COLLECTING AND CLEANING DATA

4

Collecting Data

This section describes how to use R and Python to help you with the second step of the roadmap in Section 1.1 on page 4. You are taking this step because you need to get some data.[1] However, this step assumes that you already have defined a problem you want to understand better, have laid out some hypotheses, and have identified relevant data sources, as discussed in Section 1.1; those tasks drew more on your critical thinking skills than your computational skills.

So, now you are in a situation where you know what data to collect and from where. The source can be a webpage or a file to be downloaded. Most of the time you will get files, so make sure you understand exactly what each variable means and how the values are represented in the file. This requires that you read the documentation of the data file, paying particular attention to the methodology used to collect the data.

4.1 Knowing Where Your Files Are

None of the examples in the previous chapters imported a data file, but for the rest of the book, we will only work with real data files. I recommend that from now on, you keep all your files in **Dropbox**,[2] as I suggested in Section 2.3 on page 22. The data for this book is in a folder named **BookData**, and you can use this shortened link to download it: https://goo.gl/Czi3Vh. The screen will look similar to Figure 4.1.

---

[1] Data may be collected in many different ways. Survey specialists struggle to develop adequate collection techniques to understand what is going on in society. Important examples of such works are the World Value Survey (http://www.worldvaluessurvey.org/), the General Social Survey (http://www3.norc.org/GSS+Website/), and the American National Election Studies (http://www.electionstudies.org/). This chapter does not deal with survey techniques.

[2] You are free to use an alternative repository, as long as you make the changes to the code I offer using Dropbox.

85

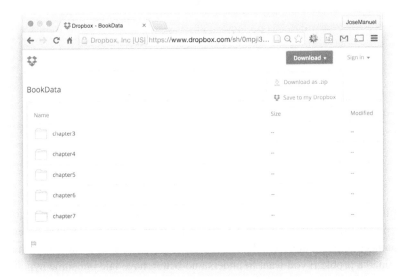

Figure 4.1 Data folder in DropBox.

If you have installed Dropbox in your machine, you only need to select the option Save to my Dropbox, which will appear after you press the Download button in the right upper corner, as also shown in Figure 4.1. I strongly recommend placing the "BookData" folder in the Dropbox *root* folder (I assume you have done so in my examples). If you do not want Dropbox, just go for the option Download as .zip and then unzip the folder in the root of your computer.[3]

Next, tell RStudio that you want to be in the "chapter4" folder and that you also want all your code to be saved there. It takes two steps to do that:

- To ensure you are actually in the "chapter4" folder (or any folder you want) take a look at Figure 4.2, which shows your destination. Click on the series of dots (where the arrow is pointing to) to find this chapter.
- To actually have your code and any extra output be saved in this folder, you need to set this folder as the RStudio *default* location, which requires that you select the option More, which you can see in the upper menu of Figure 4.2 (see the arrow). Then select the option, *Set As Working Directory*. After selecting that option, you will see this message on the RStudio console:

---

[3] Use this option only if you are experienced dealing with file locations.

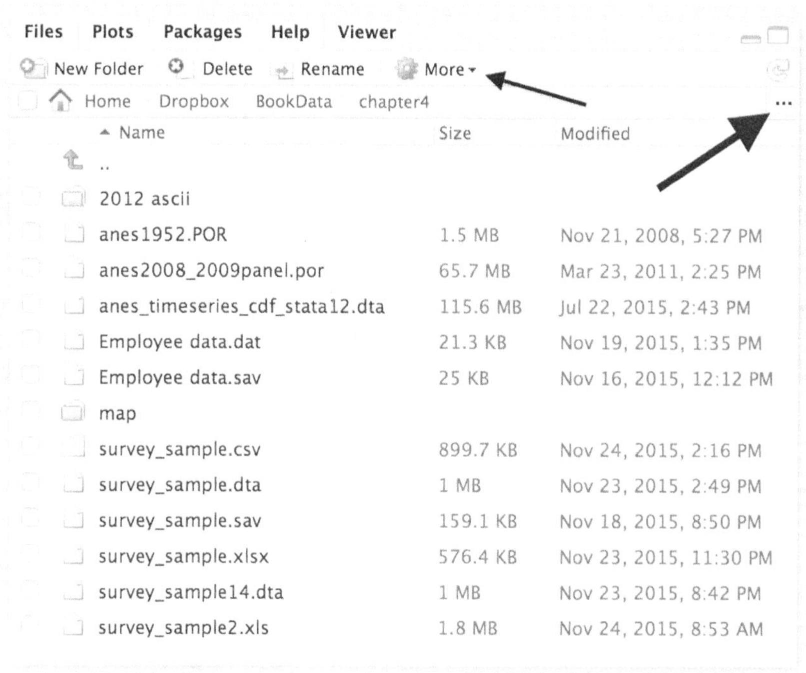

Figure 4.2 Configuring RStudio to access the data. This is how it looks on a Mac.

setwd("~/Dropbox/BookData/chapter4"). This is the command you would have had to write if you had not used the More option in RStudio; when you selected that option, RStudio "typed" that instruction for you. This confirms that "chapter4" is now your working directory and also reveals the *path* to that folder (not to the file). Remember that the results shown here are from my console; yours should be similar but not the same.

It is important to realize that knowing the path and setting a folder as the working directory are related but are not the same task. It is easy to set the working directory in RStudio, but that means you have direct access only to the data files in that folder. If you needed to get access to a file in another folder you cannot access it without knowing the actual path to that folder. To find that path, R has the command file.path, which looks in my codes like this:

```
folderData=file.path("~","Dropbox","BookData","chapter4")
```

Having to know the path to each folder is not commonly required in other software (i.e., SPSS, STATA) where you just open files from their menus. But

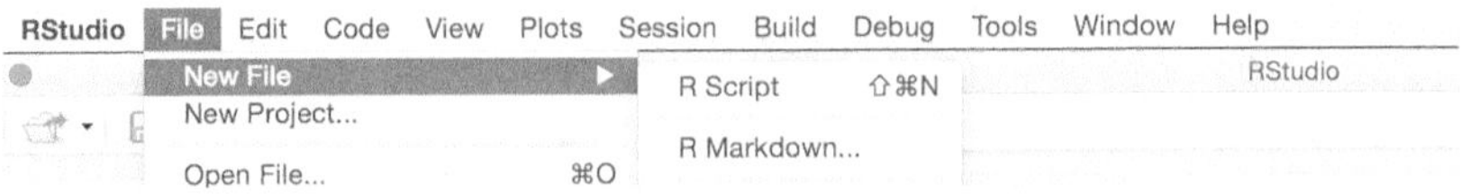

Figure 4.3 Creating a new script in RStudio.

in R (and Python) you need to actually write the path to a file that is not in your working directory. Let me share a trick to make it easier:

- Create a new *R Script* by going to the RStudio option `File` in the upper main menu. See Figure 4.3 for how to create a new script.
- On the new script, copy and paste the instruction you saw when setting the working directory :

  `setwd("~/Dropbox/BookData/chapter4")`.
- Go to the folder where the file that is not in your current working directory is located. You should use the three dots shown in Figure 4.2 again. Assume you want a file from "chapter3."
- Set that folder as your working directory.
- Copy the command you see and paste it on your empty script. It will be something like:

  `setwd("~/Dropbox/BookData/chapter3")`.
- Transform the `setwd` command into a `file.path` command. In this example, it should be:

  `file.path("~","Dropbox","BookData","chapter3")`.
- Go back to the "chapter4" folder and reset it as the working directory.[4]
- You can save your script now.

You should consider doing the same if you are using Windows. There are not many differences between the Windows and Mac versions, as you can see in Figure 4.4, where the rectangle shows you how the files are organized or located in Windows.

After setting the folder for this chapter as the working directory, my console in RStudio will send me a different *path* now that I am in Windows: `setwd("C:/Users/magajm/Dropbox/BookData/chapter4")` So again, I see the path to that folder, which guides me how to write the path to another folder (like "chapter3") using `file.path`:

`file.path("C","Users","magajm","Dropbox","BookData","chapter3")`

---

[4] In R, you can always find out what your current working directory is by typing `getwd()`. To confirm what your default folder is, it is a good practice to include this command in your script.

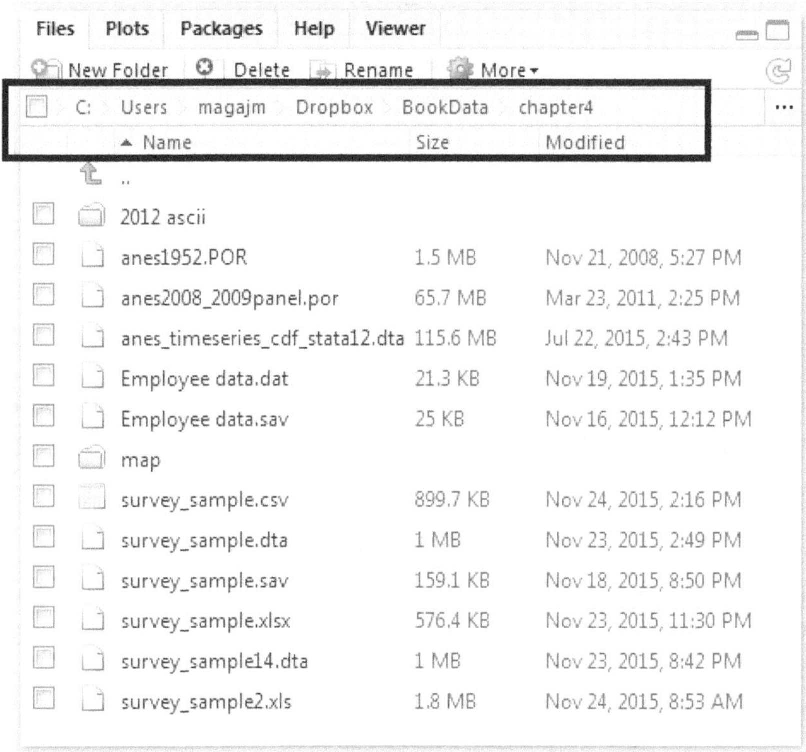

Figure 4.4 Configuring RStudio to access the data. This is how it looks in Windows.

In contrast, in Python, you will always see something like this to write a *path* to a folder:

```
import os
folderData=os.path.join("~","Dropbox","BookData","chapter4")
```

That works exactly as you just saw in R, but with the package **os**. If you want to set a folder as a working directory, you need to use the command os.chdir(). The syntax is similar to this:[5]

```
import os
os.chdir(write here the path)
```

In all cases, you need to confirm your current working directory and where the files you need are. Not knowing this information will create errors when reading or writing

---

[5] In Python, you can always find out what your current working directory is by typing os.getcwd().

	id	gender	bdate	educ	jobcat	salary	salbegin	jobtime	prevexp	minority
1	1	m	02/03/1952	15	3	$57,000	$27,000	98	144	0
2	2	m	05/23/1958	16	1	$40,200	$18,750	98	36	0
3	3	f	07/26/1929	12	1	$21,450	$12,000	98	381	0
4	4	f	04/15/1947	8	1	$21,900	$13,200	98	190	0
5	5	m	02/09/1955	15	1	$45,000	$21,000	98	138	0
6	6	m	08/22/1958	15	1	$32,100	$13,500	98	67	0
7	7	m	04/26/1956	15	1	$36,000	$18,750	98	114	0
8	8	f	05/06/1966	12	1	$21,900	$9,750	98	0	0
9	9	f	01/23/1946	15	1	$27,900	$12,750	98	115	0
10	10	f	02/13/1946	12	1	$24,000	$13,500	98	244	0

Figure 4.5 SPSS data view.

files, and your code will not work until you fix them. It is therefore very important to master this first step. After that, you will be ready to work with the rest of the examples.

4.2 Importing Data Sets

Importing data sets may be the simplest step in data collection. The following subsections describe common data file types in the public policy and social sciences literature.[6]

4.2.1 Importing Files Produced with SPSS

SPSS files are very commonly used by social scientists such as sociologists, anthropologists, and political scientists. Most national and world surveys offer a version of their data in this format. Even if the data is clean (see Chapter 5), in SPSS terms, the importing process may generate some problems. If you have an SPSS file, it can be imported in these ways:

- In R you can use **foreign** created by R Core Team (2015), which is arguably the most extensively used package for SPSS files. Alternatively, packages such as Hmisc and **memisc** by Elff (2015) can also be used.[7]
- In Python, you can rely on *pandas* to work with SPSS files. However, pandas will call R to do the job in an easier way.

The SPSS data shown in Figure 4.5 has information on an organization's personnel, which is in this chapter's folder. You can see it is not different from what you find in a spreadsheet.

---

[6] I omitted some data types that are used less frequently in the literature for social and policy sciences, such as Weka, SAS, and Matlab. However, any of these data files can be converted to CSV file types and then used inside R or Python.

[7] The package haven https://github.com/hadley/haven could also be worth considering for SPSS, STATA, and SAS.

	Name	Type	Width	Decimals	Label	Values	Missing	Columns	Align	Measure	Role
1	id	Numeric	4	0	Employee Code	None	None	4	Right	Scale	Input
2	gender	String	3	0	Gender	{f, Female}...	None	5	Left	Nominal	Input
3	bdate	Date	10	0	Date of Birth	None	None	13	Right	Scale	Input
4	educ	Numeric	2	0	Educational Level (years)	{0, 0 (Missing)}...	0	8	Right	Ordinal	Input
5	jobcat	Numeric	1	0	Employment Category	{0, 0 (Missing)}...	0	8	Right	Nominal	Input
6	salary	Dollar	8	0	Current Salary	{$0, missing}...	$0	8	Right	Scale	Input
7	salbegin	Dollar	8	0	Beginning Salary	{$0, missing}...	$0	8	Right	Scale	Input
8	jobtime	Numeric	2	0	Months since Hire	{0, missing}...	0	8	Right	Scale	Input
9	prevexp	Numeric	6	0	Previous Experience (months)	{0, missing}...	None	8	Right	Scale	Input
10	minority	Numeric	1	0	Minority Classification	{0, No}...	9	8	Right	Nominal	Input

Figure 4.6 SPSS variable view.

However, SPSS also shows the current file metadata, a somewhat sufficient description of the variables in the data set that the creator of the file included (it was not auto-generated). The metadata for the variable in the previous image can be seen in Figure 4.6.

From Figure 4.6, you can know the Type of values you have; and can understand better what the variable Name represents by reading the Label; sometimes the name of a column is not very descriptive (for instance, the name id represents Employee Code). Data can have missing values in some or all variables, and SPSS allows you to customize what values should be treated as missing values (i.e., -9999). The Values field is very important when you have categorical values, because that is where you will identify what the categories are. These previous metadata are very important when importing into R or Python. There are other fields in this view that are good to be aware of, but are not so relevant during the importation process: the designer of the data will have determined the scale of measurement of the variable, whether it should be considered an input or output variable; and the alignment of the column and its width. If you import just the data without paying attention to the information in the metadata, you increase the likelihood of bad computations. If you have SPSS installed, you will be able to compare results with R or Python, but if you do not, you may be working with corrupted data that later will cause trouble in data exploration, modeling, and visualization. Python and R packages or libraries will work to deal with those problems effectively, but may demand more dedication from you. Let's see an example to illustrate how these packages deal with corrupted data.

You should have data file *"Employee Data.sav"* saved in the Dropbox folder "chapter4" for this book. Start the importing process by creating a path to the file:

```
# Tell WHERE the file is using 'file.path'
# 'file.path' works for Windows, Linux, and Mac OS
# 'file.path' does not change your working folder

# path to the folder:
folderData=file.path("~","Dropbox","BookData","chapter4")
# path to the file:
fileSpss=file.path(folderData,"Employee Data.sav")
# notice that we have actually concatenated 'folderData'
# with 'Employee Data.sav'using 'file.path',
```

```
# we could have also written:
# fileSpss=file.path("~","Dropbox","BookData",
#                     "chapter4",'Employee Data.sav')
```

Then, let's get the SPSS file into R using `read.spss` from the package `foreign`:

```
# Calling the library needed
# This library is already installed in R,
# so no need to install it, just activate it:
library(foreign)
# 'fileSpss' is just the path to the file,
# not the file.
# 'testData' will actually be the data from SPSS:
testData = read.spss(fileSpss,to.data.frame = T)
```

When you run the command above, you may get some warnings. Do not worry about them.[8]

It is always a good idea to test if the data is finally in the format expected, in this case a data frame. To do so, use `is.data.frame`:

```
#just confirming!
is.data.frame(testData)
```

```
[1] TRUE
```

We are now sure that we have the data in a data frame. To take a look at it, just use `head(testData)`, and you will get an output like the one in Figure 4.7.

```
  id gender        bdate educ    jobcat salary salbegin jobtime prevexp minority
1  1   Male 11654150400   15   Manager  57000    27000      98     144       No
2  2   Male 11852956800   16   Clerical  40200    18750      98      36       No
3  3 Female 10943337600   12   Clerical  21450    12000      98     381       No
4  4 Female 11502518400    8   Clerical  21900    13200      98     190       No
5  5   Male 11749363200   15   Clerical  45000    21000      98     138       No
6  6   Male 11860819200   15   Clerical  32100    13500      98      67       No
```

Figure 4.7 SPSS data in R.

To work with Python, you also have to be sure you are telling Python where the files are:

```
#%% Tell WHERE the file is:
import os
folderData=os.path.join("~","Dropbox","BookData","chapter4")
fileSpss=os.path.join(folderData,"Employee Data.sav")
```

---

[8] The **foreign** package works well, but it gives a warning that the file has some information it does not understand. There are other packages that work without any warnings (but you need to install them).

The Python community does have a library to deal with SPSS files, which is named savReaderWriter[9]; however, its installation requires many detailed steps. Therefore, it is safer to call R from pandas. Calling R from Python requires that you install the library **RPy2**; for that you need to use again **PIP**.[10]

Once RPy2 is installed, run this cell code:

```
#%% Importing from R into pandas as a data frame
from rpy2.robjects import pandas2ri
from rpy2.robjects.packages import importr
foreign=importr("foreign") # this is an R library
# Using "foreign" almost as in R:
testData=foreign.read_spss(fileSpss, to_data_frame=True,
                           use_value_labels=True)
pandas2ri.activate() #activating pandas conversion
testData=pandas2ri.ri2py(testData)
```

As in R, by typing `testData.head()` in Python, you will see the same information shown in Figure 4.7.[11] Also, notice that both R and Python do not give you the metadata in a simple way. In R it is easier to recover the metadata with `attributes`:

- For all the data sets:

```
attributes(testData)$variable.labels
```

```
                         id                         gender
            "Employee Code"                       "Gender"
                      bdate                           educ
            "Date of Birth"    "Educational Level (years)"
                     jobcat                         salary
      "Employment Category"               "Current Salary"
                   salbegin                        jobtime
          "Beginning Salary"            "Months since Hire"
                    prevexp                       minority
"Previous Experience (months)"     "Minority Classification"
```

- For one variable:

```
attributes(testData)$variable.labels[["bdate"]]
```

```
[1] "Date of Birth"
```

A SPSS file could also come in a format different from the common **.sav**, as you can see in Figure 4.8. It shows a page from the American National Election Studies (ANES), where two other SPSS extensions can be found. One is the *portable* SPSS (**.por**), and the other is the fixed-width file (**.txt**), which includes some SPSS syntax files (**.sps**). In R, **memisc** offers functionality for these particular formats:

---

[9] http://pythonhosted.org/savReaderWriter/.
[10] From your environment, type in the terminal: pip install rpy2.
[11] Installing rpy2 in Windows is more complicated, and requires several steps. An explanation on how to do it is found in the webpage of rpy2 or visit this link (if it is still available): http://eurekastatistics.com/installing-rpy2.

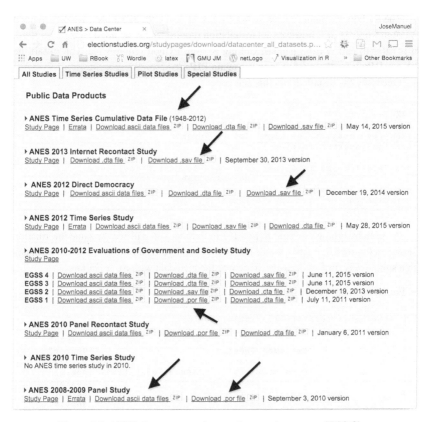

Figure 4.8 ANES data center webpage. Arrows show some SPSS files.

- **Working with a portable SPSS file**: Let's visit the ANES website and download one
  of these files.[12] This will require a free and simple signup at their Data Center link.[13]
  After that, you will have access to all their data files, as shown in Figure 4.8. For this
  example, download the *ANES 2008 2009 Panel Study*. The portable file will download
  in a zip folder. You should have that file in the folder where the data for this chapter
  is available.

  The following code will get you a data frame:

```
library(memisc)
folder=file.path("~","Dropbox","BookData","chapter4")
fileSpssPor=file.path(folder,"anes2008_2009panel.por")
fileSpssImporter = spss.portable.file(fileSpssPor)
```

---

[12] ANES (http://www.electionstudies.org/) is useful to study public opinion and political
behavior. I only show here how to collect the data, but their data follows a complex design and
its analysis requires specialized techniques, as explained in DeBell (2010).

[13] http://electionstudies.org/studypages/download/datacenter_all_NoData.php.

```
# fileSpssImporter is an "importer"
# we need to transform it into a data frame:
SpssDF=as.data.frame(data.set(fileSpssImporter[])) #getting all!
# Selecting some variables. This file has 4318 variables.
is.data.frame(SpssDF[40:42])
```

```
[1] TRUE
```

The memisc package only gives you an *importer* (fileSPSSImporter); that is, the complete data set is not in R memory yet. Only when you transform it into a data frame will it be in R memory. Notice that I am using empty square brackets for slicing, but in this case I request all the rows and columns (you could request a subset). If you do not use this slicing process, the data frame will not be produced.

- **Working with fixed-width data**: The same website also offers ASCII files. Let's download the 2012 ASCII from Figure 4.8, which gives you a zip file again. The files you need are available in our chapter folder (see Figure 4.9).

Figure 4.9 Fixed-width file folder. Notice the .sps files, where there are commands for SPSS. You will use those commands in R.

The folder in Figure 4.9 has a .txt file (this is where the fixed-width data is[14]) and other .sps files containing codes to build the fixed-width data into an SPSS format. The next R code is in charge of that:

```
#library(memisc) # you may not need to call this again.

#notice the path has a new folder
folder=file.path("~","Dropbox","BookData",
                 "chapter4","2012 ascii")
# the data are here:
dataOnly="anes_timeseries_2012_rawdata.txt"
fileTXT=file.path(folder,dataOnly)
# info about the columns
infoColumns="anes_timeseries_2012_columns.sps"
fileSPScols=file.path(folder,infoColumns)
# info about the names of variables
varNames="anes_timeseries_2012_varlabels.sps"
fileSPSVarLabels=file.path(folder,varNames)
# info about the cell values
```

[14] Fixed-width data are useful and very efficient for big files.

```
cellValues="anes_timeseries_2012_codelabelsassign.sps"
fileSPSAssignLabels=file.path(folder,cellValues)
# info about missing values
missinValuesInfo="anes_timeseries_2012_missingdata.sps"
fileSPSMissing=file.path(folder,missinValuesInfo)
# getting the importer:
fileSPSS = spss.fixed.file(fileTXT,
                    columns.file=fileSPScols,
                    varlab.file=fileSPSVarLabels,
                    codes.file=fileSPSAssignLabels,
                    missval.file=fileSPSMissing)
```

From the importer, you can get the data frame as before:

```
# fileSpss to a data frame:
SpssDF=as.data.frame(data.set(fileSpss[]))
# Just confirming:
is.data.frame(SpssDF)
```

```
[1] TRUE
```

As it is clear, R has ready-to-use tools to collect SPSS files. Collecting SPSS files in Python is beyond the scope of this book because it requires much more effort for a basic Python user. However, a frequently used strategy is to use SPSS to export a file into a more common format that Python could read, like STATA or CSV, and of course, you can import data into R and then create a file from R in a format that Python can use.[15]

4.2.2 Importing STATA Files

STATA is a very important program, commonly used by economists and policy analysts. Like SPSS, STATA has metadata, whose relevance should not be overlooked. If you have STATA installed on your machine, you may not care about metadata in STATA, but if you do not have it installed and you rely only on Python and R to understand what the data are about, you should be very careful. In general, when you open an STATA file using STATA itself, you will find something similar to Figure 4.10.

Figure 4.10 displays the information from a categorical variable (parborn). The name of the variable `parborn` may not tell you much, so STATA offers some metadata. That information could be lost when importing the data, if done carelessly.

In R, using the **foreign** package is always a basic alternative, but if the STATA file is in a version higher than **version 12**, you will NOT be able to read it.[16] I have a file in STATA version 13, which I will read with an other package, named **readstata13**:

---

[15] Or simply keep using `rpy2`.

[16] The package **memisc** can be used for STATA files, but it also does not support version above 12 (please see the help for command `Stata.file` in package `memisc`). A good alternative for a version higher than 13 is the package **haven**.

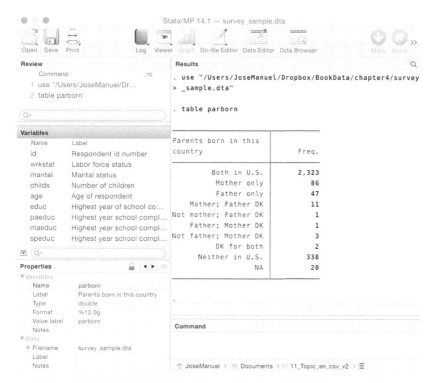

Figure 4.10 File in STATA. Notice that metadata is available in the same window (in this case, you see the details of a categorical variable).

```
folder=file.path("~","Dropbox","BookData","chapter4")
fileStata=file.path(folder,"survey_sample.dta")
# install.packages("readstata13")
library(readstata13)
dataFromStata=read.dta13(fileStata) # get Data Frame
```

In the **foreign** package I use the option to.data.frame with the read.spss command, but read.dta13 by default returns a data frame. Let's see a slice of this one:

```
# Just showing a slice of the data frame:
head(dataFromStata[,11:14])
```

```
  sex race born parborn
1   1    1    1       0
2   2    1    1       0
3   1    1    1       0
4   1    1    1       0
5   2    1    1       8
6   1    1    1       2
```

We can again use **attributes** to display more details on these variables:

```
# You can also use "attr" with different syntax
# attr(dataFromStata, "var.labels")[11:14]
attributes(dataFromStata)$var.labels[11:14]
```

```
[1] "Gender"                        "Race of respondent"
[3] "Born in this country"          "Parents born in this country"
```

The code above works as it does in SPSS, but you need to call the var.labels instead of variable.labels (only for SPSS). The code below uses an alternative command, attr, which enables R to recover some STATA metadata that the **foreign** package did not recover in SPSS:

```
# notice this is "val.labels", not "var.labels".
columnLabel=attr(dataFromStata, "val.labels")[13:14]
attr(dataFromStata, "label.table")[columnLabel]
```

```
$born
NAP Yes  No   DK   NA
 0   1    2    8    9

$parborn
                      NAP         Both in U.S.          Mother only
                       -1                    0                    1
            Father only    Mother; Father DK Not mother; Father DK
                      2                    3                    4
    Father; Mother DK Not father; Mother DK          DK for both
                      5                    6                    7
        Neither in U.S.                   NA
                      8                    9
```

Python is a good alternative for STATA, too. In particular, pandas has a function `read_stata` that retrieves the STATA file as a pandas data frame. The same file used above can be opened using this code cell in Spyder:

```
#%% Tell WHERE the file is:
import os  #package used here to control folder location
folderData=os.path.join("~","Dropbox","BookData","chapter4")
fileSTATA=os.path.join(folderData,"survey_sample.dta")

#%% Importing into Pandas as a data frame
import pandas
dataStata=pandas.read_stata(fileSTATA)
dataStata.iloc[:,10:14].head()
```

This time you will get the results in a data frame, and they will resemble a STATA file, as shown in Figure 4.11.

Pandas version 18 can open version 13 of STATA; if you need to update your version, use Navigator or go to the terminal and type **conda update pandas** (this may

```
       sex   race born            parborn
0     Male  White  Yes     Both in U.S.
1   Female  White  Yes     Both in U.S.
2     Male  White  Yes     Both in U.S.
3     Male  White  Yes     Both in U.S.
4   Female  White  Yes  Neither in U.S.
```

Figure 4.11 Python output for STATA import. Notice the difference from the R import. I ran the code with pandas version 18.

require several updates, and I recommend that you accept when prompted to do so; see Figure 4.12).

Let's now turn to less sophisticated, but very popular, data files.

4.2.3 Importing Data Tables

Large research projects often produce STATA and SPSS data files. However, most of the data you have to manage in everyday situations at work is in your computer as an spreadsheet, like the one shown in Figure 4.13.

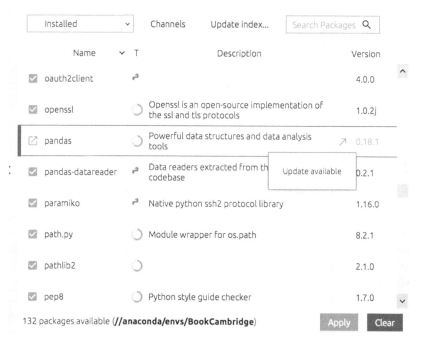

Figure 4.12 Updating from Navigator. Simply click apply, once you have selected the package to update. Notice that Anaconda will need to update several other packages as well.

	A	B	C	D	E	F	G
	Respondent id number	Labor force status	Marital status	Number of children	Age of respondent	Highest year of school completed	Highest year school completed, father
1							
2	1	Working full time	Divorced	2	80	12	12
3	2	Working part-time	Never married	0	27	17	20
4	3	Working full time	Married	2	36	12	12
5	4	Working full time	Never married	0	21	13	NAP
6	5	Working full time	Never married	0	35	16	NAP
7	6	Working full time	Divorced	1	33	16	9
8	7	Working full time	Separated	0	43	12	14
9	8	Working full time	Never married	0	29	13	16
10	9	Working part-time	Married	2	39	18	16
11	10	Working full time	Divorced	0	45	15	16
12	11	Unemployed, laid off	Never married	0	29	12	12
13	12	Working full time	Married	1	41	15	NAP
14	13	Working part-time	Divorced	2	32	14	NAP
15	14	Working full time	Married	1	48	20	12
16	15	Keeping house	Never married	0	20	12	12
17	16	Working full time	Married	5	43	16	6
18	17	Working full time	Divorced	4	27	11	6
19	18	Keeping house	Widowed	7	34	7	DK
20	19	Working full time	Separated	0	43	9	0
21	20	Working full time	Married	1	26	16	16

Figure 4.13 Spreadsheet data in Excel.

The data that you see is all the information you have when you start working; that is, the spreadsheet gives you no metadata. Fortunately, an Excel spreadsheet is very easy to import in R using the **readxl** package:

```
folder=file.path("~","Dropbox","BookData","chapter4")
fileExcel=file.path(folder,"survey_sample.xlsx")
# install.packages("readxl")
library(readxl)
dataFromExcel=read_excel(fileExcel,"data")
is.data.frame(dataFromExcel)
```

```
[1] TRUE
```

```
head(dataFromExcel[13:14])
```

```
  Born in this country Parents born in this country
1                  Yes                 Both in U.S.
2                  Yes                 Both in U.S.
3                  Yes                 Both in U.S.
4                  Yes                 Both in U.S.
5                  Yes              Neither in U.S.
6                  Yes                  Father only
```

Notice that in `read_excel` I have made explicit that I want the table (worksheet) named "data"; if you want another table, you just need to write its name. You can also retrieve the data table using numbers, so you get the tables according to their position. As you may have guessed, you can only open one data table per call. Omitting names will not give an error, but you will only get the first worksheet.

In a similar way, Python can use pandas to call a table:

```
#%% Tell WHERE the file is:
import os

folderData='/Users/JoseManuel/Dropbox/BookData/chapter4'
fileExcel=os.path.join(folderData,"survey_sample.xlsx")
```

```
#%% Importing into pandas as a data frame
import pandas

dataExcel=pandas.read_excel(fileExcel)
dataExcel.iloc[:,12:14].head()
```

Notice that in this Python code I wrote the complete path to the folder, instead of using **path.join**. This is an alternative way of telling Python where files are.

There are other file formats that are very similar to Excel spreadsheets; the most common one is the **CSV format** (*comma; separated value*). In general, CSV has become a de facto format to exchange data among many researchers and analysts. This is mainly because every software has its own proprietary data format but always export or import data in the CSV format. The following code allows you to get a data frame from a CSV data file:

```
folder=file.path("~","Dropbox","BookData","chapter4")
fileCSV=file.path(folder,"survey_sample.csv")
dataFromCSV=read.csv(fileCSV)
is.data.frame(dataFromCSV)
```

```
[1] TRUE
```

```
head(dataFromCSV[13:14])
```

```
  Born.in.this.country Parents.born.in.this.country
1                  Yes                  Both in U.S.
2                  Yes                  Both in U.S.
3                  Yes                  Both in U.S.
4                  Yes                  Both in U.S.
5                  Yes               Neither in U.S.
6                  Yes                   Father only
```

To use **read.csv** you do not need to activate any R package. In fact, this command is a wrapper for the command **read.table**. That is, you can open the same file using **read.table** while adding some parameters to the function, as shown below:

```
fileCSV=file.path(folder,"survey_sample.csv")
dataFromCSV=read.table(fileCSV,header=T,sep=",")
is.data.frame(dataFromCSV)
```

```
[1] TRUE
```

```
head(dataFromCSV[13:14])
```

```
  Born.in.this.country Parents.born.in.this.country
1                  Yes                   Father only
2                  Yes                  Both in U.S.
3                  Yes                  Both in U.S.
4                  Yes                  Both in U.S.
5                  Yes                  Both in U.S.
6                  Yes                  Both in U.S.
```

Python, via pandas, can easily import CSV files too:

```
#%% Tell WHERE the file is:
import os

folderData=os.path.join("~","Dropbox","BookData","chapter4")
fileCSV=os.path.join(folderData,"survey_sample.csv")

#%% Importing into pandas as a data frame
import pandas

dataCSV=pandas.read_csv(fileCSV)
dataCSV.iloc[:,12:14].head()
```

CSV files, in particular, and tabular data, in general, are well supported by most statistical software. However, when you download a CSV file you need to get documentation on the metadata, because standard spreadsheet-like tabular data gives no metadata in the file.

4.2.4 A Comment on PDF Tables

Sometimes, policy analysts receive data tables in PDF reports and wish to carry out more analytic work on the data. This can be done easily by contacting the creator of the report and obtaining the data in an spreadsheet-like format, or if the report itself has a link to get data. If neither of those options are available and if there are many PDF files, you may instead try to use an ad-hoc software program to prepare those files for Python and R (a basic CSV file). R and Python can deal with PDFs, but each table in a PDF can present so many different challenges that it may not be worth making a particular piece of code for each case.[17] Python has many modules that try to deal with PDF files,[18] as well as R (see package tm by Feinerer et al. (2015)); the main strategy is to convert them into an html or XML document and then use a scraping technique. If you can copy and paste the PDF table into an Excel or Google spreadsheet and obtain good results, then just save it as a data table readable in either Python or R. Another option is to use one of the many software programs that promise the capture of PDF tables into Excel or CSV files; however, because most of them are not free, it may be worth looking at the TABULA[19] project that promises the same but without cost.

4.3 Importing Maps from Shapefiles

So far we have learned how to obtain data frames. Now let's get ready to import more complex structures. This last subsection deals with shapefiles, a particular format to

---

[17] There is a standard (ISO 32000-1:2008, rev 2013), but most PDFs created before earlier 2008 do not follow it, and current files may also have incompatibilities.

[18] Visit www.binpress.com/tutorial/manipulating-pdfs-with-python/167 to read a preview by Arnold (2014).

[19] http://tabula.technology/.

represent geographical information via polygons, points, and lines. It is developed and regulated by ESRI and was used in ArcView (currently ArcGIS). A shapefile (**shp**) always comes together with other files (a **.shx**, a **.dbf**, **.prj** and so on - the first two are mandatory). All these files need to be together in the same folder for the .shp file to work properly.

To show how to import these files, I downloaded a world map from the web in a zip folder. After unzipping the folder, I renamed it as "map" and that is where the .shp file and its accompanying files will be. The .shp file is named *TM WORLD BORDERS 0.3*, so all the other files will have the same name but a different file type extension. Let's import this file into R:

```
folder=file.path("~","Dropbox","BookData","chapter4")
SHP=file.path(folder,"map","TM_WORLD_BORDERS-0.3.shp")
# You need to install:
## install.packages("gpclib")
## install.packages("maptools")

library(maptools)
gpclibPermit()
```

```
[1] TRUE
```

```
#importing:
worldmap=readShapeSpatial(SHP)
```

Now you have the shapefile in `worldmap`. Let's look at some of its details:

```
#Detailed Information of some variables
summary(worldmap[5:7])
```

```
Object of class SpatialPolygonsDataFrame
Coordinates:
     min      max
x -180 180.0000
y  -90  83.6236
Is projected: NA
proj4string : [NA]
Data attributes:
                   NAME         AREA              POP2005
<c5>land Islands:    1   Min.    :      0.0   Min.   :0.000e+00
Afghanistan     :    1   1st Qu.:     44.5   1st Qu.:1.275e+05
Albania         :    1   Median :   5515.5   Median :3.086e+06
Algeria         :    1   Mean   :  52696.1   Mean   :2.509e+07
American Samoa  :    1   3rd Qu.:  34708.8   3rd Qu.:1.240e+07
Andorra         :    1   Max.   :1638094.0   Max.   :1.313e+09
(Other)         :  240
```

```
#Just the names of the variables
attributes(worldmap@data)$names[5:7]
```

```
[1] "NAME"    "AREA"    "POP2005"
```

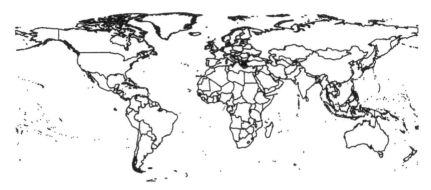

Figure 4.14 Plotting a map in R.
Source: Available at http://thematicmapping.org/downloads/world_borders.php
under a Creative Commons Attribution-Share Alike License.

```
#basic statististics of one variable
# notice the use of '@data$'
summary(worldmap@data$POP2005)
```

```
   Min.   1st Qu.   Median    Mean   3rd Qu.     Max.
0.000e+00 1.275e+05 3.086e+06 2.509e+07 1.240e+07 1.313e+09
```

Of course, in contrast to a basic data frame, this file contains the information needed to produce a map:

```
plot(worldmap)
```

Figure 4.14 is a simple plot of polygons, which represent the countries of the world. A map of the rivers of the world would use a plot of lines instead. Notice I needed to install several packages, **maptools** being the most important. When you install that package, R will ask you to install more packages on the run, which you want to do. The command `gpclibPermit()` is requested by maptools, so I included it in the code. However, it was not needed to run this lines of code, although it would be required to carry out advanced operations. Notice also that the command `summary`, this time, provides more information on the data you just imported. Precisely, it tells you that "worldmap" is a `SpatialPolygonsDataFrame`. Finally, this code enables you to access the attributes of this special data frame.

Let's turn to Python now. This example is going to use **geopandas**, which requires that I first install `conda-forge` – part now of the Anaconda channels (we set that up on page 21). Find conda-forge in the list of NOT installed packages, select it, and install it in our environment for this book.

When you install geopandas, you will see that several other packages will be installed
at the same time. When installtion is complete, the package will work as expected.[20]
Here is how you can use geopandas to read a shapefile:

```
#%% Calls
import os
import geopandas as gp
#%% Location
folder='/Users/JoseManuel/Dropbox/BookData/chapter4/map'
fileSHP=os.path.join(folder,"TM_WORLD_BORDERS-0.3.shp")
world  = gp.GeoDataFrame.from_file(fileSHP)
world.head() # as data frame!
#%% plotting
world.plot(linewidth=1,color='white')
```

As before, the code above will allow you to import the file, explore it as a data
frame, and create a simple plot. However, in both R and Python, we needed to carry
out more installations. As you may have guessed, dealing with shapefiles for R and
Python requires the participation of complex programs.

Here, I have shown how to get a shapefile into R and Python. That is the first step to
creating interesting and easy visualizations using maps. However, even though shapefiles are very common because of their connection to ESRI ArcGis, it is just one among
many map formats. If you are interested in different kinds of maps (i.e., raster) or more
web-friendly formats (for Google Earth's KML, GeoJson, TopoJson, etc.) you should
reviewing the following references: if you want to use R, see Bivand et al. (2013) and
Brunsdon and Comber (2015) or for Python, see Garrard (2016) and Lawhead (2015).

The next sections explore more complex situations where data is not ready as a file
to be downloaded, so we need to interact with webpages to get it.

4.4 Collecting via APIs

Some organizations offer mechanisms to get their data via an API (application programming interface), which is a way to access their data or subsets of data by writing a precise
query as a *URL* (an address on the web). This query must follow the guidelines the organization gives you, so that you need to read the documentation provided to create the
right code in Python or R.

One may need to work with an API when monitoring the history of some data, which
is incremented continually (daily, weekly, etc.). In some cases, you can download that
data, but the API offers you a temporary connection to the most recent data that you
need to capture to produce the reports and plots you need. To work with APIs, some
organizations require you to be a registered user. The ones that require registration

---

[20] As I am writing this book, I heard that for geopandas to work you need to *downgrade* fiona, by
simply typing in your environment console: **conda install fiona=1.1.6**. I did NOT do that, and
everything worked well for me.

```
▼<wb:countries xmlns:wb="http://www.worldbank.org" page="1" pages="4" per_page="10" total="31">
  ▼<wb:country id="AFG">
     <wb:iso2Code>AF</wb:iso2Code>
     <wb:name>Afghanistan</wb:name>
     <wb:region id="SAS">South Asia</wb:region>
     <wb:adminregion id="SAS">South Asia</wb:adminregion>
     <wb:incomeLevel id="LIC">Low income</wb:incomeLevel>
     <wb:lendingType id="IDX">IDA</wb:lendingType>
     <wb:capitalCity>Kabul</wb:capitalCity>
     <wb:longitude>69.1761</wb:longitude>
     <wb:latitude>34.5228</wb:latitude>
  </wb:country>
  ▼<wb:country id="BDI">
     <wb:iso2Code>BI</wb:iso2Code>
     <wb:name>Burundi</wb:name>
     <wb:region id="SSF">Sub-Saharan Africa (all income levels)</wb:region>
     <wb:adminregion id="SSA">Sub-Saharan Africa (developing only)</wb:adminregion>
     <wb:incomeLevel id="LIC">Low income</wb:incomeLevel>
     <wb:lendingType id="IDX">IDA</wb:lendingType>
     <wb:capitalCity>Bujumbura</wb:capitalCity>
     <wb:longitude>29.3639</wb:longitude>
     <wb:latitude>-3.3784</wb:latitude>
  </wb:country>
  ▼<wb:country id="BEN">
```

Figure 4.15 Result of an API search in XML. The browser used is Google Chrome.

often give you a **key** or **token** that you should include in your code to access the API. Let us use World Bank API, which does not require user registration and is well documented.[21] In particulr, the basic guidelines one needs for coding come from the developer's zone webpage.[22] That webpage has instructions for how to write a URL that will allow you to see in the browser the information that you want. For example, to get the names of low-income countries you can type this in your browser:

http://api.worldbank.org/countries?per_page=10&incomeLevel=LIC

That link has two parts, a unit of analysis (`countries`) and the filters. The filters start after the symbol **?**. You can have many filters by using the symbol **&**. This link is asking for 10 country records at a time. Some filters can have default values. As the website informs us, if you omit the filter `per_page`, you will get 50 records per page by default; if you do not specify a format, you will get XML by default too. Writing that URL address in your browser, produces something similar to what is shown in Figure 4.15.

4.4.1 APIs in R: Reading XML

XML is simply a way of storing some data that needs a structure more flexible than a table. A spreadsheet is a data structure where the intersection (row,column) is a cell that can have one value. We can quickly get but into trouble if that intersection needs more

---

[21] See http://data.worldbank.org/node/9.
[22] http://data.worldbank.org/developers/api-overview/basic-call-structure.

than one value. Imagine the intersection (country, language spoken); if a country speaks more than one language, you would consider creating more columns. XML has a way to do that.[23]

It is time to bring that XML data into R, following these steps:

1. Make sure you have a package that can read the data from the API; in this case, you need to install the package **XML** produced by Temple Lang and CRAN Team (2015). Activate that package, as usual.

```
library(XML) # previously: install.packages("XML")
```

2. Use the link to parse the data into R.

```
unit="http://api.worldbank.org/countries"
filters="?per_page=10&incomeLevel=LIC"
query=paste0(unit,filters) # 'paste0' concatenates without spaces
dataXML=xmlParse(query)
```

3. Convert the parsed data in XML (dataXML) into R lists. These are R structures that you know how to manipulate.

```
UNITS=xmlToList(dataXML)
```

UNITS contains several lists of lists.

4. Try to get a basic understanding of the organization of the data you have.

```
summary(UNITS)
```

```
        Length Class  Mode
country 10     -none- list
country 10     -none- list
country 10     -none- list
country 10     -none- list
country 10     -none- list
country 10     -none- list
country 10     -none- list
country 10     -none- list
country 10     -none- list
country 10     -none- list
.attrs  4      -none- character
```

This tells you that you have 11 elements (lists): 10 countries, where each country is also composed of 10 lists, and one list of metadata (.attrs) that is made up by simple strings.

---

[23] XML data bases are part of the **NOSQL** family. For a brief summary, visit http://www
.w3schools.com/xml/xml_whatis.asp.

5. Read and understand the metadata available. The last element you can see when typing UNITS is the metadata. If you want to see it directly, just type:

```
UNITS$.attrs

   page     pages  per_page    total
   "1"       "4"    "10"       "31"
```

This metadata tells you that there are 31 countries for that filter. However, you only have 10. If wanted all 31, you need to change the filter. Simply omit the "per page" filter, which allows you to obtain up to 50 results. If you had more results, say 12,000, you would need to use the filter again, requesting 12,000 per page, or you would need to write a code to read several pages.

6. Show the information you have for each country:

```
options(width=40) # to see result in two columns
names(UNITS[[1]])

[1] "iso2Code"     "name"
[3] "region"       "adminregion"
[5] "incomeLevel"  "lendingType"
[7] "capitalCity"  "longitude"
[9] "latitude"     ".attrs"
```

7. Take a look at the data. Now that you know you have countries as lists of lists, and one list of metada, see how they look. For that simply write UNITS. Figure 4.16 shows you the 10th country.

You knew you have 10 countries as lists and that each country has 10 lists inside, so Figure 4.16 shows in bold typeface each one of those inside lists (iso2Code, name, region, etc.). As you see four lists have subelements (text and .attr), as, for example, region or incomeLevel.

8. Access the field you want in this list:

```
# name of the country?
UNITS[[1]]$name

[1] "Afghanistan"
```

```
# region of the country?
UNITS[[1]]$region$text

[1] "South Asia"
```

Now, we can create our data frame in R:

```
# number of records I have:
nRecords=10
# initializing empty vectors for country names and
# their regions
Names=vector()
```

```
$country
$country$iso2Code
[1] "GN"

$country$name
[1] "Guinea"

$country$region
$country$region$text
[1] "Sub-Saharan Africa (all income levels)"
$country$region$.attrs
 id
"SSF"

$country$adminregion
$country$adminregion$text
[1] "Sub-Saharan Africa (developing only)"
$country$adminregion$.attrs
 id
"SSA"

$country$incomeLevel
$country$incomeLevel$text
[1] "Low income"
$country$incomeLevel$.attrs
 id
"LIC"

$country$lendingType
$country$lendingType$text
[1] "IDA"
$country$lendingType$.attrs
 id
"IDX"

$country$capitalCity
[1] "Conakry"

$country$longitude
[1] "-13.7"

$country$latitude
[1] "9.51667"

$country$.attrs
 id
"GIN"
```

Figure 4.16 A record in parsed XML into R lists. I edited the output text, so each internal list is in bold typeface.

```
Regions=vector()
# Getting each country name, and appending it to the vector
for (i in seq(nRecords)){

  # getting name and region of a country
  thisCountryName=(UNITS[[i]]$name)
  thisCountryRegion=(UNITS[[i]]$region$text)
```

```
# Updating vectors.
# You can use 'append' instead of 'c':
Names=c(Names,thisCountryName)
Regions=c(Regions,thisCountryRegion)
}
# Creating data frame with vectors:
options(width=50) # width of screen
# If you use 'as.data.frame' you will get an error
# as it does not allow duplicate values
# and Region has duplicates.
LowIncomeCountries=data.frame(Names,Regions)
# This data frame has only 10 countries,
# you should try as an exercise to get the 31.
```

4.4.2 APIs in Python: Reading XML

The strategy I shared here is simple: understand how the data in the API query is organized and identify progressively what data structures are present, so you can find out how to retrieve the information you want. I follow the same approach, with some more level of detail, in these Python code cells:

1. Prepare the query to obtain all the data:

```
#%% Building the query:
unit="http://api.worldbank.org/countries"
filters="?per_page=31&incomeLevel=LIC"
query=unit+filters
```

2. Use the query to import the data to your computer from the web:

```
#%% Getting the data using the query
import requests
webpage = requests.get(query)
```

You should have the package **requests** in Anaconda, but if it is not installed in your environment, install it.[24] The command get will fetch the webpage. Now you have the XML you saw in Figure 4.15.

3. Translate the XML into a Python data structure:

```
#%% Parsing the data into a Python dictionary:
import xmltodict
UNITS = xmltodict.parse(webpage.content)
```

You know that there are lists of lists, so you need a good structure that allows you to manipulate keys and values: a Python dictionary is the right choice (choosing other structure increases the risk of losing information). You used that earlier using xmltodict.parse, so please install xmltodict in your environment.[25]

---

[24] If not, go to the terminal and write (always in your environment) pip install requests.

4. Check the keys of the dictionary you produced in the last step:

```
#%% Finding keys of this Data
UNITS.keys()
```

Here you know that you only have one element: **wb:countries**. It should be very complex, because it is storing all the XML data, but in a different format.

5. You need to know what structure the element **wb:countries** has:

```
#%% what is this:
type(UNITS['wb:countries'])
```

It is another dictionary (OrderedDict).

6. Now that you know the type of structure you have, obtain the keys:

```
#%% Finding keys for this internal object:
UNITS['wb:countries'].keys()
```

Here you have keys that offer you the data and the metadata.

7. See the metadata:

```
#%% Inspecting meta data
UNITS['wb:countries']['@page']  #1
UNITS['wb:countries']['@pages']  #4
UNITS['wb:countries']['@per_page']  #10
UNITS['wb:countries']['@total']  #31
```

8. Understand how the data units are organized:

```
#%% What type of element is each country?
type(UNITS['wb:countries']['wb:country'])
```

Each country is a list. To see the first element use:

```
#%% See first element:
UNITS['wb:countries']['wb:country'][0]
```

Then each element of the list should be a dictionary:

```
#%% What is an element of this list:
type(UNITS['wb:countries']['wb:country'][0])
```

In Figure 4.17 you can see the structure and values of this element (country).

---

[25] If you do not find it, type **pip install xmltodict** in the terminal.

```
OrderedDict([(u'@id', u'AFG'),
             (u'wb:iso2Code', u'AF'),
             (u'wb:name', u'Afghanistan'),
             (u'wb:region',
              OrderedDict([(u'@id', u'SAS'), ('#text', u'South Asia')])),
             (u'wb:adminregion',
              OrderedDict([(u'@id', u'SAS'), ('#text', u'South Asia')])),
             (u'wb:incomeLevel',
              OrderedDict([(u'@id', u'LIC'), ('#text', u'Low income')])),
             (u'wb:lendingType',
              OrderedDict([(u'@id', u'IDX'), ('#text', u'IDA')])),
             (u'wb:capitalCity', u'Kabul'),
             (u'wb:longitude', u'69.1761'),
             (u'wb:latitude', u'34.5228')])
```

Figure 4.17 Structure of a country when recovered using the API.

9. Explore the structure of each dictionary in the list:

```
#%% Key of the element of list:
UNITS['wb:countries']['wb:country'][0].keys()
```

Based on the information from Figure 4.17 and the last code, you are now able to get the name and region of the country:

```
#%% Getting the name of that country:
UNITS['wb:countries']['wb:country'][0]['wb:name']

#%% Getting the region of that country:
UNITS['wb:countries']['wb:country'][0]['wb:region']['#text']
```

10. Make a list of the names and regions of all the countries you have. To do that you have two strategies in Python:

- Using a FOR-LOOP, which you are familiar with:

```
#%% List of country names and regions (I): Looping
allUnits=UNITS['wb:countries']['wb:country']
Names=[];Regions=[]
for unit in allUnits:
    Names.append(unit['wb:name'])
    Regions.append(unit['wb:region']['#text'])
```

- Using a list comprehension:

```
#%% List of country names (II): using List comprehension:
Names=[unit['wb:name'] for unit in allUnits]
Regions=[unit['wb:region']['#text'] for unit in allUnits]
```

List comprehension will give you the same list, while saving coding space and speeding up the process (you can only realize the difference in speed if you are processing a big list).

11. Finally, build the data frame:

```
#%% Your data frame in pandas
import pandas
ColumnsAsDict={'NAME':Names, 'REGION':Regions}
LowIncomeCountries= pandas.DataFrame.from_dict(ColumnsAsDict)
```

I could have chosen to get the data using packages that hide all the coding and offer straightforward ways to interact with the World Bank API:

- In Python, you have the package **wbdata**[26] created by Sherouse (2014), and the package **webpy**[27] created by Duck (2013).
- In R, there is a package named **WDI** created by Arel-Bundock (2013).[28]

These packages can facilitate the process of getting information from the World Bank. They have different functions to collect the data you need. However, my purpose in this section was to guide you through the reasoning needed in each situation, so you can apply that in other situations where similar packages are not available.

4.4.3 APIs in R and Python: Reading JSON

When you start working with XML, you can be confident that other NOSQLs (beyond spreadsheet model) formats will be easy to handle too. JSON is an important format of this kind, also known as a *document-oriented data base*. In this section I show you how to import data in JSON from an other API, the one from **Socrata**.

The API from Socrata does not need a key or token for authorization, but it is recommended to get one if you plan to use the data often and professionally. To obtain an authorization key or token, register here: https://opendata.socrata.com/login

Socrata has a video about the registration process and how to get the token: https://dev.socrata.com/blog/2014/10/15/\app-tokens-registrations-developer-spotlight .html

However, in this example I will proceed without a token.

Socrata has open data services for several organizations. In this example, visit the city of Seattle at https://data.seattle.gov/

There, you will be offered several data topics. Please select **public safety**. This link will take you to several data files; one is **Seattle Police Department 911 Incident Response**, which stores "all the Police responses to 9-1-1 calls within the city." Visit that link.

---

[26] Basic documentation is here: https://github.com/oliversherouse/wbdata.
[27] Basic documentation is here: https://github.com/mattduck/wbpy.
[28] Basic documentation is here: https://github.com/vincentarelbundock/WDI.

When you are at the webpage of the 9-1-1 calls, you are offered options to view or download the data, as well as options listed under *others*. One of those options is **API**. Select API, and you will be given some information on using the API. Choose the link to *API Docs*, which provides you all the instructions you will need.

You can read all those instructions if you are really interested. But what you need to know is the *link to the data API*, which is also known as the **endpoint**:

https://data.seattle.gov/resource/pu5n-trf4.json

This link will give you ALL the data that can be shared.[29] Now we can use R to get it:

```
library(jsonlite)
endPoint="https://data.seattle.gov/resource/pu5n-trf4.json"
data911 = fromJSON(endPoint)
names(data911)
```

```
 [1] ":@computed_region_kuhn_3gp2"
 [2] ":@computed_region_q256_3sug"
 [3] "at_scene_time"
 [4] "cad_cdw_id"
 [5] "cad_event_number"
 [6] "census_tract"
 [7] "district_sector"
 [8] "event_clearance_code"
 [9] "event_clearance_date"
[10] "event_clearance_description"
[11] "event_clearance_group"
[12] "event_clearance_subgroup"
[13] "general_offense_number"
[14] "hundred_block_location"
[15] "incident_location"
[16] "initial_type_description"
[17] "initial_type_group"
[18] "initial_type_subgroup"
[19] "latitude"
[20] "longitude"
[21] "zone_beat"
[22] ":@computed_region_2day_rhn5"
[23] ":@computed_region_cyqu_gs94"
```

As you see, we have all the data in an R data frame. In bigger data sets you can filter some rows or request some columns, but you need to prepare queries for that as you did in the World Bank API.[30] And remember that you may want to use the authorization token, which is not present in our current `endPoint`. You can do the same in Python using pandas:

---

[29] Pay attention to the documentation about the data; it will mention some limitations for the sake of ethical or privacy concerns.

[30] You may want to review their guide to filtering: https://dev.socrata.com/docs/filtering.html and queries: https://dev.socrata.com/docs/queries/.

```
import pandas as pd

endPoint = "https://data.seattle.gov/resource/pu5n-trf4.json"
data911 = pd.read_json(endPoint )
```

And again, you have all the data in a pandas data frame.

4.5 Collecting Tabular Data by Scraping

When you have an API, it means the organization that owns the data is offering you a way to collect its data. But when you want to organize some data that some pages offer without an API, you need to start a scraping project. Scraping data is a way to automate data collection instead of having a research assistant spend hours copying and pasting data. However, if the data is in one webpage, it may be wiser not to omit copying and pasting.

In general, when scraping websites, you cannot assume that the data is well structured. APIs may not offer a data table (XML or a similar format is used for that reason), but if the data is nevertheless well structured and organized, you do not need to scrape in that situation. If there is a way to avoid scraping, it is a good idea to consider it. Becoming a good scraper requires becoming familiar with web terminology, such as JSON, HTTPS, CSS, Client-Server, and so on, which is beyond the scope of this section. After completing this section, if you would like to know more about scraping, I recommend reading the book by Munzert (2014) and the work of Danneman and Heimann (2014) for R or the books of Mitchell (2015) and the one from Lawson (2015) for Python.

In this section, I focus on scraping data tables from Wikipedia. Learning to scrape *wiki tables* has proven important in my teaching because they contain interesting social information built from different sources. The fact the information is in a table helps you see some structure; in addition, the data may include pictures, hyperlinks, footnotes, or even different and nonstandard ways to let you know a value is missing or unknown. This time R and Python are used differently to achieve the same. In this guided example, I work with the Wikipedia page shown in Figure 4.18 about border wars – conflicts involving two or more countries.

4.5.1 Scraping Tabular Data with R

You can scrape the web using tools that are available online,[31] but here we are going to build a simple tool. First let's do it with R, which has some functions for that. The basic principle of scraping is that it involves interacting with the server and the code behind the webpage. If you understand that, the rest will be easier. Keep in

---

[31] Just search for *scraping tools* in your browser.

19th century [edit]

Start	Finish	Conflict	Combatants	Fatalities
1846	1848	Mexican–American War	United States v. Mexico	~29,000
1879	1883	War of the Pacific	Chile v. Bolivia and Peru	13,000+

20th century before World War II [edit]

Start	Finish	Conflict	Combatants	Fatalities
1910	1918	Border War	United States v. Mexico	100+
1932	1935	Chaco War	Bolivia v. Paraguay	~100,000
1938	1938	Battle of Lake Khasan	Soviet Union v. Japan	~1,300
1939	1939	Slovak–Hungarian War	Slovakia v. Hungary	66
1939	1939	Battle of Khalkhin Gol	Soviet Union and Mongolia v. Japan and Manchukuo	~16,000

1945–2000 [edit]

Start	Finish	Conflict	Combatants	Fatalities
1947	1948	Indo-Pakistani War of 1947	Pakistan v. India	~3,000
1950	Ongoing (ceasefire signed in 1953)	Korean War	South Korea v. North Korea	2 419 010+
1962	1962	Sino-Indian War	PRC v. India	~4,000
1965	1965	Indo-Pakistani War of 1965	Pakistan v. India	~6,800
1966	1989	South African Border War	Angola v. South Africa	Unknown
1967	1967	Chola incident	India v. People's Republic of China	~5
1969	1969	Sino-Soviet border conflict	PRC v. Soviet Union	Unknown
1971	1971	Indo-Pakistani War of 1971	Pakistan v. India	~4,000+
1979	1990	Sino-Vietnamese conflicts 1979–1990	Vietnam v. China	Unclear
1980	1988	Iran–Iraq War	Iran v. Iraq	1–2 million[1]
1981	1981	Paquisha War	Ecuador v. Peru	~10
1982	1982	1982 Ethiopian–Somali Border War	Ethiopia v. Somalia	Unknown
1984	1987	Siachen Conflict	Pakistan v. India	~2,400.
1985	1985	Agacher Strip War	Burkina Faso v. Mali	179
1987	1987	1987 Sino-Indian skirmish	India v. People's Republic of China	Unknown
1987	1988	Thai–Laotian Border War	Thailand v. Laos	~1,000
1989	1991	Mauritania–Senegal Border War	Mauritania v. Senegal	Unknown
1995	1995	Cenepa War	Ecuador v. Peru	~450
1998	2000	Eritrean-Ethiopian War	Ethiopia v. Eritrea	~70,000
1999	1999	Kargil War	India v. Pakistan	~4,500

Figure 4.18 Wikipedia table to be scraped.
Source: This data may be used under a CC Attribution Share Alike license.
Available at https://en.wikipedia.org/wiki/List_of_border_conflicts.

mind that HTML, JSON, and other formats can give you a data-frame like structure, but they can go beyond rectangular or tabular formats for data. However, because we have a wiki table, we can try to get the data into a tabular format. To take a look behind the scenes, please see the HTML source code for one of the wiki tables[32] in Figure 4.19.

There are different tags in Figure 4.19 that indicate when some portion of the data starts and ends:

---

[32] All browsers can show you the webpage source; these links share the instructions for most browsers: http://www.computerhope.com/issues/ch000746.htm or also http://www.wikihow.com/View-Source-Code.

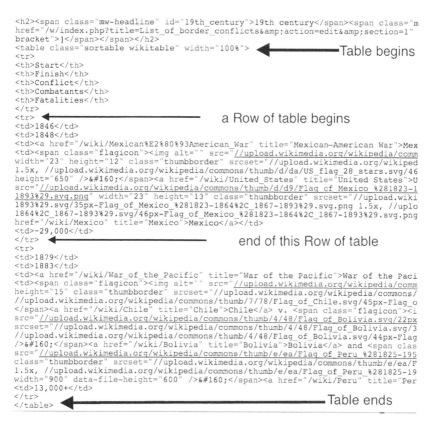

```
<h2><span class="mw-headline" id="19th_century">19th century</span><span class="m
href="/w/index.php?title=List_of_border_conflicts&amp;action=edit&amp;section=1"
bracket">]</span></span></h2>
<table class="sortable wikitable" width="100%">        ◄————————Table begins
<tr>
<th>Start</th>
<th>Finish</th>
<th>Conflict</th>
<th>Combatants</th>
<th>Fatalities</th>
</tr>
<tr> ◄————————————————— a Row of table begins
<td>1846</td>
<td>1848</td>
<td><a href="/wiki/Mexican%E2%80%93American_War" title="Mexican–American War">Mex
<td><span class="flagicon"><img alt="" src="//upload.wikimedia.org/wikipedia/comm
width="23" height="12" class="thumbborder" srcset="//upload.wikimedia.org/wikiped
1.5x, //upload.wikimedia.org/wikipedia/commons/d/da/US_flag_28_stars.svg/46
height="650" /> </span><a href="/wiki/United_States" title="United States">U
src="//upload.wikimedia.org/wikipedia/commons/thumb/d/d9/Flag_of_Mexico_%281823-1
1893%29.svg.png" width="23" height="13" class="thumbborder" srcset="//upload.wiki
1893%29.svg/35px-Flag_of_Mexico_%281823-1864%2C_1867-1893%29.svg.png 1.5x, //uplo
1864%2C_1867-1893%29.svg/46px-Flag_of_Mexico_%281823-1864%2C_1867-1893%29.svg.png
href="/wiki/Mexico" title="Mexico">Mexico</a></td>
<td>-29,000</td>
</tr> ◄————————————— end of this Row of table
<tr>
<td>1879</td>
<td>1883</td>
<td><a href="/wiki/War_of_the_Pacific" title="War of the Pacific">War of the Paci
<td><span class="flagicon"><img alt="" src="//upload.wikimedia.org/wikipedia/comm
height="15" class="thumbborder" srcset="//upload.wikimedia.org/wikipedia/commons/
//upload.wikimedia.org/wikipedia/commons/thumb/7/78/Flag_of_Chile.svg/45px-Flag_o
</span><a href="/wiki/Chile" title="Chile">Chile</a> v. <span class="flagicon"><i
src="//upload.wikimedia.org/wikipedia/commons/thumb/4/48/Flag_of_Bolivia.svg/22px
srcset="//upload.wikimedia.org/wikipedia/commons/thumb/4/48/Flag_of_Bolivia.svg/3
//upload.wikimedia.org/wikipedia/commons/thumb/4/48/Flag_of_Bolivia.svg/44px-Flag
/> </span><a href="/wiki/Bolivia" title="Bolivia">Bolivia</a> and <span clas
src="//upload.wikimedia.org/wikipedia/commons/thumb/e/ea/Flag_of_Peru_%281825-195
class="thumbborder" srcset="//upload.wikimedia.org/wikipedia/commons/thumb/e/ea/F
1.5x, //upload.wikimedia.org/wikipedia/commons/thumb/e/ea/Flag_of_Peru_%281825-19
width="900" data-file-height="600" /> </span><a href="/wiki/Peru" title="Per
<td>13,000+</td>
</tr>
</table> ◄——————————————————————— Table ends
```

Figure 4.19 HMTL behind a webpage. This is how the data from Figure 4.18 looks in HTML.

- `<table>` and `</table>` show when that table start and ends. If you have several tables, as in this example, you should have one pair of these tags for each one.

- `<tr>` and `</tr>` limit the values of a whole row in the table.

- `<td>` and `</td>` indicate one value and are in general within a row.

- `<th>` and `</th>` indicate titles (headers).

- `<a>` and `</a>` hold hyperlinks and the text shown in the webpage, respectively, for that link (you will see this in Figure 4.22).

There are other important tags that you may need to look for when you face a particular scraping problem. But the ones presented are enough for our scraping example. Let's use R to start working. First install RCurl (created by Temple Lang and the CRAN team (2015a)). We have not used it yet, but without it, you might get errors or warnings for different reasons (firewall, VPN, https, etc.). Most examples in the web tutorial do

not use it, and you are welcome to go ahead without installing it. However, by using
RCurl you will avoid spending time later trying to figure out what went wrong.[33]

```
library(XML) # you may not need to run this if it is active
#install.packages("RCurl")
library(RCurl)
wiki = "https://en.wikipedia.org/wiki/"
link ="List_of_border_wars"
wikiPage = getURL(paste0(wiki,link))
# GETTING THE DATA
wikiTables = readHTMLTable(wikiPage)
```

The code above apparently has the tables we want, but first check if you have a data
frame:

```
is.data.frame(wikiTables)
```

```
[1] FALSE
```

This tells us that, although we may want a data frame, we do not have one yet. We cannot
expect one, because there are several tables, so maybe we have a list of tables instead:

```
is.list(wikiTables)
```

```
[1] TRUE
```

This wikipage has four tables, and these are in a list. Let's confirm that one element of
the list is a data frame:

```
is.data.frame(wikiTables[[1]])
```

```
[1] TRUE
```

If the tables are similar, they should have the same headings (variable names); let's
check two of them:

```
names(wikiTables[[1]])
```

```
[1] "Start"      "Finish"      "Conflict"
[4] "Combatants" "Fatalities"
```

```
names(wikiTables[[4]])
```

```
[1] "Start"      "Finish"      "Conflict"
[4] "Combatants" "Fatalities"
```

Then, you can integrate all tables into one data frame:

---

[33] Once you become familiar and more interested in scraping, I recommend taking a look at the
package rvest.

```
conflictDF=rbind(wikiTables[[1]], wikiTables[[2]],
                 wikiTables[[3]],wikiTables[[4]])
# Alternative way:   conflictDF= do.call('rbind', wikiTables)
```

I have followed a very simple process for the sake of not overwhelming you with many details.[34] In the next chapter on cleaning, the code will be more complex. It would be good to request str(conflictDF) to ensure that all the data frame columns are factors, which is not something you necessarily want every time. Then, you will see that indeed cleaning will be needed soon.

4.5.2 Scraping Tabular Data with Python

It is now Python's turn. The main package we will use is BeautifulSoup created by Richardson (2015); it is flexible enough to scrape webpages. Let's follow a very detailed approach to this scraping:

1. The first code cell allows you to get the Wikipedia webpage:

```
#%%# Getting webpage
wikiLink='http://en.wikipedia.org/wiki/List_of_border_wars'
identification = { 'User-Agent' : 'Mozilla/5.0'}

from requests import get
wikiPage = get(wikiLink, headers=identification)
```

Notice I propose using an **identification**. I did not use it before, because APIs are programmed to let you take their data, but some webpages may not be amenable to scraping. To stop bots form collecting massive amounts of data, Wikipedia only allows access to a recognized user agent. In this case, you are not telling Wikipedia *you are* a Python code, but rather that you are the Mozilla search engine, which is an accepted bot for Wikipedia.[35]

2. Give the webpage to BeautifulSoup (BS).

```
#%% BS will interpret the html
from bs4 import BeautifulSoup as BS
Wiki= BS(wikiPage.content,'html.parser')
allTables = Wiki.findAll('table', {'class': 'sortable wikitable'})
```

From this code, Wiki has the HTML you want. But it is the whole HTML code from the URL provided. That is why the code includes allTables; that is, holding only the tables from that wiki page. In this case, BS has looked for all the

---

[34] You can see that I have commented on a code that uses do.call, which will glue all the data frames in one step. I explain that in the next chapter.

[35] Allowing or restricting search engines could be a complex decision. The more you allow, the more visible a page could become, but then users may experience slower service; the less you allow, the less prone the page is to malware.

HTML sections that have been declared as tables with class *sortable wikitable* (see the top arrow that indicates the beginning of the table in Figure 4.19) and captured the HTML codes where this filter is true. Noticed I have not used `xmltodict`; in fact you could use it, and then the whole wikipage would be a dict now. But we do not need everything into a dict, because we will need to see the dictionary and understand every key and content to build the data frame. BS will use the HTML tags to make this process much easier and productive. Let's see what we have inside the wiki tables:

- Find out how many tables there are:

```
len(allTables)
```

This confirms we have four tables. In R each of these was converted to a list; and, in this case, BS has created a *ResultSet*, a structure similar to a list, which is holding every table in `allTables`.[36]

- Find out how many elements the last table has:

```
len(allTables[3])
```

The last table in the wikipage has seven wars[37]; that means that you expect eight rows, including the titles of the table column. But my table has 17 rows, which means there are other elements you do not see in the Wikipedia page, but that are present in the HTML code.

- Tell BS to get only the rows from that table and count them:

```
allRows=allTables[3].find_all("tr")
len(allRows)
```

Now we got the result we expected: only the rows of the wars of the current century. In this case `find_all` is acting as a kind of filter, because it only recovers the elements that are between the HTML tags `<tr></tr>` (as you saw in Figure 4.19). So the strategy is clear with BS: you need to know what to get using HTML tags as filters.

- Confirm that the first row represents the titles for that table:

```
allRows[0]
```

The column titles are in a row (the first one), so the previous command fetched them along the other rows. When you run the command above, you will get some HTML code, including the tags you used as filters. This will tell you that you are

---

[36] You would get `bs4.element.ResultSet` if you now write the command `type(Tables)`.
[37] There may be more wars if there are more conflicts among countries after this book is published.

```
<tr>
<th>Start</th>
<th>Finish</th>
<th>Conflict</th>
<th>Combatants</th>
<th>Fatalities</th>
</tr>
```

Figure 4.20 Exploring results from BeautifulSoup (I)
Source: https://en.wikipedia.org/wiki/List_of_border_conflicts.

still working with HTML, it is there in the object `allTables` and `allRows`, and we are just filtering specific HTML sections. The last command output is similar to what is shown in Figure 4.20.

- Visit and understand the structure of the last row in this table:

```
allRows[6]
```

You will get something similar to Figure 4.21.

```
<tr>
<td>2012</td>
<td>2014</td>
<td><a href="/wiki/Syrian%E2%80%93Turkish_border_clashes_(2012%E2%80%9314)"
title="Syrian–Turkish border clashes (2012–14)">Syrian–Turkish border clashes
(2012–14)</a></td>
<td><span class="flagicon"><img alt="" class="thumbborder" data-file-
height="600" data-file-width="900" height="15"
src="//upload.wikimedia.org/wikipedia/commons/thumb/5/53/Flag_of_Syria.svg/23px
-Flag_of_Syria.svg.png"
srcset="//upload.wikimedia.org/wikipedia/commons/thumb/5/53/Flag_of_Syria.svg/3
5px-Flag_of_Syria.svg.png 1.5x,
//upload.wikimedia.org/wikipedia/commons/thumb/5/53/Flag_of_Syria.svg/45px-
Flag_of_Syria.svg.png 2x" width="23"/> </span><a href="/wiki/Syria"
title="Syria">Syria</a> v. <span class="flagicon"><img alt=""
class="thumbborder" data-file-height="800" data-file-width="1200" height="15"
src="//upload.wikimedia.org/wikipedia/commons/thumb/b/b4/Flag_of_Turkey.svg/23p
x-Flag_of_Turkey.svg.png"
srcset="//upload.wikimedia.org/wikipedia/commons/thumb/b/b4/Flag_of_Turkey.svg/
35px-Flag_of_Turkey.svg.png 1.5x,
//upload.wikimedia.org/wikipedia/commons/thumb/b/b4/Flag_of_Turkey.svg/45px-
Flag_of_Turkey.svg.png 2x" width="23"/> </span><a href="/wiki/Turkey"
title="Turkey">Turkey</a></td>
<td>17</td>
</tr>
```

Figure 4.21 Exploring results from BeautifulSoup (II)
Source: https://en.wikipedia.org/wiki/List_of_border_conflicts.

Figure 4.22 provides a better look at the details shown in Figure 4.21.

\<td\> 2012 **\</td\>**

\<td\> 2014 **\</td\>**

\<td\> \<a href="/wiki/Syrian%E2%80%93Turkish_border_clashes_(2012%E2%80%9314)"

title="Syrian–Turkish border clashes (2012-14)" \>

Syrian–Turkish border clashes (2012–14)

\</a\> **\</td\>**

\<td\> \<span class="flagicon" \>

\<img alt="" class="thumbborder" data-file-height="600" data-file-width="900" height="15"

src="//upload.wikimedia.org/wikipedia/commons/thumb/5/53/Flag_of_Syria.svg/23px-Flag_of_Syria.svg.png"

srcset="//upload.wikimedia.org/wikipedia/commons/thumb/5/53/Flag_of_Syria.svg/35px-Flag_of_Syria.svg.png 1.5x,

//upload.wikimedia.org/wikipedia/commons/thumb/5/53/Flag_of_Syria.svg/45px-Flag_of_Syria.svg.png 2x"

width="23"\>

\</span\>

\<a href="/wiki/Syria" title="Syria"\>

Syria

\</a\>

v.

\<span class="flagicon"\>

\<img alt="" class="thumbborder" data-file-height="800" data-file-width="1200" height="15"

src="//upload.wikimedia.org/wikipedia/commons/thumb/b/b4/Flag_of_Turkey.svg/23px-Flag_of_Turkey.svg.png"

srcset="//upload.wikimedia.org/wikipedia/commons/thumb/b/b4/Flag_of_Turkey.svg/35px-Flag_of_Turkey.svg.png 1.5x,

//upload.wikimedia.org/wikipedia/commons/thumb/b/b4/Flag_of_Turkey.svg/45px-Flag_of_Turkey.svg.png 2x"

width="23"\>

\</span\>

\<a href="/wiki/Turkey" title="Turkey"\>Turkey\</a\> **\</td\>**

\<td\> 17 **\</td\>**

Figure 4.22 Understanding tags in HTML.

3. Build a list for each column, using the tags from Figure 4.22 in *BeautifulSoup*:

```
#%% Converting each column in wikitable into a list

# Columns are created here as empty lists ('initialized').
start=[]; end=[]
conflict=[] ; combatants=[] ; fatalities=[]

# Do this for each table
for table in allTables:
    allRows=table.find_all("tr") # Get all the rows

    # Do this for each Row in the current table
    for row in allRows[1:]: # omitting  first row (titles)
        allCells = row.find_all("td") # Get the cells

        ## Fill each column with a particular value of cell:
        start.append(allCells[0].get_text()) # text of cell 1
        end.append(allCells[1].get_text())   # text of cell 2
        conflict.append(allCells[2].get_text()) # text of cell 3

        # 4th cell has many values (and in hyperlinks)
        countries=allCells[3].find_all('a') # countries in cell 4
        # List of combatant countries (text only)
        combatants.append([value.get_text() for value in countries])

        fatalities.append(allCells[4].get_text())# text of cell 5
```

After initializing the columns, you can see a good example of *nested* loops. We have one *for-loop* to visit every table, and another *for-loop* inside of this one to visit every

```
                Combatants              Conflict  End Fatalities Start
0   [United States, Mexico]  Mexican-American War  1848   ~29,000  1846
1      [Chile, Bolivia, Peru]    War of the Pacific  1883   ~10,000  1879
2   [United States, Mexico]            Border War  1918      100+  1910
3        [Bolivia, Paraguay]            Chaco War  1935  ~100,000  1932
4     [Soviet Union, Japan]  Battle of Lake Khasan  1938    ~1,300  1938
```

Figure 4.23 Data frame from scraping in Python.
Source: https://en.wikipedia.org/wiki/List_of_border_conflicts.

row of a table. Every time we visit a `table`, we get all its rows by using `find_all`. The result is saved in `allRows`, from where we use `allCells`, which is possible because cell values are within the `td` tag in each `row`. The values for our data frame are in those cells, so we visit cell by cell. I do not use a *for-loop* here; instead, I access each value in `allCells` using indexes. Because it is a table, I know what is in the first, second, third, fourth, and fifth cells. Then, I visit each and extract the text in that cell using `get_text`. This is a critical function in the scraping process because it helps you recover the values you actually see in a webpage, not the HTML code behind it. So every text extraction is saved into the lists (columns). Once you have columns as lists, you can create the data frame.

4. Let's make the data frame. The lists are organized into a dictionary to make the process straightforward:

```
ColumnsAsDicts={'Start':start,'End':end,
                'Conflict':conflict, 'Combatants':combatants,
                'Fatalities':fatalities}

from pandas import DataFrame as DF
# Creation of data frame
conflictDF = DF.from_dict(ColumnsAsDicts)

conflictDF.head() # inspecting
```

Notice that in the code above, I wrote `from pandas import DataFrame as DF`. This is useful if you want to use pandas for a particular function and not load the whole pandas. It avoids writing the following:

```
import pandas
conflictDF = pandas.DataFrame.from_dict(ColumnsAsDicts)
```

In addition, I invented an acronym on the run: `DataFrame as DF`. Now I no longer need to write `DataFrame.from_dict(ColumnsAsDicts)`. At the end, you have a data frame with the values collected, as shown in Figure 4.23.

However, Figure 4.23 gives you a data frame with a strange order of columns. We input the lists in the right order, but the data frame received them in a different order. Dicts work that way, which is why they do not have indexes but keys. We could change in pandas by moving the columns in the data frame. But if you want a

```
In [10]: conflictDF_O.head()
Out[10]:
   Start   End              Conflict                 Combatants Fatalities
0  1846  1848     Mexican-American War  [United States, Mexico]    ~29,000
1  1879  1883      War of the Pacific   [Chile, Bolivia, Peru]     13,000+
2  1910  1918             Border War    [United States, Mexico]       100+
3  1932  1935             Chaco War     [Bolivia, Paraguay]       ~100,000
4  1938  1938  Battle of Lake Khasan    [Soviet Union, Japan]       ~1,300
```

Figure 4.24 First lines of Pandas data frame built from an ordered dict.
Source: https://en.wikipedia.org/wiki/List_of_border_conflicts.

structure like a dict to respect the order in which you inputted the columns, you need
to use an *ordered dictionary*, which is created with tuples:

```
#%% Alternative: Data frame from ordered dict of lists

# here we set the order
ColumnsAsTuples=(('Start',start),('End',end),
                 ('Conflict',conflict),('Combatants',combatants),
                 ('Fatalities',fatalities))

# here we confirm the order:
from collections import OrderedDict as OD
ColumnsAsDicts_Ordered= OD(ColumnsAsTuples)

# Creation of data frame from dict (as usual)
conflictDF_Ordered= DF.from_dict(ColumnsAsDicts_Ordered)
```

The resulting data frame, has the columns in the correct order, as shown in
Figure 4.24.

There may be more ways of doing this, but let me show you one other way. The
previous strategy created a list for every column and then created a simple dict with
the lists as its elements. However, because dicts may not preserve the order you want,
we created tuples to make an ordered dict. An interesting alternative is to save row
by row in a list:

```
Rows=[] # 'Rows' is created as an empty list ('initialized').

# Do this for each table
for table in allTables:
    allRows=table.find_all("tr") # Get all the rows

    # Do this for each Row in the current table
    for row in allRows[1:]: # omitting first row (titles)
        allCells = row.find_all("td") # Get the cells

        ## get text for each cell:
        start= allCells[0].get_text(); end=allCells[1].get_text()
        conflict=allCells[2].get_text()
        # 4th cell has many values: the combatant countries...so:
        countries=allCells[3].find_all('a')  # countries in cell
        # List of combatant countries (text only)
        combatants=[value.get_text() for value in countries]
        fatalities=allCells[4].get_text()# text of cell 5
```

```
# HERE we update the Rows list contents:
Rows.append((start, end,conflict, combatants, fatalities))
```

Then, I only create a list with the rows, and tell pandas DF the column names. The code to make the data frame could be as follows:

```
from pandas import DataFrame as DF

# create list of names:
columnNames=['start','end','conflict','combatants', 'fatalities']

# create data frame:
conflictDF_fromRows=DF(Rows, columns=columnNames)

conflictDF_fromRows.head() # inspecting
```

You end up with the same data frame in Python and in R, but we did not use the same strategy to create it. R uses a function that recovers tables from wiki pages. Python uses a package to access webpages using the tags these they contain for organizing their content. However, all the data frames we produced from our collection stage may have problems specially the ones derived from scraping. Let's see in the next chapter how R and Python can help us clean these data frames.

5

Cleaning Data

Data cleaning is an iterative process. However, this chapter is more concerned with explaining the cleaning steps than the order in which you should do them. It reviews each data frame created in Chapter 4, performs a basic data exploration, and then cleans the "dirty" values, – those that have some anomalies caused during the process of importing the data into R or Python or because the original values were not ready to be imported into a different software. I focus on missing values, encoding, and, especially, symbols that were not imported correctly.

5.1 Dealing with Missing Values

Missing values are likely to be present in every data set. Data related to engineering activities can get lost, but, in general, a missing value indicates that a sensor did not record a particular data value. In social data, however, you will not only find an "NA" representing missing values but they may be coded with other values representing varieties of "missingness." The coding of missing values is well covered by licensed software such as STATA or SPSS, but not explicitly covered in standard R or Python. As we learned in the last chapter, the *memisc* and *foreign* packages can import SPSS data very well into R (although there is less support from Python[1]) and that Python and R can import without problems STATA files and the other formats we explored. Let's see how Python and R deal with missing data.

---

[1] We showed how to used R code inside Python, because the installation of savReaderWriter can be cumbersome (http://pythonhosted.org/savReaderWriter/).

Table 5.1. *Example of missing values with ANES 2012 sav file*

Code[a]	Value label
−1	Inapplicable
−2	Missing, see documentation
−3	Restricted access
−4	Error, see documentation
−5	Not asked, terminated (breakoff)
−6	Not asked, unit nonresponse
−7	Deleted due to partial interview
−8	Don't know
−9	Refused

[a] See further details in page 36 of the survey cookbook (ANES 2014)

5.1.1 Identifying and Setting Missing Values: Codebooks

Finding a data set without missing values is rare. The problem is knowing whether the missing values are clearly identifiable or not. In general, if your data set comes with a codebook, then that means that you will know all the metadata needed. If you scrape the data, you may not know if you are missing values or not.

The SPSS data from ANES is a good example of the varieties of missing data in social science research. Table 5.1 from ANES time series for 2012 shows clearly which values should not enter into the calculations, but are nevertheless informative. That table was created using the codebook provided by ANES:

Table 5.1 has many values that should be considered missing values, and we have the codebook to identify them.[2] SPSS offers labels for the missing values (sixth column in Figure 4.6 on page 91), and also a way to flag those values as missing (seventh column in Figure 4.6).

Let's start with R, using the ANES 2012 data from page 95, but this time with the *sav* version. Let's use some functions from *memisc*:

```
library(memisc)
# setting up the folder:
folder=file.path("~","Dropbox","BookData","chapter5")
```

[2] Sometimes, the codebook may instruct how to treat missing values that the SPSS data is not treating as missing; therefore you always need to read the codebook, even if you only work in SPSS.

```
fileSpssSav=file.path(folder,"anes_timeseries_2012.sav")
# getting the info
fileSpss = spss.system.file(fileSpssSav)
```

This file has many variables, so making a summary of them all is not useful. However, social science researchers are in general interested in only a small number of variables. In this example, imagine you are interested in the subset of questions related to *Liberal-conservative placement*, which ask respondents, pre- and post-election, to place themselves on a seven-point scale ranging from "extremely liberal" to "extremely conservative." The answers are stored in the variables named `libcpre_self` and `libcpo_self`. Let's see the set of answers for one of these questions:

```
labels(fileSpss$libcpre_self)
```

```
Values and labels:

  -9 '-9. Refused'
  -8 '-8. Don't know'
  -2 '-2. Haven't thought much about this'
   1 '1. Extremely liberal'
   2 '2. Liberal'
   3 '3. Slightly liberal'
   4 '4. Moderate; middle of the road'
   5 '5. Slightly conservative'
   6 '6. Conservative'

   7 '7. Extremely conservative'
```

From the results above, you see that all the possible responses are shown, even the ones identified as missing values in Table 5.1. A question may not generate any missing values; in this case there were only three kinds of missing values. The important thing to ensure here is that R "knows" what the missing values are in that data:

```
missing.values(fileSpss$libcpre_self)
```

```
NULL
```

As you see, R is not aware that these files have missing values. If you do not set the missing values, whatever analysis you carry out later will be based on invalid values. It is important to note that missing values are not the fault of *memisc* or ANES. The importing process did not set the missing values in the data set, but you cannot start analyzing data without having read the metada, which, fortunately, you have in the ANES codebook. However, *memisc* can set the missing values now:

```
# setting for each variable we want:
missing.values(fileSpss$libcpre_self) = c(-9:-1)
missing.values(fileSpss$libcpo_self) = c(-9:-1)
# Let's see what we get now:
missing.values(fileSpss$libcpre_self)
```

```
-9, -8, -7, -6, -5, -4, -3, -2, -1
```

This is a nice way to identify the missing values. These values will become "NA" later, but it is good to know you can control those values from here. Now let's get those variables from the large data set (fileSpss is just the "importer"):

```
subANES2012 = subset(fileSpss,
                     select=c(libcpre_self,libcpo_self))
```

Using subset we have subANES2012, a *data.set*, which is structure similar to a data frame that works with *memisc* commands and that can keep track of the missing values and other metadata:

```
codebook(subANES2012$libcpre_self)
```

The result from the last command is shown in Figure 5.1.

R is now fully aware how these data should be treated. Notice the tag **M** (for missing) next to the negative values. Let's turn this data set into a simple R data frame and get the frequencies again:

```
#memisc 'data set' into a data frame:
subANES2012DF=as.data.frame(subANES2012)
frequencies_LibPre=table(subANES2012DF$libcpre_self)
# install.packages("plyr") # install if needed
library(plyr)
count(subANES2012DF,'libcpre_self')
```

```
                  libcpre_self freq
1            1. Extremely liberal  195
2                     2. Liberal  638
3             3. Slightly liberal  641
4 4. Moderate; middle of the road 1828
5         5. Slightly conservative  789
6                 6. Conservative 1001
7          7. Extremely conservative  208
8                            <NA>  614
```

As you can see, the missing values have been identified, aggregated, and set as "NA." Thus, the *memisc* package proved useful in identifying and setting the

```
> codebook(subANES2012$libcpre_self)
========================================================

subANES2012$libcpre_self 'PRE: 7pt scale
Liberal/conservative self-placement'

--------------------------------------------------------

Storage mode: double
Measurement: nominal
Missing values: -9, -8, -7, -6, -5, -4, -3, -2, -1

        Values and labels       N       Percent

  -9 M 'Refused'               32           0.5
  -8 M 'DK'                    26           0.4
  -2 M 'NotThought'           556           9.4
   1   'xLiberal'             195      3.7   3.3
   2   'Liberal'              638     12.0  10.8
   3   'sLiberal'             641     12.1  10.8
   4   'Moderate'            1828     34.5  30.9
   5   'sConservative'        789     14.9  13.3
   6   'Conservative'        1001     18.9  16.9
   7   'xConservative'        208      3.9   3.5
```

Figure 5.1 Looking for missing data in an SPSS file.

missing values. You can even convert the *memisc* 's *dataset* into an standard data frame, which will inherit the missing value setting.

Let's work now with an SPSS file where the missing values have already been set (we used this data set in Section 4.2.3 on page 99); this time let's use the basic functionality of the *foreign* package. First let's see all the values:

```
library(foreign)
folder=file.path("~","Dropbox","BookData","chapter5")
fileSpssSav=file.path(folder,"survey_sample.sav")
surveyDF=read.spss(fileSpssSav,
                   use.missings=F, #without this!
                   to.data.frame=T,
                   use.value.labels = T
)
# install.packages("plyr")
library(plyr)
count(surveyDF,'rincome')
```

```
       rincome  freq
1          NAP   597
2    LT $1000    42
3  $1000 TO 2999  42
4  $3000 TO 3999  40
5  $4000 TO 4999  27
```

```
 6   $5000 TO 5999   32
 7   $6000 TO 6999   43
 8   $7000 TO 7999   41
 9   $8000 TO 9999   63
10  $10000  - 14999  199
11  $15000  - 19999  198
12  $20000  - 24999  238
13  $25000 or more   884
14          Refused  118
15               DK   26
16               NA  242
```

You can guess which are the missing values (the first one and the last three ones). But R does not know which ones are missing because I did not import missing value information (see comment in the code). Now let me try to import those values:

```r
surveyDF=read.spss(fileSpssSav,
                   use.missings=T, # changing this!
                   to.data.frame=T,
                   use.value.labels = T
)
# install.packages("plyr")
library(plyr)
count(surveyDF,'rincome')
```

```
          rincome freq
1        LT $1000   42
2   $1000 TO 2999   42
3   $3000 TO 3999   40
4   $4000 TO 4999   27
5   $5000 TO 5999   32
6   $6000 TO 6999   43
7   $7000 TO 7999   41
8   $8000 TO 9999   63
9   $10000 - 14999  199
10  $15000 - 19999  198
11  $20000 - 24999  238
12  $25000 or more  884
13            <NA>  983
```

R knows now which values have to be treated as missing. I recommend using (changing) the parameters in this case, so that you can see the differences and be sure what you are dealing with.

Opening and setting the missing values in the 2012 ANES survey, in the Stata version offered in the website, will be similar using R:

```r
library(foreign)
folder=file.path("~","Dropbox","BookData","chapter5")
filename="anes_timeseries_2012_stata12.dta"
fileSTA=file.path(folder,filename)
surveyDF=read.dta(fileSTA,
                  convert.factors = T,
```

```
                missing.type = T,
                convert.underscore = FALSE,
                warn.missing.labels = TRUE)
    library(plyr)
    count(surveyDF,'libcpo_self')
```

Out[1]:
nonunion   1417
union   461
.   368
dtype: int64

Figure 5.2 Missing data in Python (I): NAs are present but are not ready for Python.

However, as this book was written, *memisc* and *foreign* can only import up to version 12 (currently STATA is in version 14).[3]

Let's use Python this time for STATA. As we will see, Python, via pandas, has the basic functionality we need to identify and set the missing values. First, I will use a demo file that comes in STATA, "nlsw88.dta," which is part of the U.S. National Longitudinal Survey for employed women in 1988.

```
#%%
from pandas import read_stata
from os.path  import join
folderData=join("~","Dropbox","BookData","chapter5")
fileSTATA1=join(folderData,"nlsw88.dta")
surveyW88=read_stata(fileSTATA1,
                convert_categoricals=True,
                # see original missing values codes
                convert_missing=True)
#frequencies:
surveyW88['union'].value_counts()
```

Figure 5.2 shows the frequencies of every value present in STATA. In the parameters of the function read_stata, I first request to see the labels of the categories and then to see the missing values. If the missing values have been set as such in STATA, then you will see how many there are. Python shows the frequencies of the non-missing values, and the missing ones are represented using the symbol ".". However, pandas, in this situation, will count the "." as valid. The next code will set the missing values as NaN (the valid value for missing data in Python) wherever the "." from Stata is present:

---

[3] When you download from the ANES website, the folder will give you the last version of STATA and a copy in version 12.

```
nonunion    1417
union        461
dtype: int64
```

Figure 5.3 Missing data in Python (II): NAs are present and ready for Python.

```
#%%
surveyW88=read_stata(fileSTATA1,
                     convert_categoricals=True,
                     # missing is replaced by NaN
                     convert_missing=False)
surveyW88['union'].value_counts()
```

In Figure 5.3, the missing values are present in the pandas data frame, but only the non-missing values are shown with their frequency count. We could request to see them, but missing values are hidden by default.

Let's look at the ANES data sets we already used Remember that ANES 2012 coded the missing values using negative integer values among the categories of the variable libcpo_self. Here is the code:

```
#%%
fileSTATA2=join(folderData,"anes_timeseries_2012.dta")
anes2012=read_stata(fileSTATA2,
                    convert_categoricals=True,
                    # see original missing values codes
                    convert_missing=True)
anes2012['libcpo_self'].value_counts()
```

And Figure 5.4 shows the results.

So, in contrast to how we handled the data in the file nlsw88.dta, we need to define what a missing value is in the ANES 2012 data file. The codebook instructs you that this is needed, but those values have not been set as

```
4. Moderate; middle of the road   1756
6. Conservative                     975
5. Slightly conservative            671
2. Liberal                          646
3. Slightly liberal                 639
-2.0                                410
-6.0                                252
7. Extremely conservative           188
1. Extremely liberal                166
-7.0                                152
-9.0                                 36
-8.0                                 23
```

Figure 5.4 Missing data in Python (III): NAs are present but not recognized by Python.

4.0	1756
6.0	975
NaN	873
5.0	671
2.0	646
3.0	639
7.0	188
1.0	166

Figure 5.5 Missing data in Python (IV): NAs are present and recognized by Python.

missing in STATA, as they were SPSS. (There is no "." symbol in the original data file.) The next code will recode the missing values, this time changing the default of value_counts to show NaNs in the frequency counts. Notice that I use the package *numpy* to add the NaN value and that I set convert_categoricals=False:

```
#%%
anes2012=read_stata(fileSTATA2,
                # no labels, just integers
                convert_categoricals=False,
                convert_missing=False)
anes2012['libcpo_self'].value_counts()

# RECODING
from numpy import nan
missVals=range(-9,0) # ALL MISSING VALUES
anes2012=anes2012.replace(missVals, nan) # RECODING

# Frequencies including NaNs:
anes2012['libcpo_self'].value_counts(dropna=False)
```

Setting convert_categoricals as False facilitated the recoding process, but erased the labels, as you can see in Figure 5.5.

I recommend that you run the command **describe** varying the parameters (for example, anes2012['libcpo_self'].describe()) to see the different results that can be obtained. It is a good practice to see what pandas is counting as valid before going further.

5.1.2 Identifying and Setting Missing Values: No Codebooks

In the previous cases, we worked with data that came from well-known sources that follow coding plans and share codebooks, so you knew beforehand what the missing values were in your data. However, you might encounter situations where institutions do not offer codebooks or the source where you get the data has no standard way to represent missing values, and you need to discover them by yourself.

Let's take a look at the data from the *shapefile* we saw in Section 4.3 on page 102. For this case, we only need to use the **.dbf** file related to the shapefile:

```
library(foreign) # a familiar library by now
#location
folder=file.path("~","Dropbox","BookData","chapter5","map")
filename="TM_WORLD_BORDERS-0.3.dbf"
fileMapDBF=file.path(folder,filename)
# reading in the data:
mapData=read.dbf(fileMapDBF)
# do this for every column:
for (i in seq_along(mapData)){
    # print column , print if column has a missing value:
    cat(names(mapData[i]),anyNA(mapData[i]),'\n')
}
```

```
FIPS TRUE
ISO2 FALSE
ISO3 FALSE
UN FALSE
NAME FALSE
AREA FALSE
POP2005 FALSE
REGION FALSE
SUBREGION FALSE
LON FALSE
LAT FALSE
```

The **.dbf** file is similar to a spreadsheet. In the code above, we visited every column by its index **i**, which will take each of the values returned by seq_along(mapData); that is, a vector of integers from 1 to 11.[4] From the output, we see that some values in the second columns are TRUE, which is the result of applying anyNA() to that column; this means that at least one cell in that column is a missing value. Keep in mind that *.dbf* files use the value *null* to represent missingness, so R has transformed those into NAs. This only means that R has detected the "official" missing values, but there might be others that are "hidden" in the columns that apparently have no missing values. For example, would you expect a zero in the population of a country (POP2005)?

```
#finding missing value:
sum(mapData$POP2005 == 0) #or length(which(mapData$POP2005==0))
```

```
[1] 18
```

---

[4] You can use seq_along(mapData) to get a list of indexes that correspond to every column. It is the same as writing seq(1,length(mapData)) or seq(1,ncol(mapData)). If you want the row indexes, you can write seq(1,nrow(mapData)).

As you just saw, we have 18 countries with no population:

```
mapData[mapData$POP2005==0,]$NAME
```

```
 [1] Mayotte                                  \xc5land Islands
 [3] Norfolk Island                           Cocos (Keeling) Islands
 [5] Antarctica                               Bouvet Island
 [7] French Southern and Antarctic Lands      Heard Island and McDonald Islands
 [9] British Indian Ocean Territory           Christmas Island
[11] United States Minor Outlying Islands     Svalbard
[13] Saint Martin                             Saint Barthelemy
[15] Guernsey                                 Jersey
[17] South Georgia South Sandwich Islands     Taiwan

246 Levels: \xc5land Islands Afghanistan Albania Algeria ... Zimbabwe
```

As the output shows, Taiwan, among other islands, has no population. This tells us something very important that you should know by now: you cannot rely on data collected from the web. When you download this file, you will get a readme.txt file, that will tell you that this and other columns of data have been collected from other data sets. It is probable that the zeroes are the coding they decided to use to represent missing values; it is therefore wise to set those zeroes as missing values in population.[5] It is important to know that shapefiles do not behave properly if there are missing values, so some value has to be written in every cell of the **.dbf** file.[6] Therefore, if you are a basic user of shapefiles in public policy, you need to have complete data.[7] In this situation, we could write the next code to set the zeroes as missing values like this and update (save) the file (but not yet):

```
#setting missing values:
mapData$POP2005[mapData$POP2005==0] = NA
write.dbf(mapData,fileMapDBF) #saving updated file
```

When you run the code above you will alter the **.dbf**, file, so that when you rerun the previous codes you will not see the original "mistakes." If you want to restore the original file, the zip file TM_WORLD_BORDERS-0.3.zip with the original files is in the folder of this chapter. However, we may not need to change the cell values, but be aware that plotting or computing statistics, will require some slicing or subsetting to omit the invalid values. For example, to know the mean of the world population, you could write:

---

[5] It may be wiser to look for a more reliable data source, but you will have to go through the same exploration to decide what source to keep.

[6] http://desktop.arcgis.com/en/desktop/latest/manage-data/shapefiles/geoprocessing-considerations-for-shapefile-output.htm.

[7] Certainly you can work with other data formats that are more flexible than ESRI's shapefiles (XML, GeoJSON, SVG, etc.).

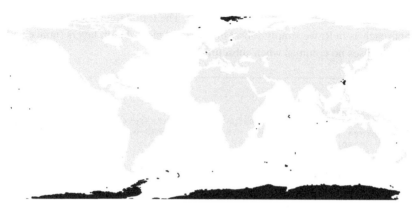

Figure 5.6 Plotting a map with NAs in R.
Source: This figure may be used under a CC Attribution Share Alike license, available at http://thematicmapping.org/downloads/world_borders.php.

```
mean(mapData$POP2005[mapData$POP2005 > 0])
```

```
[1] 27068954
```

The code above avoids using zeroes, which will bias the mean to a lower value:

```
mean(mapData$POP2005) # Wrong results:
```

```
[1] 25088299
```

You can use the same strategy for plotting. In Figure 5.6, I subset the shapefile into two layers and printed each one in a different color (one with countries with valid population information and another without it). This code does the subsetting:

```
library(maptools)
SHP=file.path(folder,"TM_WORLD_BORDERS-0.3.shp")
worldmap=readShapeSpatial(SHP)
validPopCountries=worldmap[worldmap@data$POP2005>0,]
missingPopCountries=worldmap[worldmap@data$POP2005≤0,]
```

This code does the plotting, which plots both layers in one figure:

```
# This is the first layer
plot(validPopCountries, col="grey", border=NA) # no borders
# This is the second layer (added)
plot(missingPopCountries, col="black",add=TRUE)
```

A similar plot can be obtained in Python. The following code uses the same approach as in R: we simply subset the data and plotted both layers (notice that Python uses no commas when subsetting).

```
#%% Importing modules and getting data
import os
import geopandas as gp
folder='/Users/JoseManuel/Dropbox/BookData/chapter5/map'
fileSHP=os.path.join(folder,"TM_WORLD_BORDERS-0.3.shp")
world   = gp.read_file(fileSHP)
#%% Subsetting
goodWorld=world[world['POP2005']>0]
badWorld=world[world['POP2005']≤0]
#%% Plotting
base = goodWorld.plot(linewidth=0,color='grey')
badWorld.plot(ax=base, linewidth=0,color='black')
```

Let's turn our attention to **spreadsheets**, which, are much easier to work with than shapefiles; however, they can bring some interesting challenges. Let's get the data for the Human Development Index (HDI) from one of the United Nations webpages (hdr.undp.org/en/data) and download the Excel file with *All 2015 data by indicator, year and country.*[8] This file is saved in the folder of this chapter. When you open this data set, you will immediately see some problems, as shown in Figure 5.7.

The "dirty" elements in Figure 5.7 occur very frequently. These elements and some other ones are described below:

- Presentation: Reports in Excel may not have the headers (column names) in the first row; instead, the title of the table or spreadsheet and sometimes even logos may be in the top row.
- Broken names: The names of a variable may not be contained in one cell.
- Non-standard missing values: An empty cell is easily interpreted as a missing value in these kind of data sets, but in these reports you may see a different symbology for missing values.
- Section names: Some reports, contain rows that have been combined or merged to include a subtitle for a section of the data.
- Calls and footnotes: The some symbols are used as *calls* among the data to reference footnotes. You may find the text of footnotes at the end of the spreadsheet.
- Definitions: Texts that define defining concepts may be found at the end of the document.

---

[8] hdr.undp.org/sites/default/files/2015_statistical_annex_tables_all.xls.

	A	B	C	D	E	F	G	H
3		Table 1: Human Development Index and its components				} Presentation		
6			Human Development Index (HDI)		Life expectancy at birth		Expected years of schooling	
7	HDI rank	Country	Value		(years)		(years)	
8			2014		2014		2014	a
9	VERY HIGH HUMAN DEVELOPMENT							
10	1	Norway	0.944		81.6		17.5	
11	2	Australia	0.935		82.4		20.2	c
12	3	Switzerland	0.930		83.0		15.8	
13	4	Denmark	SECTION NAME 0.923		80.2		18.7	c
14	5	Netherlands	0.922		81.6		17.9	
15	6	Germany	0.916		80.9		16.5	
16	7	Ireland	0.916		80.9		18.6	c
17	8	United States	0.915		79.1		16.5 CALLS	
18	9	Canada	0.913		82.0		15.9	
19	10	New Zealand	0.913		81.8		19.2	c
20	11	Singapore	0.912		83.0		15.4	f
21	12	Hong Kong, China (SAR)	0.910		84.0		15.6	
22	13	Liechtenstein	0.908		80.0	h	15.0	
23	14	Sweden	0.907		82.2		15.8	
24	15	United Kingdom	0.907		80.7		16.2	
25	16	Iceland	0.899		82.6		19.0	c
26	17	Korea (Republic of)	0.898		81.9		16.9	

◀ ▶ Table 1   Table 2   Table 3   Table 4   Table 5   Table 6   Table 7   Table 8   +

Figure 5.7 Some dirtiness in a spreadsheet. You can see here headers, footnote calls, and rows used for section names. Notice this file has multiple sheets (tables).

Some of these issues can be solved inside Excel; if you are not skilled at using macros or Visual Basic programming, it could take you a large amount of time to address these problems. Let's work with R first:

```
# Setting up
library(xlsx)
folder=file.path("~","Dropbox","BookData","chapter5")
filename="2015_statistical_annex_tables_all.xls"
fileHDI=file.path(folder,filename)
# Initial FILTERS:
firstRow=10    #to SKIP PRESENTATION
lastRow=208   # to OMIT FOOTNOTES
colsOK=c(2,seq(3,11,2)) # OMIT COLUMNS WITH CALLS
# Getting what we need:
Data = read.xlsx(fileHDI,"Table 1",
                 startRow=firstRow,endRow=lastRow,
                 stringsAsFactors=F, #see below
                 header=F # No Column titles
                 )[colsOK]
# Giving names to the 6 columns (we have no 'header'):
names(Data)=c('Country','HDI','LEB','EYS','MYS','GNI')
```

I had to include some filters, because the spreadsheet report had cells we did not need.[9] One particular filter to remember is the setting of **stringsAsFactors** as *False*. This is critical, because it will conserve every value, but in text format; that is, a number like 3 will be read as "3." This may look weird, but it avoids the problem that occurs when people use nonstandard text to represent a missing value in a spreadsheet (i.e., "N/A", "?","X", "...", "-", and so on). If R finds such text in a column with numbers, and **stringsAsFactors=True**, then all the items in the column will be coerced to the factor (categorical) type; and if, in fact, that column represented numbers, its conversion into a numeric type will cause extra work.[10] With all those settings, we still have work to do, so let's first take care of the rows used as *section names*, step by step:

- We have a data frame with six columns (Data). The section name occupies only the first column, and adjacent cells in the other columns are empty. Empty cells are read as NA in R by default, so we need to work on those five columns (from the second to the sixth one):

```
# Columns of interest (all but first):
columnsToClean=Data[,-1]
```

- We have a slice of the original data frame (Data) named columnsToClean, where we have the same data frame, but without the first column. Now, I want to know if a cell in columnsToClean is NA or not.

```
# Data frame with TRUE and FALSE values (TRUE means cell is NA)
ColumnsTrueFalse = data.frame(lapply(columnsToClean,is.na))
```

I obtained ColumnsTrueFalse, and it looks like this (only showing rows 47–53):

```
      HDI    LEB    EYS    MYS    GNI
47  FALSE  FALSE  FALSE  FALSE  FALSE
48  FALSE  FALSE  FALSE  FALSE  FALSE
49  FALSE  FALSE  FALSE  FALSE  FALSE
50   TRUE   TRUE   TRUE   TRUE   TRUE
51  FALSE  FALSE  FALSE  FALSE  FALSE
52  FALSE  FALSE  FALSE  FALSE  FALSE
53  FALSE  FALSE  FALSE  FALSE  FALSE
```

- If you see TRUE in a cell, it means that this cell from ColumnsTrueFalse was empty in the spreadsheet (and now R put an NA there). When all the cells in the same row are TRUE, that row has a section name. If you remember

---

[9] In case you want to directly set a row as a header you can use:
```
names(DF)=as.vector(unlist(DF[row number,]))
```
[10] I should have used this setting when scraping, but I will use it later to show you how it changes the results.

logic, if would be fine to apply the logic operator **AND** to the set of values of each row, because it will return **TRUE** when all are true. We can do that using:

```
# Keep rows where ALL are NAs (these are positions)
RowsTrueFalse = Reduce("&",ColumnsTrueFalse)
```

We got one column with the logic result (showing the first 60 results):

```
 [1] FALSE FALSE FALSE FALSE FALSE FALSE FALSE FALSE FALSE
[10] FALSE FALSE FALSE FALSE FALSE FALSE FALSE FALSE FALSE
[19] FALSE FALSE FALSE FALSE FALSE FALSE FALSE FALSE FALSE
[28] FALSE FALSE FALSE FALSE FALSE FALSE FALSE FALSE FALSE
[37] FALSE FALSE FALSE FALSE FALSE FALSE FALSE FALSE FALSE
[46] FALSE FALSE FALSE FALSE  TRUE FALSE FALSE FALSE FALSE

[55] FALSE FALSE FALSE FALSE FALSE FALSE
```

- The last result tells you which rows have all the cells as true. This is useful, because these logical values can be used as a logical filter. Let's filter the original data frame `Data`, so that we keep only the rows that are true. Let's see how it looks:

```
Data[RowsTrueFalse,]
```

```
                        Country HDI  LEB  EYS  MYS  GNI
50          HIGH HUMAN DEVELOPMENT <NA> <NA> <NA> <NA> <NA>
107       MEDIUM HUMAN DEVELOPMENT <NA> <NA> <NA> <NA> <NA>
147          LOW HUMAN DEVELOPMENT <NA> <NA> <NA> <NA> <NA>
192 OTHER COUNTRIES OR TERRITORIES <NA> <NA> <NA> <NA> <NA>
```

We see in this output that we finally have created section names. Now we know where they are, but we really want the other rows, where the data is located. We can find those rows easily by *complementing* `RowsTrueFalse` by using the operator `!`:

```
Data = Data[!RowsTrueFalse,]  # using '!' to negate
```

Take a look the rows of section names above. You can see that they occupied the rows 50, 107, 147, and 192. If our last code was successful, those rows should not be present now. So, if I call those rows in the data frame `Data`, the data frame should give me the rows that are occupying their places. Pay attention here, because I will get row 51, when I request row 50 (row 51 now occupies the 50th place and is the one after row 49 in this case); then I will get row 109 when I request row 107, because now we do not have either row 50 or row 107, and so on:

```
Data[c(50, 107, 147,192),]
```

```
      Country         HDI             LEB  EYS      MYS
51    Belarus 0.79836651789255 71.3 15.66023 11.97681
```

```
109  Moldova (Republic of) 0.693302690570274  71.6  11.86843  11.1860714
150              Pakistan 0.538381761878611  66.2   7.78876  4.733353615
196                Nauru                       ..    ..   9.34942        ..
                 GNI
51  16676.09012
109  5223.032475
150  4866.183604

196       ..
```

You see that the rows requested are not available anymore. Then, the updated version of our data frame Data has no more section names.

This is a long process, but I want to be sure you understand the output of each step. In the next chapter, I use the complete.case() function (on page 211), but only because I already know these data. Sometimes simple approaches can give you incorrect results, and you should only apply them after you know the data file organization well. Next, let's find out the missing values representation in the spreadsheet. We do not have empty cells now, but we still have all our numbers as text:

```
mean(Data$HDI,na.rm = T)
```

In the command above, I requested the mean and got no good result, even though I instructed it not to consider missing values (na.rm = T). The problem is that Data$HDI is not yet a column of numbers, but is still a column of characters. We could try to convert all those values into numbers, but if there is a symbol representing missing values different from NA, R will still read the column as a cells of characters. We first need to identify those symbols and set them as NAs[11]:

```
# some object to represent important values
colsToCheck=seq(2,ncol(Data))
rowsToVisit=seq(1:nrow(Data))
# For-Loop
symbolsForNA=c()    # empty vector to be filled
for (i in rowsToVisit){
  for (j in colsToCheck){
    # Got an NA when trying to convert value to number?
    if (is.na(as.numeric(Data[i,j]))) { # WARNINGS!!!
    # if I got NA, I append that value
      symbolsForNA = c(symbolsForNA , as.character(Data[i,j]))
    }
  }
}
# Deleting repeated values:
symbolsForNA=unique(symbolsForNA)
```

---

[11] Replacing a string with NA is very easy, but you need to know what symbols are used instead of NA.

We got some warnings because the command as.numeric was applied to a non-numeric value.[12] When you try to turn a non-numeric symbol into a number using is.na(as.numeric(Data[i,j])), you will get a warning and the result will be NA. I used that result to find out the position (row i and column j) of the non-numeric value and the symbols used for missing values. Then, once this value is discovered, I append that non-numeric value to my vector. In this case, I only found one symbol: ".."; however, the code above is useful when there were more non-numeric symbols in a numeric column. Of course, a symbol can appear many times, but I need it just once in my vector; that is why I applied unique at the end to delete repeated symbols.

The strategy now is to replace every cell that has that symbol with NA, column by column. Notice that the next code will work if you have more than one non-numeric value:

```
#setting NAs
Data[2:6]=lapply(Data[2:6], # column by column
                 #replace value if it is in 'symbolsForNA':
                 function(x)
                 replace(x,x%in%symbolsForNA, NA))
```

The key function is replace, which will receive the content of a cell, x, and if x is equal to any of the elements in the vector of symbols for non-standard missing values (in our case symbolsForNA), R will replace the entire cell content, x, writing NA instead.

However, because we set stringsAsFactors as False when we read the data initially, the numeric values should still be text instead of numbers:

```
# I a using here some parameters in str(),
# so that the output is printed within
# the book margins:

str(Data,width = 70,strict.width = "cut")
```

```
'data.frame': 195 obs. of  6 variables:
 $ Country: chr  "Norway" "Australia" "Switzerland" "Denmark" ...
 $ HDI    : chr  "0.94387728002259" "0.934958250222263" "0.92961313"..
 $ LEB    : chr  "81.6" "82.4" "83" "80.2" ...
 $ EYS    : chr  "17.49259" "20.22107" "15.79043" "18.68933" ...
 $ MYS    : chr  "12.631" "12.96338081" "12.82348463" "12.72938824" ..
 $ GNI    : chr  "64992.34046" "42260.61295" "56431.06833" "44025.4"..
```

As you see, all the column value are non-numeric (characters). They are easily converted into numeric type (that would not be the case if their type were

---

[12] This will give no warning as.numeric ("3"), but this command as.numeric(",") will send a warning and the output will be precisely NA.

factor). We simply apply the function as.numeric to the data frame, column by column:

```
#Now chars into numbers
Data[2:6]=lapply(Data[2:6], # data frame
                as.numeric) # column by column
```

Notice the use of **lapply**. I introduced this command on page 67, but in a simpler way, because the function in that subsection had a different look, something like lapply(Data[2:6], sum), which will take every column and compute the sum of each of them (the function will return as many values as there are columns). That line of code will give a valid sum if there are no NA values in the column.[13] In the simpler form, lapply receives a data frame and applies a function to each column. **The output depends on the function.** In our previous example (using lapply and replace), we needed to make changes to *each* cell. That is why I wrote function (x), which allows lapply to apply the function to each element of the column, so we get one result per cell, column by column. I could have done this using a combination of **for** and **if**, but this was a good case to make use of this command and, improve readability. The last code worked differently because, as.numeric works with the whole column, altering all its values at once.

Up to this point we have a clean data frame. If you request a summary, you will get the correct results:

```
summary(Data)
```

```
    Country            HDI               LEB               EYS
 Length:195       Min.   :0.3483    Min.   :49.00    Min.   : 4.10
 Class :character 1st Qu.:0.5738    1st Qu.:65.22    1st Qu.:11.07
 Mode  :character Median :0.7241    Median :73.10    Median :13.07
                  Mean   :0.6924    Mean   :71.02    Mean   :12.86
                  3rd Qu.:0.8166    3rd Qu.:76.80    3rd Qu.:15.02
                  Max.   :0.9439    Max.   :84.00    Max.   :20.22
                  NA's   :7         NA's   :5        NA's   :6
       MYS              GNI
 Min.   : 1.374   Min.   :    580.7
 1st Qu.: 5.570   1st Qu.:   3752.8
 Median : 8.460   Median :  10558.7
 Mean   : 8.107   Mean   :  16888.1
 3rd Qu.:10.727   3rd Qu.:  22659.6
 Max.   :13.067   Max.   : 123124.4
 NA's   :7        NA's   :5
```

---

[13] If you had NAs in the column, you will need to write **lapply(Data[2:6],sum,na.rm=T)** to get the sum of the non-missing values.

Let's try to accomplish the same task using Python. This is relatively easy, because it uses a similar logic as in R:

- Let's set the location:

```
#%% Setting up
from pandas import read_excel
from os.path import join
folder='/Users/JoseManuel/Dropbox/BookData/chapter5'
filename="2015_statistical_annex_tables_all.xls"
fileXLS=join(folder,filename)
```

As you see, separating the folder and file name improves readability.
- Set some filters:

```
#%% Initial FILTERS:
FirstRow=9        # Remember Python Index starts in '0'
RowsToSkipFromBottom=68 # omit these rows from bottom up
colsOK=[1] + range(2,11,2) # columns to select
```

- Read in the file:

```
#%% Read in the data
Data=read_excel(fileXLS,"Table 1",
                skiprows=FirstRow,
                skip_footer=RowsToSkipFromBottom,
                parse_cols=colsOK,
                header=None, #No variable names!
                convert_float=False #keep floats!
                )
Data.columns=['Country','HDI','LEB','EYS','MYS','GNI']
```

Notice that the function `read_excel` has parameters that are similar to its R counterpart. The main difference is that to get the last row, you need to indicate how many rows to omit from the last row up.
- Let's build the data frame without section names:

```
#%% (I) Building data frame without section names:

# Columns of interest (all but first):
columnsToClean=Data.iloc[:,1:]

# Keep row when last five columns are NOT NaN:
Data=Data[columnsToClean.notnull().all(axis=1)]
```

The key to understand this simple code is `all(axis=1)`. This command, which you may see often, tells Python to apply the function `all` by rows (if `axis=0`, then the function is applied by column). Notice the use of `notnull`, which signals if a cell has a non-missing value (true) or not (false). The use of these functions made implementing this step really quick.

- Let's get the list of symbols that are used to represent the missing values. We already know it is just one symbol ('..'), so the approach is the same as in R:

```
#%% (II) Building list of symbols used as missing

rowsToVisit, colsToCheck=Data.shape
symbolsForNA=[] # list of NAs

for i in range(1,rowsToVisit):
    for j in range(1,colsToCheck):
        # is this symbol a character?
        if isinstance(Data.iloc[i,j],(basestring)):
            # append that symbol to my list of NAs
            symbolsForNA.append(Data.iloc[i,j])
# Deleting repeated values:
symbolsForNA=list(set(symbolsForNA))   #set works as unique in R
```

The key function here is isinstance, which asks if an element belongs to a particular kind. Here, to find out if a cell value is not a number, I am asking if the value in Data.iloc[i,j] is of type basestring.[14]

- Get the final version of the data frame, with the proper values (nan) where values are missing:

```
#%% (III) Replacing those symbols with NaN

import numpy as np
Data= Data.replace(symbolsForNA, np.nan)
```

Python does this step quicker than R, which cannot change all the values in the data frame at once, but must visit column by column.

After the code above is run, you can describe the data set and get the statistics you expect when your columns are numbers. Notice that the command describe will give statistics only for numerical values by default; because we have one column (Country) that is categorical, you may want to override the default and add include='all'. This is shown in Figure 5.8.

The Excel file from the United Nations had no codebook, but the functions of R and Python were able to deal with the common problems found in this kind of report. Now let's turn our attention to data scraped from the web. These data are always peculiar, so each case is a challenge. Let's use again the data from the example in Section 4.5.1 on page 118, using R.

```
# Collecting:
library(XML)
library(RCurl)
wiki = "https://en.wikipedia.org/wiki/"
link ="List_of_border_wars"
```

[14] In Python 3, str is used instead of basestring.

```
wikiPage = getURL(paste0(wiki,link))
wikiTables = readHTMLTable(wikiPage,
                        stringsAsFactors=FALSE) # FALSE!!
conflictDF=do.call('rbind', wikiTables)
```

```
Data.describe(include='all')
                       Country         HDI          LEB          EYS          MYS  \
count                      195  188.000000   190.000000   189.000000   188.000000
unique                     195         NaN          NaN          NaN          NaN
top         Russian Federation         NaN          NaN          NaN          NaN
freq                         1         NaN          NaN          NaN          NaN
mean                       NaN    0.692439    71.017789    12.862920     8.107455
std                        NaN    0.154702     8.416365     2.872384     3.092735
min                        NaN    0.348254    49.000000     4.100000     1.373855
25%                        NaN    0.582300    65.750000    11.106245     5.858860
50%                        NaN    0.727136    73.300000    13.279740     8.552604
75%                        NaN    0.831137    77.250000    15.186046    10.876732
max                        NaN    0.943877    84.000000    20.221070    13.066777

                      GNI
count          190.000000
unique                NaN
top                   NaN
freq                  NaN
mean         16888.135787
std          18734.508996
min            580.731815
25%           3830.446006
50%          10939.006000
75%          23900.309645
max         123124.359600
```

Figure 5.8 Clean summary with NaNs in Python.
Source: From http://hdr.undp.org/fr/data.

We are reading again that data from Wikipedia, but I have made a few changes to the code we used originally. Now, I ensure that my non-numeric values are not considered factors in R (stringsAsFactors=FALSE) and construct a data frame by binding other data frames at once using the function do.call, which is simpler than what we did on page 118. The command do.call is intuitive: It applies a function to a list of elements. This list of data frames (wikiTables) is the output of the function readHTMLTables.[15] It is important that every data frame in the list has the same headers, so that rbind will work. We made the headers consistent before, so I am able now to use do.call; that is, I would not use this function if I had not confirmed that the tables (data frames) had the same headers and were in the same locations. Let's request the first rows:

---

[15] This is different than lapply, which applies a function to each element.

```
> head(conflictDF)
          Start Finish              Conflict             Combatants Fatalities
NULL.1    1846   1848    Mexican-American War    United States v.  Mexico   ~29,000
NULL.2    1879   1883     War of the Pacific Chile v.  Bolivia and  Peru    ~10,000
NULL.11   1910   1918            Border War     United States v.  Mexico      100+
NULL.21   1932   1935            Chaco War          Bolivia v.  Paraguay   ~100,000
NULL.3    1938   1938 Battle of Lake Khasan    Soviet Union v.  Japan      ~1,300
NULL.4    1939   1939  Slovak-Hungarian War       Slovakia v.  Hungary        66
```

The result you see has weird row names, which were produced during the *binding* process. It is easy to reset the row names (you want to run `str(conflictDF)` immediately after to check what you have so far):

```
rownames(conflictDF)=NULL   # resetting the row names
```

We do not have "section names" in these data, so our first step is identifying the non-numeric symbols in the columns 1, 2, and 5, where the numbers, currently set as *characters*, are. To identify those symbols, I create two data frames, one for the symbols and the other to save the column where a character was found:

```
colsToCheck=c(1,2,5)
NAsymbols=c() # to save symbols
NAsymbolsColumns=c() # to save positions
for (i in seq(1:nrow(conflictDF))){
    for (j in colsToCheck){
        if (is.na(as.numeric(conflictDF[i,j]))) {
            # found a character I could not convert to number!
            # add character to NAsymbols and
            # its position to NAsymbolsColumns:
            NAsymbolsColumns = c(NAsymbolsColumns,as.numeric(j))
            NAsymbols    = c(NAsymbols, as.character(conflictDF[i,j]))
        }
    }
} # you will get some warnings, don't worry!
NAs=data.frame(Column=NAsymbolsColumns,
               Symbol=NAsymbols)
# dropping rows where symbols repeat:
NAs=NAs[!duplicated(NAs$Symbol),]
#sorting by 'Column' location:
NAs=NAs[order(NAs$Column), ]
```

The code above follows the same strategy used for the same purpose. It uses the command **duplicated** to inform, using TRUE or FALSE, which values in the column NAs$Symbol have already appeared. As before, the brackets help me subset the NAs data frame. I also use **order**, which allows me to sort a data frame by a specific column value; here, I sorted the data frame by the value of

```
> NAs
     Column    Symbol
1         5   ~29,000
2         5   ~10,000
3         5      100+
4         5  ~100,000
5         5    ~1,300
6         5   ~16,000
7         5    ~3,000
8         5    ~4,000
9         5     ~6,80
10        5   ~4,000+
11        5   ~2,400.
12        5   Unknown
13        5    ~4,500
14        5   262-322
15        5   150-200
```

Figure 5.9 NAs obtained in a scraped table. Each row says in what column the symbol is located. I omitted the row number.
Source: https://en.wikipedia.org/wiki/List_of_border_conflicts.

the column where the symbol was found. There are 15 values that could not be converted to numbers,[16] as shown in Figure 5.9.

Figure 5.9 is very important. There you see that only one of the three columns, the fifth column (*Fatalities*), has values that could not be converted to numbers (the other two columns still have numbers as characters, but we know they can be converted into numeric type). Most of the values on fatalities could be "recovered" under some assumptions. You can get the mean of the cells showing an interval (262–362), you can omit the approximation symbol (~), and so on. The strategy you use has to be well reasoned according to the case, unless you simply want to turn them all into NA. The most clear candidate for NAs is Unknown. For the purpose of this section, let's just set all those non-numeric symbols, as NA. As before, we visit every value in a column and set each value that is in the set of non-numeric symbols as NA; then every value of the columns is set as a number.

```
#setting NAs
conflictDF[c(2,5)]=lapply(conflictDF[c(2,5)],
               #setting as NA if is 'x'is a symbol:
               function(x) replace(x,x%in%NAs$Symbol, NA))
#Now chars into numbers
conflictDF[c(2,5)]=lapply(conflictDF[c(2,5)],
               #coercing x into numeric
               function(x) as.numeric(x))
```

[16] Remember that this value may be different by the time you read this book.

The reasoning was simple, but we have lost a lot of information in the last code. We could have done better, but let's return to this later.

The same result can be obtained in Python. The code below starts with the creation of the data frame (step 4 on page 123):

```
#%% Creating data frame
from collections import OrderedDict as OD
from pandas import DataFrame as DF
import numpy as np
#Data frame
wikiTablesTuples=(('Start',start),('End',end),
                 ('Conflict',conflict),
                 ('Combatants',combatants),
                 ('Fatalities',fatalities))
wikiTablesDict= OD(wikiTablesTuples)
conflictDF= DF.from_dict(wikiTablesDict)
```

I start by creating an *ordered dictionary*, where the order of creation is respected. The next step is to create the data frame with the non-numeric symbols:

```
#%% Identifying non-numeric symbols

Nrows,Ncols=conflictDF.shape
colsToCheck=[0,1,4] # 1st, 2nd and 5th column
NAsymbols=[]
NAsymbolsColumns=[]

for i in range(Nrows):
    for j in colsToCheck:
        try:
            # try to convert cell value into a number:
            float (conflictDF.iloc[i,j])
        except ValueError:
            # this happens if conversion fails:
            NAsymbols.append(conflictDF.iloc[i,j])
            NAsymbolsColumns.append(j)

## create data frame using the two lists:
NAs=DF.from_dict({'Column':NAsymbolsColumns,
                  'Symbol':NAsymbols})
# data frame without duplicates
NAs=NAs.drop_duplicates('Symbol',False).sort('Column')
```

This time, I do not use **if**, but *exceptions* (review this topic from page 76). When you try to set a non-numeric symbol as a number, an error/warning is generated in R, which lets you know you have a non-numeric symbol in R. In this case, I am using the warnings/errors: when the coercion of a value to a float fails, I save (append to a list) that value and its column. The duplicates in NAs are then erased, and the whole data is sorted by the values in Column.

The last step is simply to replace the values in the data frame that are in the set of non-numeric symbols by NaN:

```
#%% Setting all non-numeric symbols as NaN:

badValues=list(set(NAsymbolsColumns))   #uniques
goodValues=np.nan

conflictDF.replace(badValues, goodValues,inplace=True)
```

5.1.3 Missing Values Plan

Once missing values are set, you can do all the basic statistical work without a problem, because those values will not be considered in the computations. However, because your data is going to be used to test complex hypotheses that make some inferences about the population, you may want to assess how a particular technique you are planning to use could be affected by the missing values. In particular, missing data should be evaluated to decide if it does not affect our analysis (ignorable) and could be **deleted** or omitted. If that is not the case, then we need to decide how to replace or **impute** them.

According to Allison (2002), there are two ways to delete NAs: the list-wise and the pairwise approaches. In both cases rows are deleted; however, the listwise approach considers the whole data set, whereas the pairwise approach only addresses the particular set of variables used in the analysis. Python and R have flexible ways to subset the data set, and particular techniques will provide options on how to treat the missing data in either approach. However, deleting rows may be a very weak way to deal with missing data.

The replacement of missing values is sometimes a must. There are some simple practices like replacing a missing value by one of the averages (mean, median, mode and the like) of its variable. However, as Raghunathan (2015) makes clear, one needs to understand very well the nature of the missing value to make a good plan on how to treat it, rather than simply replacing it at will. That is why missing value imputation is an important topic, and currently there are several advanced techniques to understand the nature of the missing values and propose a particular technique for their treatment.

All these techniques are beyond the scope of this book,[17] but what is clear is that our data needs to be as complete as possible. Therefore, the rest of the chapter presents more cleaning approaches to avoiding an overpopulation of missing values.

---

[17] For a user-friendly presentation of the topic, read the book *Missing Values Analysis and Data Imputation* by David Garson (it is currently free on Amazon Kindle's unlimited program).

5.2 Dirty Values

In the previous section we identified what values could not fit in the column type and decided to turn them into NA in R, or into NaN in Python. That was a good way to proceed in the UN spreadsheet case because the symbol identified actually was the symbol for missingness. However, that same approach applied to the case of scraping Wikipedia was the worst approach ever. If listwise deleting of missing values were applied, only 20% of the data would remain. This section examines ways to clean values that are dirty; that is, surrounded by symbols that make it difficult to coerce the value into the "appropriate" type. Remember that the computer cannot tell you what is the appropriate type; you need to decide that. We have not yet addressed that issue explicitly, but will focus on it beginning in this section. Once we are sure of the data type and what it is representing/measuring, we can start planning the cleaning of dirty values.

5.2.1 A Note on Encoding

Computers understand binary language, so there is a need to create mappings between what you write and read, and the computer. Therefore, you can understand *encoding* as a way to translate each character from a human alphabet into a sequence that the computer can understand. Dirtiness in your data can happen if R or Python is assuming an encoding that does not correspond to the language used in the characters of the data collected. The worst case is when you think something is a misspelled string when it is not; that is, you see an arguably "bad typed" string, but that is because it is an incorrect translation of the string, and you decide to "clean" data that is not really dirty, but is just wrongly encoded. For instance, when reading a file in Chinese; if you do not set the *GB 18030* encoding, you will see most of the document as dirty when it is not, because the encoding limits the amount of characters handled. There are many programmers and software addressing this issue, but Unicode is working in unifying the different encodings into a global one. In the following section, I explicitly request UTF-8 encoding, because it deals with most characters (it is the standard in the Internet). It may not work in every case for you, so before you start cleaning, be sure you have understood the encoding of your data.

5.2.2 Removal of Dirty Elements: Regular Expressions

In this subsection, I make use of **regular expressions** (or *regex*). The table scraped from Wikipedia before is a good candidate for doing some cleaning with them. Let's start by figuring out the data types for this kind of data:

- The data on years (`start`, `end`) and `Fatalities` should be numbers.
- The `conflict` and `Combatants` values are strings, which can include alphabets and non-alphabet symbols (punctuation symbols and other symbology).

Let's keep this in mind as we redo the cleaning of the border conflict data using R.

```
library(XML)
library(RCurl)
wiki = "https://en.wikipedia.org/wiki/"
link ="List_of_border_wars"
wikiPage = getURL(paste0(wiki,link))
wikiTables = readHTMLTable(wikiPage,
                           encoding="UTF-8", # encoding!
                           stringsAsFactors=FALSE)
ConfDirty=do.call("rbind", wikiTables)
rownames(ConfDirty)=NULL # resetting indexes
```

Notice that I am explicitly requesting the UTF−8 encoding and setting *stringsAsFactors* as false again. This will help me avoid having so many missing values. Another important thing to consider is that data from Wikipedia is continually updated, so by the time you read this book, there may be more information on the wikipage than in this example. So, to enable you to replicate it, I added a CSV file with these data:

```
file=file.path("~","Dropbox","BookData","chapter5","ConfDirty.csv")
ConfDirty=read.csv(file)
```

From this point on, you are now working with a new `ConfDirty`. Now, I will go into each cell of this data frame and find a way to obtain the numeric values, which you know from Figure 5.9 are surrounded by non-numeric characters. A naive approach would be to get the position of each cell with dirty values and write customized commands, such as the following:

```
# NOT GOOD:
if (valueOfCell == '~100,000'){
  valueOfCell=100000 }
```

However, if there were several cases like this, you would need to write a command for each case, which would take too much of your time. We need a better computational approach, and this is when regular expressions, or *regex*,[18] come in handy. Let me show you a simple example:

---

[18] Regular expressions is a very important topic; for detailed explanations read Goyvaerts and Levithan (2012) or Forta (2000).

```
#install.packages("stringi")
library(stringi)
# example VECTOR, I need to clean the last element:
YEARS=c("1950", "1970", "1985", "around 1990")
# STEP 1
## write the pattern to look for (regular expression, or regex):
pattern = "\\d+" #this means 'consecutive digits'
# STEP 2
## extract the pattern from every value:
YEARSonly=stri_extract_first_regex(YEARS,pattern)
# see result:
YEARSonly
```

```
[1] "1950" "1970" "1985" "1990"
```

The example above is very simple, but informative. The most important step is to provide the right `pattern`, and then a function like `stri_extract_first_regex` can do the rest.[19] This function simply visits each value in the vector and returns digits, as long the digits are consecutive:`"\\d+"`.

The column "Fatalities" has a similar but more complex problem than in the example just shown. In that column, for example, there is the value ~29,000; using my previous strategy will just return 29, because in this cell, the ",", breaks the continuity. There may be more symbols that have that effect, so I propose to explore this column, to find out exactly which values are different from numbers. The strategy here is to replace all the digits with nothing (' or " "), thereby revealing whatever is not a digit.

```
# 'pattern' is the same as above
# replacement
nothing=""
Dirt=stri_replace_all_regex(ConfDirty$Fatalities,
                            pattern,
                            nothing)
Dirt=unique(Dirt)
```

Now `Dirt` will reveal what this symbols are:

```
> Dirt
[1] "~,"        "+"         " "         "~,+"
[5] "~,."       "Unknown"   "-"         " - "
```

---

[19] There are different functions from other packages, but they all require that you input a *pattern*. Therefore the main problem is determining this *pattern*.

Let's understand this output:

1. There are approximations: ∼.
2. There are values greater than (or at least): +.
3. There are intervals using the *hyphen-minus* (or minus) - and the *en dash* −
   (a symbol bigger than the hyphen-minus but smaller than the *em dash*).
4. There are dots (.), which may be a character without much meaning because
   the variable is an integer. However, this may be true for the United States,
   but is not a global rule, where the . can be used also to separate thousands
   (while the comma is used for the decimal position).[20]
5. There are commas (,), which in this case represent thousands, but remember,
   from the previous bullet, that this is not a global rule.

Let's do some reasoning for this particular case. Wars either have a definite
or approximate number of deaths. When there is an approximate value around a
number, extra characters are used (∼, +). When the approximation has possible
lower and upper limits, an interval is used (with two different symbols: "−−"
and "-") . Trying to replace all the non-numeric symbols with nothing will
not work with intervals, because both values will be concatenated; for example, 150-200 will turn into 150200, when we replace the hyphen-minus with
nothing (remember that the symbol for the intervals is different for the two
cells in this case). Let me give you some examples that will be useful for creating our code:

- How can we recover two *numbers* from a *string* representing an interval, like
  150-200? Here we need to learn how to split a string, which is simple if you
  know what to use as the splitting character(s):

```
cell="150-200"
splittingCharacter="-"
splittedCell=strsplit(cell,splittingCharacter)
# RESULT:
splittedCell
```
```
[[1]]
[1] "150" "200"
```

The code above gave us what we wanted. Then, once we have the two values,
I need to decide if I keep one of them, using min or max, or should obtain
an average, like the *median*, the *mean* or the *mode*. Given that I need to use
these values in a math function, let me use the function mean:

---

[20] Visit https://en.wikipedia.org/wiki/Decimal_mark.

```
mean(splittedCell)
```
```
[1] NA
```

The last result is obviously incorrect, which means I made a mistake. What did I do wrong? The problem is that the function mean does not have as input a pair of numbers, but instead it has a list with one element:

```
str(splittedCell)
```
```
List of 1
 $ : chr [1:2] "150" "200"
```

To access the first (and only) element of this list, we simply write:

```
splittedCell[[1]]
```
```
[1] "150" "200"
```

However, those values are still texts:

```
mean(splittedCell[[1]])
```
```
[1] NA
```

A simple operation will turn those strings into numbers:

```
mean(as.numeric(splittedCell[[1]]))
```
```
[1] 175
```

This should have been the initial code for this situation:

```
cell="150-200" #also works for "150 - 200"
splittingCharacter="-"
splittedCell = strsplit(cell,splittingCharacter)[[1]]
mean(as.numeric(splittedCell))
```

The code above also works if you had "150 - 200", because as.numeric will discard those white spaces (I discuss this in more detail later).

• How can I apply the previous function (strsplit) when I have different splitting characters? Remember that we have cells with strings as intervals using a different kind of "dash" to separate both values. The smart thing to do is to create a regular expression pattern. We could create a vector of all the splitting characters, but because it may be difficult to type characters using your keyboard, we should consider using their Unicode representation to be more precise:

```
cells=c("262-322","150-200" )
Dashes=c('\u2013','\u002D') # (en-dash, hyphen-minus)
DashesPattern=paste(Dashes,collapse="|")
splittedCell=strsplit(cells,DashesPattern)
```

```
#
# success?
splittedCell
```

```
[[1]]
[1] "262" "322"

[[2]]

[1] "150" "200"
```

Our regular expression worked very well. The vector of dashes was concatenated with the symbol |, which means **OR**, so `strsplit` will split when either symbol is found in the string. However, there is a weak element in this approach: there are many kind of dashes/hyphens,[21] and they are difficult to differentiate visually. Fortunately, there are some powerful regular expressions to deal with this situation:

```
DashesPattern="\\p{Pd}" # all dashes and hyphens
splittedCell=strsplit(cells,DashesPattern,perl=TRUE)
#
# same success?
splittedCell
```

```
[[1]]
[1] "262" "322"

[[2]]

[1] "150" "200"
```

This last code is the one we need. Notice that in the function `strsplit` we set the argument `perl=TRUE` (the default setting is FALSE), which can interpret this particular kind of pattern.[22]

- How can I extract the numbers from a string in which numeric and non-numeric symbols are combined in different ways? First replace non-numeric values with `nothing`:

```
cell="~4,000+"
pattern="\\D" # opposite of "\\d"
nothing=''
stri_replace_all_regex(cell,pattern,nothing)
```

```
[1] "4000"
```

The code gives us a great strategy to recover the numbers: omitting non-numeric values. Again, the most important element here is the pattern. This simple regex pattern detects which single elements are **NOT** numeric values in the string. The function `stri_replace_all_regex` (also from the *stringi* package) has a name that is very descriptive of what it does. R has

---

[21] At http://www.fileformat.info/info/unicode/category/Pd/list.htm you can find the Unicodes for hyphens and dashes.

[22] At http://www.regular-expressions.info/unicode.html you can see this and other similar regex.

also a basic function named gsub. You can use this function by just writing gsub(pattern,nothing,cell) instead.

From the explanations given earlier, I can now offer a unified code to clean that column. I prepare a code that will read *each* value of the column, *splits* it, and recovers its *first* element. Then, I will *count* how many strings I got. *If* I get two strings, I will compute the mean of the two numbers because I found an interval. And if the splitting gives as output just one element, it means I have a cell with one value, which I will clean. Take a look at this unified code:

```
# regex patterns
Dashes="\\p{Pd}"
NonNumeric="\\D"
nothing=""
#
# for storing clean output
cleanCells=c()
#
# for EACH ELEMENT in the COLUMN
for (cell in ConfDirty$Fatalities){
  # keeping first element of list...
  splittedCell=strsplit(cell,Dashes,perl=T)[[1]]
  sizeOf_splittedCell=length(splittedCell)
  #
  # if I get two strings
  if (sizeOf_splittedCell==2){
    averageClean=mean(as.numeric(splittedCell))
    cleanCells=c(cleanCells,averageClean)
  }else{
    # if I did not get two strings
    cellClean=gsub(NonNumeric,nothing,splittedCell) #'Unknown' to ''
    cleanCells=c(cleanCells,as.numeric(cellClean))  # '' to NA
  }
}
```

The end of the code also took care of Unknown, which first was turned into nothing by gsub and then turned into NA by as.numeric:

```
cleanCells
```

```
 [1] 29000 10000   100 100000  1300    66 16000  3000
4000    680
[11]  4000  2400    NA   4500    30    20   144    42
 292     17
[21]   175
```

This vector needs to replace the whole column to finish our job:

```
ConfDirty$Fatalities=cleanCells
```

The same result can be obtained using Python, but you first need to install the package **regex** in your environment (It is in Anaconda, but if you do not find it, go to the terminal and type **pip install regex**). Then, use the CSV file provided to replicate this example.

```
#%% Collecting

# packages needed
import os
import pandas as pd

#location
folderData='/Users/JoseManuel/Dropbox/BookData/chapter5'
fileCSV=os.path.join(folderData ,"ConfDirty.csv")

# reading in, with encoding
ConfDirty=pd.read_csv(fileCSV,encoding='utf-8')
```

Then, I follow the previous strategy (coded in R) to clean the column in Python:

```
#%% Cleaning

# packages needed
import regex as re
import numpy as np

# regex patterns
Dashes=re.compile(u"\\p{Pd}")
NonNumeric = re.compile(u"\\D")
nothing=""

# for storing clean output
cleanCells=[]

# for EACH ELEMENT in the COLUMN
for cell in ConfDirty.Fatalities:

    # keeping first element of list...
    splittedCell=re.split(Dashes,cell)
    sizeOf_splittedCell=len(splittedCell)

    # if I get two strings
    if sizeOf_splittedCell==2:
        averageClean=np.mean(map(int,splittedCell))
        cleanCells.append(averageClean)
    else:
    # if I did not get two strings
        cellClean=NonNumeric.sub(nothing,splittedCell[0])
        cleanCells.append(cellClean)
```

Unlike in R, I opened the CSV file in Python using the encoding "utf-8." The CSV file was produced in R, so I made sure pandas read it appropriately. In fact, if you omit that step, the code will fail. The packages `regex` and `numpy`

are the only external aids we need to produce a similar code as in R, which I
was able to do with only some minor differences:

- Notice that the patterns have a letter **u** next to them, which indicates we are
  reading its Unicode form.
- The patterns are being *compiled*; that is, we used re.compile to prepare the
  patterns to be used later by other functions that can read regular expressions.
- The command re.split(Dashes,cell) returns a simple list of elements.
  In R, you received a list with a different structure, which required that you
  access its first element with [[1]]. Python is simpler to use in this case.
- The map function, introduced on page 79, was in charge of coercing the interval bounds into integers, so that the function mean could be applied (we used
  as.numeric in R).
- The function sub does the same as its equivalent in R (gsub), but its syntax
  is different. Note that you apply this function to splittedCell when it has
  a single value, but sub does not need the list, only its first element. That is
  why I used [0] to access the first, and only, element.

The output, splittedCell, has the right values but in the wrong types, and
we still need to transform Unknown, which now is nothing, into an NA. This
code completes the work:

```
#%% Updating column:

ConfDirty.Fatalities=pd.to_numeric(cleanCells, errors='coerce')
```

The function to_numeric converts our list into the right type, coerces nothing
into NaN, and replaces the column values in the data frame. To see the result,
simply run the command ConfDirty.describe(include='all').

In this section I presented the basic approach to cleaning data using R and
Python. Everything we have seen will be used again in the next chapters,
and new challenges will appear while we keep advancing in our knowledge
and skills.

PART THREE

FORMATTING AND STORING DATA

6

Formatting the "Clean" Data

The last subsection dealt with erasing inappropriate characters that prevented a value from being read properly. For that, concepts like encoding and regular expressions proved useful for recovering the actual value of the cell and cleaning it. However, there is still so much to do. Formatting will deal with issues that occur during and after the cleaning stage =. The data can be clean, but may still need to respect some constraints to be useful for the next stages.

It is not enough that a value looks clean; you may need to coerce it into the appropriate data type. This can be done only if you are knowledgeable about the different ways a value can be represented. Table 6.1 lists various data types in Python and R.

Values can be expressed in several different data types. For example, the word "High" could mean many things. It can be a string (a last name?), or you may need it as a ordered category/factor for a variable ("High," "Medium,"

Table 6.1. *Data types in Python and R*

Data Types			
Group	Subgroup	Python 2.7	R
String	Non-alphabets	basestring	character
	Alphabets	basestring	character
Dichotomous		category	factor
Polytomous	Nominal	category	factor
	Ordinal	ordered category	ordered factor
Counts		integer/date	integer/date
Magnitude	Interval	float/integer	float/integer
	Ratio	float	float

Table 6.2. *Start dates of calendars in different programs*

Program	Start of Calendar	Counting
R	January 1, 1970	Number of days
SPSS	October 14, 1582	Number of seconds
STATA	January 1, 1960	Number of days
Excel	January 1, 1900 (1904 for Mac)	Number of days
Open Office	January 1, 1900	Number of days
Python	October 15, 1582	Number of days
SAS	January 1, 1960	Number of seconds

"Low"). These values may be represented by numbers (for example, 1,3,5) that are restricted to a particular set of math operations. All measures of central tendency can be computed for values in a ratio scale, but not if they are in interval scale. The data may be clean, but not be in the right type, and neither R nor Python can figure out what are the right types for your data: You need to do that. Your *research design* and theoretical background should always support and justify the decisions you have to make.

This chapter focuses on formatting cleaned data, which involves more than setting cell values; it also covers how to organize the structure of the data frame into a more complex one. For instance, I will show how to format data from data frames into a *network*.

6.1 Formatting Dates

6.1.1 Pre-Formatted Dates

The representation of dates is tricky, so let me address them first. A date formatted for a particular program may not be well read in another one. Each program has different configurations to treat and interpret dates, as shown in Table 6.2.[1]

For example, in Figure 4.7 on page 92, you will see a problem with dates (column bdate) that occurred when I imported the SPSS file "Employee Data." As you can see in that figure, while bdate is properly formatted in SPSS, a different format (simple number) appears in the data frame created. The problem originates in the package foreign, which does not have an option to recover dates properly. To correct it, you have two options:

---

[1] I recommend to always search for this information, because it may vary with new releases. Always run a small test on the data to see if the standards from Table 6.2 are still working.

- Keep using the `foreign` package and create the code to produce the right format.
- Use a different package.

Let me take the easy way now, the second option, using the package `Hmisc` to solve this issue:

```
library(Hmisc)
folderData=file.path("~","Dropbox","BookData","chapter6")
fileSpss=file.path(folderData,"Employee Data.sav")
#
# EXPLICITING which column is a date:
testData=spss.get(fileSpss, datevars=c('bdate'))
#
# Veryfying:
class(testData$bdate)
```

```
[1] "Date"
```

You see that this gives you the right type, but also some warnings. No need to worry. You can now check that you have dates:

```
# Re-Veryfying:
head(testData$bdate)
```

```
[1] "1952-02-03" "1958-05-23" "1929-07-26" "1947-04-15" "1955-02-09"
[6] "1958-08-22"
```

Fortunately, `read.dta()`, in the `foreign` package, does read date format into R by default, so if you have an STATA file, you can use that package and that function (as long it is in version 12 or lower).[2] It is the same in Python: STATA files read with pandas can interpret well the dates by default.

However, there are cases that could be a little more challenging. I have a file from the European Central Bank (ECB)[3] named `EuroDollarTime.csv` in the folder of this chapter. Please open this spreadsheet in Excel or a similar program to see how it looks, and let's use R at the same time:

```
# Get data:
folderData=file.path("~","Dropbox","BookData","chapter6")
fileCSV=file.path(folderData,"EuroDollarTime.csv")
ratesEuroDollar = read.csv(fileCSV,skip=4, stringsAsFactors =F)
#
# A simple look:
head(ratesEuroDollar)
```

---

[2] Install haven for higher versions. Follow the instructions at https://github.com/hadley/haven.
[3] The ECB data warehouse is available at http://sdw.ecb.europa.eu.

```
      Period.Unit. X.US.dollar..
 1       30/11/15       1.0579
 2       27/11/15       1.058
 3       26/11/15       1.0612
 4       25/11/15       1.0586
 5       24/11/15       1.0651

 6       23/11/15       1.0631
```

As you see, the numeric values look fine, but the dates are in the European format. The names are also weird. Let's change the names and then see how R is interpreting them:

```
names(ratesEuroDollar)=c("date","dollarRate")
str(ratesEuroDollar)
```

```
'data.frame':   4133 obs. of  2 variables:
 $ date      : chr  "30/11/15" "27/11/15" "26/11/15" "25/11/15" ...
 $ dollarRate: chr  "1.0579" "1.058" "1.0612" "1.0586" ...
```

For R, both are merely strings. Do not think this happens because you applied the setting `stringsAsFactors` =F. Applying that setting does NOT mean that everything has to be read as a string. If a column is full of clean numbers, then numbers should be recovered; R is interpreting the numbers as strings in this instance because some character is provoking that action.

Let's first format the column for the dates:

```
formatInEurope="%d/%m/%y" #for dd/mm/yy
dateChanged=strptime(ratesEuroDollar[,1],format=formatInEurope)
ratesEuroDollar[,1]=as.Date(dateChanged)
```

If the code above worked, we should be able to apply math operations to the dates:

```
ratesEuroDollar[1,1]-1 # day before 2015-11-30
```

```
[1] "2015-11-29"
```

The code worked well. One key operation was the formatting of the dates (`formatInEurope`). In general, you can vary that format because programming languages accept these symbols and their connectors (/, -, etc.) in different combinations:

- \%d-\%m-\%y for dd-mm-yy (mm is month as a pair of digits)
- \%d-\%B-\%y for dd-(full month name)-yy

- \%d-\%b-\%y for dd-(short name of month)-yy
- \%d-\%b-\%YY for dd-mm-yyyy (yyyy is the year including the century)
- Other combinations including hour (\%h), minute (\%M), etc.[4]

Finally, let's clean and format the second column.

```
ratesEuroDollar[,2]=as.numeric(ratesEuroDollar[,2])
```

You got some warnings, because there were some cell values that could not be coerced into numeric form and so were converted to NA (those cells were the reason this column was interpreted as strings). Please note that the code below will NOT work:

```
ratesEuroDollar[,2]=as.numeric(ratesEuroDollar[2])
```

The function as.numeric reads vectors, so ratesEuroDollar $dollarRate and ratesEuroDollar[,2] are accepted because both are vectors. However, if you input this data frame: ratesEuroDollar[2], it causes an error.

Let's see how we can clean and format this data using Python:

```
#%%  COLLECTING and FORMATTING

import os, pandas as pd   # two imports!!

# Location:
folderData=os.path.join("~","Dropbox","BookData","chapter6")
fileCSV=os.path.join(folderData,"EuroDollarTime.csv")

# Arguments:
firstRow=4 ; columnsWithDates=[0]
newNames=['date','dollarRate']

# Reading
ratesEuroDollar=pd.read_csv(fileCSV, header=firstRow,
                        parse_dates = columnsWithDates,
                        dayfirst=True, # Dates in European format?
                        names=newNames)
```

We have two key arguments here, parse_dates and dayfirst, that eliminate the need to write code. The former receives a list with the column positions of the dates, and the latter requires True if the dates are in European format (as are our dates). Finally, let's convert the last column to numbers:

---

[4] Please type ?strptime on your RStudio console for all the details on date formats.

```
#%% CLEANING

change=ratesEuroDollar.dollarRate
ratesEuroDollar.dollarRate=pd.to_numeric(change, errors='coerce')

# Remember that 'ratesEuroDollar.dollarRate' is equal to:
# ratesEuroDollar['dollarRate']
# ratesEuroDollar[2]
# ratesEuroDollar.iloc[:,1]
```

The formatting into numbers is also straightforward. Notice that we need the argument errors='coerce' in to_numeric to convert into NaN whatever was not convertible into a number.

6.1.2 Building Dates

There is an interesting Wikipedia page that shows the dates when countries gained their independence. (list of national independence days). Let's retrieve it using R:

```
library(XML)
library(RCurl)
wiki="https://en.wikipedia.org/wiki/"
link="List_of_national_independence_days"
wikiPage = getURL(paste0(wiki,link))
wikiTables = readHTMLTable(wikiPage,
                           encoding="UTF-8",
                           stringsAsFactors=FALSE)
# first table!
Indep=wikiTables[[1]][c(1:3)] # SLICING
# renaming columns
names(Indep)=c("Country","MonthDay","Year")
```

As I noted earlier, each scraping project is unique. In this case, the output has a structure that is difficult to deal with, as shown in Figure 6.1. In that figure, readHTMLTable could not read well the rows where a country has two independence days. It also recovered the second column MonthDay with a pair of values, separated by !: one with the date in numeric style and the other in alphanumeric style.

These results would require either that we dive deeper into R or that we find an alternative function. Fortunately, another package named htmltab (Rubba (2016)) can deal with this situation. Let me show you the code:

```
# install.packages("htmltab") # Installation needed
# LINK (same as before)
wiki="https://en.wikipedia.org/wiki/"
page="List_of_national_independence_days"
```

```
wikipage = paste0(wiki,page)
newNames=c("Country","MonthDay","Year")
#
# COLLECTING
library(htmltab) # which: first table!
Indep = htmltab(doc = wikipage, which = 1)[c(1:3)] #SLICING
#
# RENAMING
names(Indep)=newNames
```

```
> head(Indep,15)
                  Country        MonthDay                                                          Year
1              Afghanistan    08-19 !August 19                                                    1919
2                  Albania   11-28 !November 28                                                   1912
3                  Algeria      07-05 !July 5                                                     1962
4                   Angola   11-11 !November 11                                                   1975
5                 Anguilla     05-30 !May 30                                                      1967
6       Antigua and Barbuda   11-01 !November 1                                                   1981
7                Argentina      07-09 !July 9                                                      1816
8                  Armenia     05-28 !May 28                                                       1918
9      09-21 !September 21            1991            Independence from the Soviet Union in 1991
10                 Austria   10-26 !October 26                                                    1955
11               Azerbaijan    05-28 !May 28                                                      1918
12     10-18 !October 18              1991 Independence re-declared from the Soviet Union in 1991
13                  Bahamas     07-10 !July 10                                                    1973
14                  Bahrain   12-16 !December 16                                                  1971
15               Bangladesh    03-26 !March 26                                                    1971
```

Figure 6.1 Defective scraping output. This was produced using readHTMLTable.
Only the first 15 rows are displayed.

Again, I saved the data I collected in a file. To get the file to replicate the example, use this code:

```
# Location
folderData=file.path("~","Dropbox","BookData","chapter6")
fileCSV=file.path(folderData,"independenceDay.csv")
#opening the file
Indep = read.csv(fileCSV,stringsAsFactors =F)
```

First, let me create a function to clean a very hidden dirty element, the *space* or blanks. This element is hidden because spaces can have several representations beyond the simple bar space; for example, the space known as the no break space or *nbsp*, whose HTML version is . So, it is better to always replace it by " " (bar space). Let me show you how to do this with a simple example:

```
# Packages needed:
require(stringr)
require(stringi)
#
# for regex:
```

```
pattern="\\s+"
test=" Bolivia , and Peru in      1990     . "
barspace=" "
stri_replace_all(test,regex=pattern,barspace)
```

| [1] " Bolivia , and Peru in 1990 . "

With this code I replaced all kinds of spaces, even a series of them (the + symbol means one or more), with bar space. However, there are still some leading and trailing spaces that need treatment:

```
cleaner=stri_replace_all(test,regex=pattern," ") #previous
str_trim(cleaner) # new result:
```

| [1] "Bolivia , and Peru in 1990 ."

Now you see that there are still spaces between a word and a punctuation mark, so let's take care of that:

```
nothing=""
pattern="\\s(?=[,.!?:])" # space followed by ONE of these
clean=str_trim(cleaner) #previous
stri_replace_all(clean,regex=pattern,nothing) # newest result:
```

| [1] "Bolivia, and Peru in 1990."

The final cleaning step wrote nothing where there was a space before a punctuation mark. With this we can make a function to clean the column of a data frame:

```
cleanSpaces=function(aColumn){
  require(stringr)
  require(stringi)
  pattern1="\\s+"
  pattern2="\\s(?=[,.!?:])"
  barspace=" "
  nothing=''
  cleanColumn=c()
  for (aCell in aColumn){
    # Multiple spaces by one bar space
    clean=stri_replace_all(aCell,regex=pattern1,barspace)
    # Bye trailing and leading spaces
    cleaner=str_trim(clean)
    # Bye spaces before punctuation
    cleanest=stri_replace_all(cleaner,regex=pattern2,nothing)
    cleanColumn=c(cleanColumn,cleanest)
  }
  return (cleanColumn)
}
```

I can apply this function that I created to the whole data frame and coerce the result (which is a list) into one frame:

```
cleanButList=lapply(Indep,cleanSpaces)
Indep=as.data.frame(cleanButList,stringsAsFactors = F)
```

Our Indep data frame looks much better than the one scraped with readHTMLTable. Now let's pay attention now to the type of data we have obtained. First, I want to confirm if Year has been interpreted as a number:

```
class(Indep$Year)
```

```
[1] "character"
```

If the column Year has been interpreted as a string, it means that there is at least one cell with non-numeric values. This is a problem that needs to be solved. Follow these steps to convert years into numbers.

- We need to know where are the values that prevent this column from being read as a vector of numbers. Let's find the cells that have a non-numeric character:

```
# some arguments:
pattern="\\D" # not a number
where=Indep$Year
cellContent=TRUE
cellRowIndex=FALSE
# USING REGEX:
grep(pattern,where,value=cellContent)
```

```
[1] "1810 and 1819" "5708 (1948)"
```

I now introduce the function grep, which saves a lot of time. In the previous chapter we used loops and conditionals for similar issues, but because you are becoming more familiar with regular expressions, I am adding this one. As you just saw, the pattern represents a non-numeric value. So grep visits the column (vector) and sees if the pattern is present in that cell; if so, grep will return either the actual content of the cell (value=TRUE) or the cell row index (value=FALSE). That is, this will give you the row positions of the cell:

```
# USING REGEX:
grep(pattern,where,value=cellRowIndex)
```

```
[1] 37 80
```

- You need to decide what information you will want from the cleaned-up cells, so you can visit the Wikipage to learn more about these cases. Let's just use the indexes to see the dirty rows:

```
# Get Row Indexes of dirty rows:
rowIndexesDirty=grep(pattern,where,value=cellRowIndex)
```

```
> Indep[indexesDirty,]
     Country                                                              MonthDay        Year
37 Colombia                                               July 20 and August 7 1810 and 1819
80   Israel Iyar 5 (On or between April 15 and May 15, depending on the Hebrew calendar).  5708 (1948)
```

You are cleaning this wikipage because you want to do some operations; for example, finding the country that won its independence most recently. Then, you realize that some countries have more than one date. You can decide to keep one (you will delete one date) or both. So, let's go the hard way and keep both.

- Recover the year in a clean format, and save the extra year in another column. We now need to visit a cell and to take the years from that cell; that means we need to look ONLY for sequences of numbers in each cell. Let me show you the use of gregexpr :

```
pattern="\\d{4}"
gregexpr(pattern, Indep$Year[c(37,80)]) # dirty rows
[[1]]
[1]  1 10
attr(,"match.length")
[1] 4 4
attr(,"useBytes")
[1] TRUE

[[2]]
[1]  1 7
attr(,"match.length")
[1] 4 4
attr(,"useBytes")
[1] TRUE
```

The function gregexpr received the pattern \\d{4}, which looks for four consecutive digits in the cells 37 and 80. As you see, it returns a list with two elements (the amount of cells inspected), and each element in the list has three subelements. The first element ([[1]]) tells you where the pattern was found in cell 37: Because there are two values (1 10), you know the pattern was found twice; if no matches were found, it would return -1. Another important attribute we should pay attention to is "match.length": It tells you how many characters are in the match. In this case we requested that the match had size 4, but I could be more flexible in the next code:

```
pattern="\\d{1,4}"    # from year 0 to 9999
positions=gregexpr(pattern, Indep$Year[c(37,80)])
regmatches(Indep$Year[c(37,80)],positions)
```
```
[[1]]
[1] "1810" "1819"

[[2]]
[1] "5708" "1948"
```

This time I have changed my pattern so that years with fewer digits can be matched. I use the function regmatches now, which recovers the actual values returned by gregexpr. You see that you obtained the expected values. Let's create the two columns:

```
yearsGood=c()
yearsExtra=c()
for (cell in Indep$Year){
  posi=gregexpr("\\d{1,4}", cell)
  years=regmatches(cell,posi)[[1]]
  yearsGood=c(yearsGood,years[1])
  # if NO second element, a NA is written by default.
  yearsExtra=c(yearsExtra,years[2])
}
```

Let's create YearClean with the vector yearsGood and a new column YearExtra with yearsExtra. This is very simple:

```
Indep$YearClean=yearsGood
Indep$YearExtra=yearsExtra
```

Let's work with the column MonthDay. Because there was more than one year, it is also possible that there is more than one month-day combination in a cell. Let's do this step by step:

• Extract the first month-day combination. From the first few lines you could assume that there is a month followed by a day. Let's use a regular expression to recover that pair. Here is a simple example to show how it works:

```
pattern="^\\w+\\s*\\d+"
string1 = "December 26 and June 25"
string2 = "December26 and June 25"
string3 = "December    26 and June 25"
```

The pattern above has an important character, the *caret* (^), which requests that our pattern be at the beginning of the string; without this caret, *all* the good matches are returned. Other key characters are the plus sign + and the star sign * . The former finds a pattern one or more times, while the latter allows for zero or more times. So we are saying that we need a match that starts at the beginning of the strings and is composed of one or more character words (\\w+), zero or more blank spaces (\\s*), and a number with one or more digits (\\d+). Let me show you the results, which come in a list:

```
positions=gregexpr(pattern, string1,perl = T)
regmatches(string1,positions)
```
```
[[1]]
```
```
[1] "December 26"
```
```
positions=gregexpr(pattern, string2,perl = T)
regmatches(string2,positions)
```
```
[[1]]
```
```
[1] "December26"
```
```
positions=gregexpr(pattern, string3,perl = T)
regmatches(string3,positions)
```
```
[[1]]
```
```
[1] "December    26"
```

So, the month-day combination is extracted with this code:

```
pattern="^\\w+\\s*\\d+"
positions=gregexpr(pattern, Indep$MonthDay)
#
# regmatches returns a list...
resultAsList=regmatches(Indep$MonthDay,positions)
# UNLIST will turn output into a vector!!!
MonthDayVector=unlist(resultAsList)
```

- To recover the second month-day combination I propose to delete the match we found previously in Indep$MonthDay and create a temporal vector with the result, so that we can apply the previous function to it. Here, deleting the match means finding the previous pattern and replacing it with nothing.

```
library(stringi)
toReplace="^\\w+\\s*\\d+"
nothing=''
temporalMonthDay=stri_replace_all_regex(Indep$MonthDay,
                                        toReplace,
                                        nothing)
```

We need to get the other combinations of month-day from temporalMonthDay, if available (not necessarily at the beginning):

```
pattern="\\w+\\s+\\d+"
newDate=c()
for (cell in temporalMonthDay){

  positions=gregexpr(pattern, cell)
  if (positions[[1]][1]==-1){
    newDate=c(newDate,NA)
```

```
}else{
  value=unlist(regmatches(cell,positions))
  # if there is more than one date
  # we are losing it, as we only collect
  # the first one
  newDate=c(newDate,value[1])
}
}
```

From here we can create an additional column `MonthDayExtra`:

```
Indep$MonthDayExtra=newDate
```

- Are you sure that all the cells in `MonthDayVector` has the same structure? We believe that we have every month-day combination, but we have not tested that. We have recovered two components as strings, but we do not know if there is a space or is nothing between them (our regex pattern,\\s*, recovered it so). We need to check that, so that the code will work for all the cells. Let's test that:

```
for (cell in MonthDayVector){
  barspace=" "
  # split cell by bar space
  parts=strsplit(cell,barspace)
  # count the amount of elements
  countParts=length(parts[[1]])
  if (countParts!=2){
    # print the cells that do not have 2 elements
    print (cell)
  }
}
```

```
[1] "September15"
```

As you see, there was one bad cell (`Mexico`). Should we change it or write a code instead? Consider that in other data you may find lots of these bad cells, so I think it is better to rebuild the whole column. Let's create two vectors, one for months and another for days.

```
pattern1="\\D+" # NOT numbers- opposite of \\d+
positions=gregexpr(pattern1, MonthDayVector)
months=unlist(regmatches(MonthDayVector,positions))
# months may include leading and trailing spaces, so:
months=str_trim(months) # needs library(stringr)
pattern2="\\d+"
positions=gregexpr(pattern2, MonthDayVector)
days=unlist(regmatches(MonthDayVector,positions))
```

The `pattern1` is requesting a sequence that does not have digits; because bar spaces are not digits, they may be included in the match. Then, our new `MonthDay` is `MonthDayClean`:

```
# I am CONCATENATING with a "-"
Indep$MonthDayClean=paste(months,days,sep="-")
# Verifying:
Indep[Indep$Country=="Mexico",]$MonthDayClean
```
```
[1] "September-15"
```

I have concatenated this line with the hyphen-minus to ease the final step.

Now that we have columns with clean data, it is time to build the dates. We have one column with this pattern *month-day*, where the month is the full name of the month and the day goes from 1 to 31. We also have another column with year, where year is represented with century information (four digits). We need to concatenate the month-day with the year, using the same separator that is between month and day (-)[5]:

```
# First concatenate the last two columns
DateOfIndependence=paste(Indep$MonthDayClean,
                         Indep$YearClean,
                         sep="-")
# Get the date from the string:
## %B for complete name of month
## %Y for year with century

# FORMATTING:
myFormat="%B-%d-%Y"
Indep$Date=as.Date(DateOfIndependence,
                   format=myFormat)
#
# Confirming:
class(Indep$Date)
```
```
[1] "Date"
```

Now that cleaning and formatting are done, I can write a query that returns the last country that obtained its independence. Let's see what works:

```
# This is bad but gives no error
Indep[which(Indep$Year==max(Indep$Year,na.rm = T)),]$Country
```
```
[1] "Israel"
```

```
# This is good
Indep[which(Indep$Date==max(Indep$Date,na.rm = T)),]$Country
```
```
[1] "South Sudan"
```

---

[5] You can also choose the separator / instead.

For how long has Peru been independent?

```
# This is right
datePeruInd=Indep[Indep$Country=='Peru',]$Date
today = as.Date(Sys.Date(),format=myFormat)
# result (in days):
today-datePeruInd
```

| Time difference of 71354 days

If you need to know more about operations with dates, read more about the package lubridate (Grolemund et al., 2016):

```
# install.packages("lubridate")
library(lubridate)
year(today)-year(datePeruInd)
```

| [1] 195

Let us now see how Python works on the original problem shown in Figure 6.1 on page 169. I will not use the CSV file I used in R, but the original HTML from the webpage, so that I can show you the versatility of Python and the package beautiful soup.

First, I want to retrieve the data as we have done before with other wikipages:

```
#%% # COLLECTING

from requests import get
from bs4 import BeautifulSoup as BS
#%%
# Location
wikibase="http://en.wikipedia.org/wiki/"
place="List_of_national_independence_days"
wikiLink=wikibase+place

# avoid rejection from server
identification = {"User-Agent":"Mozilla/5.0"}

# contact server
wikiPage =get(wikiLink, headers=identification)

# BS gets wikipedia page as html
wikiSoup =BS(wikiPage.content,"html.parser")

# BS extracts the whole table (it is html)
wikiTable=wikiSoup.find("table",{"class":"wikitable sortable"})
```

The HTML contents are in wikiPage.content. Most likely when you visit this wikipage, it will have been updated. Because I want you to replicate my results, I prepared a file with the HTML in wikiPage.content, which is in the folder of this chapter under the name IndepHtml.txt. The code below tells you how to open a *.txt* file like this one:

```
#%% Reading file and retrieving table:

import os
folderData='/Users/JoseManuel/Dropbox/BookData/chapter6'
fileHTML=os.path.join(folderData ,"IndepHtml.txt")

f = open(fileHTML, 'r')    # open the file
wikiPageFile=f.read()      # get contents, you have the data now
f.close()                  # close file (you have the data now)

# Use file in beautiful soup, and get the table:
wikiSoup =BS(wikiPageFile,"html.parser")
wikiTable=wikiSoup.find("table",{"class":"wikitable sortable"})
```

The object wikiPageFile is exactly the same as wikiPage.content. Although the data is now in a file instead of being downloaded from the web, it has the same problems. If the wikitable had not had any issues, you could have used this code to get the table as a data frame:

```
#%% CREATE DATA FRAME

# headersHtml is simply the first row of the table
headersHtml=wikiTable.find_all('tr')[0]
# headersList is a list with the column titles as elements
headersList=[name.get_text() for name in headersHtml.find_all('th')]

# rowsHtml_asList has the data of the table, except the Headers
rowsHtml_asList=wikiTable.find_all('tr')[1:]
# rowsList is a list of rows, and each row is a list of cells
rowsList=[] # list of cell lists
for row in rowsHtml_asList:
    rowsList.append([cell.get_text() for cell in row.find_all('td')])

# Data frame creation
import pandas as pd

# making a data frame from list of lists!
Indep = pd.DataFrame(data=rowsList, columns=headersList)
```

Let me explain what this last code does, because we will use part of it later.

- **headersHtml** extracts the first HTML row from the wikitable. In this row, we have the column titles in HTML. This is a list of one element.
- **headersList** gets every element with the tag **th** (header) and extracts only the text. Each title is an element of the list. No more HTML here.
- **rowsHtml** extracts all but the first HTML rows from the wikitable. These rows are the contents in HTML, and each row is an element of this list.

```
108  <tr style="vertical-align: top;">  ◄ ── Row starts
109  <td><span class="flagicon"><img alt=""  ) ◄ ── span
     src="//upload.wikimedia.org/wikipedia/commons/thumb/1/1a/Flag_of_Argentina.
     svg/23px-Flag_of_Argentina.svg.png" width="23" height="14"
     class="thumbborder"
     srcset="//upload.wikimedia.org/wikipedia/commons/thumb/1/1a/Flag_of_Argenti
     na.svg/35px-Flag_of_Argentina.svg.png 1.5x,
     //upload.wikimedia.org/wikipedia/commons/thumb/1/1a/Flag_of_Argentina.svg/4
     6px-Flag_of_Argentina.svg.png 2x" data-file-width="800" data-file-
     height="500" /> </span><a href="/wiki/Argentina"
     title="Argentina">Argentina</a></td>
110  <td><span style="display:none;" class="sortkey">07-09 !</span><span
     class="sorttext">July 9</span></td>
111  <td>1816</td>
112  <td><a href="/wiki/Argentine_Declaration_of_Independence" title="Argentine
     Declaration of Independence">Independence</a> declared from the <a
     href="/wiki/Spanish_Empire" title="Spanish Empire">Spanish Empire</a> in
     1816.</td>
113  <td></td>  ◄ ── Empty cell
114  </tr>  ◄ ── Row ends
```

Figure 6.2 Understanding rowspan issues when scraping (I). In this row, which shows data from Argentina, there is only simple span in each cell. This is the HTML as shown in Google Chrome; seven elements are shown (108 to 114).

- **rowsList** reads each element from **rowsHtml** to make a list of rows, but also visits each row to extract the text from every element with the tag **td** (data cell). So it is a list of lists. No more HTML here.
- A data frame is created using the lists created.

These were the steps to get the wikitable formatted as a data frame; unfortunately, we know it still has problems. If you request the first 15 rows of the three leftmost columns with **Indep.iloc[:,:3].head(n=15)**, you will get the same data as in Figure 6.1 on page 169.

Python has enough functionalities to deal in a simple way with this situation. But we need to understand very well what the problem is, so that we can create an effective code. Because R users are not expected to be programmers, the R developers are building tools to make things easier; that is why, the function we found in R (**htmltab**) prevented us from reading the HTML code. In Python, however, you must take a look at the HTML to find the structure and then decide what to do. Let us compare a case without issues to one with problems, taking a look at a "good" row in HTML (see Figure 6.2):

Figure 6.2 shows the HTML contents of one row in the wikitable as obtained using the Google Chrome browser and gives you the information about Argentina. As you see, this row starts and ends with the same kind of tag (**tr**). Between those tags there are data organized into cells, and each cell is identified by the **td** tag. Because this is a table, in general, each row should have the same amount of cells (so that the table looks like a spreadsheet), and of course, the position of each cell should respect the order of the headers of the

```
115  <tr style="vertical-align: top;">  ◄- - Row starts
116  <td rowspan="2"><span class="flagicon"><img alt=""        ◄- -rowspan
     src="//upload.wikimedia.org/wikipedia/commons/thumb/2/2f/Flag_of_Armenia.s
     g/23px-Flag_of_Armenia.svg.png" width="23" height="12" class="thumbborder"
     srcset="//upload.wikimedia.org/wikipedia/commons/thumb/2/2f/Flag_of_Armenia
     .svg/35px-Flag_of_Armenia.svg.png 1.5x,
     //upload.wikimedia.org/wikipedia/commons/thumb/2/2f/Flag_of_Armenia.svg/46p
     x-Flag_of_Armenia.svg.png 2x" data-file-width="1200" data-file-height="600"
     /> </span><a href="/wiki/Armenia" title="Armenia">Armenia</a></td>
117  <td><span style="display:none;" class="sortkey">05-28 !</span><span
     class="sorttext">May 28</span></td>
118  <td>1918</td>
119  <td>Declaration of independence from <a href="/wiki/Russian_Empire"
     title="Russian Empire">Russian Empire</a> in 1918.</td>
120  <td></td>
121  </tr>
122  <tr style="vertical-align: top;">◄- - Row starts          ► ◄No Country
123  <td><span style="display:none;" class="sortkey">09-21 !</span><span
     class="sorttext">September 21</span></td>
124  <td>1991</td>
125  <td>Independence from the <a href="/wiki/Soviet_Union" title="Soviet
     Union">Soviet Union</a> in 1991.</td>
126  <td>National Day</td>
127  </tr> ◄-·- Row ends
```

Figure 6.3 Understanding rowspan issues when scraping (II). In this case, one row, which shows the data from Armenia, seems incomplete, but a cell with rowspan has to appear again in the same position in the next row. This is the HTML as shown in Google Chrome; 14 elements are shown (115 to 127).

table. Then, if a cell has no information, you must leave the cell empty (which will be considered a missing value). In the case of Argentina we see that the last cell is empty (no data between the tags). If you compare the visual representation of this wikitable with the HTML code, you can easily find each cell's values. Pay particular attention to the name of the country, in this case element 109 (the first one from the top). You can see that the country name cell has a tag span after the td at the beginning; with this tag, you can add more information to the cell that may or may not be visible when you visit a particular wikipage. In this case, the span allows the adding of the flag icon. In contrast element 111, which holds the year of independence, has no tags in that cell. This is a simple row.

From Figure 6.1 on page 169, we knew that the Argentina data had no problems, but that Armenia had one. As you could see in that figure, Armenia appeared to take up two rows on the Wikipedia page (when you see it in the browser) because there are two different dates for two different historical events. If you go to the HTML and compare it to the visual you get on the Wikipedia page, you realize that there are two blocks for Armenia, but the second one is incomplete. This is clearer in Figure 6.3.

The tag rowspan is useful when a cell value has to appear in more than one row. But, when we scrape, we the text from the HTML extracts the contents by cells. So, as we saw, it is possible to retrieve one or more rows that are missing one cell, thereby making all the cells move to the left. So, let's plan the strategy to prevent that shift.

1. Every row should have the same amount of cells. We first visit a row and then visit every cell in that row. The row and cell should be in HTML (they come from (rowsHtml_asList in the previous code).
2. If the cell above has the tag rowspan, it means that all the rows under its influence will lack one element. The rowspan tag indicates how many times the cell value appears: If the value is three, it means that two rows will lack that cell (the rowspan in Figure 6.3 is two). Remember that we are reading all this information from an HTML source, so that the tags can be identified (rowsHtml_asList in the previous code).
3. We act once we find a row with rowspan. We then save the **position of the row** in the table, **the position of the cell** in that row, the **value** of the tag rowspan, and the **text** of that row, which will be inserted in the next one(s).
4. With the information collected in the last step, we can modify the rows affected. The rows to be modified are the ones in plain text format (not HTML); that is, rowList in our previous code.
5. When the *list of cell lists* (rowList) is updated, we create the data frame as in the previous code.

The code below shows the implementation of our strategy:

```
#%% REPAIRING TABLE EXTRACTED

#HTML lists;
theHeaders=wikiTable.find_all('tr')[0]
rowsHtml_asList=wikiTable.find_all('tr')[1:]

# PLAIN TEXT lists
headersList=[name.get_text() for name in theHeaders.find_all('th')]
rowsList=[]
for row in rowsHtml_asList:
    rowsList.append([cell.get_text() for cell in row.find_all('td')])

# visit the HTML rows, get position and contents in HTML
for rowPosition,rowHTML in enumerate(rowsHtml_asList):

    # visit the HTML cells, get position and contents in HTML
    for cellPosition,cellHTML in enumerate(rowHTML .find_all('td')):

        if cellHTML.has_attr('rowspan'): # TIME TO ACT!!

            # saving information to complete rows affected
            issue={'row':rowPosition,
                   'column':cellPosition,
                   'value':int(cellHTML['rowspan']), #repetitions
                   'text':cellHTML.get_text()}
```

```
        # xrange starts in '1' to make changes in the next row
        for offset in xrange(1, issue['value']):

            # issue['row'] is rowPosition
            # so the rows to modify
            # are in the positions next to that
            whatRow=issue['row']+offset

            # complete the row by inserting the text of the issue
            # in the right column
            rowsList[whatRow].insert(issue['column'],issue['text'])

# Data frame creation
import pandas as pd
Indep = pd.DataFrame(data=rowsList, columns=headersList)
```

The code above has used most of the functions we have seen so far, with the exception of the function `enumerate`. This function saves coding because when applied to a lists,

```
enumerate(rowsHtml_asList)
```

it will give you two values: The first one is the position of the value currently read, and the second one is the actual value. It eliminates the need to use indexes to make the code more readable. We use it above to access the HTML elements, which are in lists, so we can keep track of their row and column position. Figure 6.4 gives you a simple example of this function's use.

So, by now you have a data set with cells in place. However, having the cells in place does not mean the values are clean or formatted. You can see the first three rows of the three leftmost columns in Figure 6.5.

```
In [1]: listExample=['a','b','c']
   ...: x=enumerate(listExample)
   ...: for a,b in x:
   ...:     print a,b
   ...:
   ...:
   ...:
   ...:
0 a
1 b
2 c
```

Figure 6.4 Using enumerate in Python.

```
Indep.iloc[:,:3].head(15)
```

```
                    Country    Date of holiday Year celebrated
0               Afghanistan      08-19 !August 19           1919
1                   Albania    11-28 !November 28           1912
2                   Algeria        07-05 !July 5           1962
3                    Angola    11-11 !November 11           1975
4                  Anguilla        05-30 !May 30           1967
5       Antigua and Barbuda    11-01 !November 1           1981
6                 Argentina        07-09 !July 9           1816
7                   Armenia        05-28 !May 28           1918
8                   Armenia   09-21 !September 21           1991
9                   Austria     10-26 !October 26           1955
10               Azerbaijan        05-28 !May 28           1918
11               Azerbaijan     10-18 !October 18           1991
12                  Bahamas       07-10 !July 10           1973
13                  Bahrain    12-16 !December 16           1971
14               Bangladesh       03-26 !March 26           1971
```

Figure 6.5 Scraped table repaired in Python. The table values are not yet clean nor formatted.

We need to create and format a new column named Date, and for that, the columns that serve as input (the second and third columns from Figure 6.5) should be clean. Here is the step-by-step process to create and format a new column.

- We see in Figure 6.5 that the second column has a ! separating the dates (that was also visible in Figure 6.1 on page 169, but now the table is well shaped). I now use that character to split NOT only that column but also, every column in the data frame, and I will keep the left side:

```
#%% Split and keep left side

# x is a cell, split it using "!"
# splitting returns a list, so left side is first element.
# DEFENSIVE CODE: "if x!= None else None", that is
# DO NOT apply split if cell is empty
KeepLeftSide=lambda x: x.split('!')[0] if x!= None else None

# apply function cell by cell:
Indep=Indep.applymap(KeepLeftSide)
```

The code above created a function using the *lambda* approach, which was introduced on page 79. The new function created, KeepLeftSide, is applied to every cell in the data frame with the help applymap (introduced on page 69).

- Now, we need to get rid of the leading and trailing spaces:

```
#%% Trim leading and trailing white spaces

# x is a cell,
# "strip" deletes leading/trailing spaces in cell
TrimCell=lambda x: x.strip() if x!= None else None

# apply function cell by cell
Indep=Indep.applymap(TrimCell)
```

- From the third column, we need to recover the year.

```
#%% Extract year in column "Year celebrated"

# "str.extract" will search pattern and extract it
# extract needs grouping: using "()"

pattern='(^\\d+)'

# You can replace Indep.iloc[:,2] by Indep['Year celebrated']
Indep.iloc[:,2]=Indep.iloc[:,2].str.extract(pattern)
```

The last code altered the original third column.

- Finally, you create the column with the correctly formatted date:

```
#%% Create DATE column

# create a string from concatenating
# 'Date of holiday' and 'Year celebrated'
# as 'Date of holiday' has a hyphen minus
# we used the same when 'Year celebrated' is added
dateAsString=Indep.iloc[:,1]+'-'+Indep.iloc[:,2]

# use "to_datetime" to convert dateAsString into
# a proper format, and create new column

Indep['Date']= pd.to_datetime(dateAsString,
                              format="%m-%d-%Y",
                              errors='coerce') # outbounds dates!
```

Our job is done here. Just type Indep.dtypes if you want to confirm you have dates, and you will see that our new column is of type datetime64[ns]. One very important fact to consider is that some countries won their independence centuries earlier than the internal valid dates in pandas. In this case, you will see the value NaT, the missing value for dates: The function to_datetime has an argument errors, which produces an NaT when it cannot convert a string into a date. Python can allow you to change that, but it requires some extra coding that is not relevant for this example.[6]

---

[6] pandas-docs.github.io/pandas-docs-travis/timeseries.html#timeseries-oob has the steps to follow if you ever need to work with very old dates (before 09-22-1677, Pandas minimum time stamp). Notice that Table 6.2 on page 164 does not indicate the time stamps, but rather the value to consider when you convert a date stored as a number.

6.2 Focusing on Categorical Data

This section focuses on factors/categorical data, particularly the ordered ones. Let me retrieve a wikitable that offers information on three important *measures of freedom* around the world. Let's use R to get the table from the webpage[7]:

```
# Getting the webpage
library(XML)
library(RCurl)
library(stringi)
wiki="https://en.wikipedia.org/wiki/"
link = "List_of_freedom_indices"
wikiPage = getURL(paste0(wiki,link))
# Getting the tables:
wikiTables = readHTMLTable(wikiPage,
                           encoding="UTF-8",
                           stringsAsFactors=FALSE)
# Getting the indexes of freedom (3rd table):
IDXs=wikiTables[[3]]
```

As I have done before when dealing with wikipages, I have the file with the data I am using for this case (year 2016), so that you can replicate my examples:

```
folder=file.path("~","Dropbox","BookData","chapter6")
filename="IDX2016.csv"
fileCSV=file.path(folder,filename)
#
# I will use 'check.names' so that R does not attempt
# to adapt the headers.
IDXs=read.csv(fileCSV,stringsAsFactors=F,check.names = F)
```

The first problem is in the headers:

```
# names have some dirt:
names(IDXs)
```

```
Country
Freedom in the World 2016[6]
2016 Index of Economic Freedom[7]
2016 Press Freedom Index[10]
```

- Headers are too long, so let's get rid of the year and the spaces.
- Headers have footnotes, which must also be deleted.

---

[7] http://en.wikipedia.org/wiki/List_of_Indices_of_Freedom.

Remember that it is very common to have footnotes in tables somewhere in the spreadsheet example on page 138, but in a different column, so this is a good time to try our cleaning tools:

```
# a footnote is like:
# one opening bracket: \\[
# one or more numbers \\d+
# one closing bracket \\]
# one or more spaces: \\s+
# OR: |
pattern='\\s+|\\d+|\\[|\\]'
nothing=''
test='abc IN [1968] '
gsub(pattern,nothing,test)
```

```
| [1] "abcIN"
```

We see the regex worked well (you should always do some trial and error). Then, we can clean the headers:

```
names(IDXs)=gsub(pattern,nothing,names(IDXs))
```

Let's check each variable in a frequency table to explore the distribution of categories. First, take a look at the *Freedom in the World* index:

```
library(plyr)
count(IDXs,'FreedomintheWorld')
```

```
  FreedomintheWorld freq
1            1 free   89
2     3 partly free   63
3        5 not free   57
4              n/a    4
```

The numbers give a sense of order, the highest being the worst situation for this variable. The "n/a" is a value that needs to be set as NA. Let's look now at the *Index of Economic Freedom*:

```
count(IDXs,'IndexofEconomicFreedom')
```

```
  IndexofEconomicFreedom freq
1                1 free     5
2         2 mostly free    33
3     3 moderately free    55
4       4 mostly unfree    62
5            5 repressed    24
6                  n/a    34
```

This variable has the same missing value coding and shows that the higher the number, the less economic freedom. Let's visit the last variable:

```
count(IDXs,'PressFreedomIndex')
```

```
        PressFreedomIndex  freq
1             1 good situation    16
2 2 satisfactory situation    49
3     3 noticeable problems    60
4       4 difficult situation    51
5 5 very serious situation    18
6                        n/a    19
```

As in the previous cases, the same value is used for missing data, and the numbers increase to represent a scale from good to bad. I can easily convert all this information into a numeric data frame, this time creating a function to help me do it (notice I am not using `return` which in R will return the *last* object):

```
## Create function:
ExtractConvert_toNum=function(x) {
    library(stringi)
    pattern = "\\d+"
    # extract
    numberExtracted=stri_extract_first_regex(x,pattern)
    # convert (n/a will be tranformed to proper NA)
    as.numeric(numberExtracted) # LAST OBJECT
    }
#
# Applying:
IDXs[,c(2:4)]=lapply(IDXs[,c(2:4)],ExtractConvert_toNum)
# See the summary
summary(IDXs[,c(2:4)])
```

```
 FreedomintheWorld IndexofEconomicFreedom PressFreedomIndex
 Min.   :1.000     Min.   :1.000          Min.   :1.000
 1st Qu.:1.000     1st Qu.:3.000          1st Qu.:2.000
 Median :3.000     Median :3.000          Median :3.000
 Mean   :2.694     Mean   :3.374          Mean   :3.031
 3rd Qu.:5.000     3rd Qu.:4.000          3rd Qu.:4.000
 Max.   :5.000     Max.   :5.000          Max.   :5.000
 NA's   :4         NA's   :34             NA's   :19
```

The summary makes it clear that we need to make a decision about whether the variables should be ordinal or numeric. These three variables are ordinal, but R assumes that they are numbers (the mean has been computed). For modeling purposes, there is a difference in the outputs if you keep these variables as numeric. The function `factor` transforms a single value or a vector of values into a factor (category) and has an argument to set the values into ordinal type. In this moment, our data is in numeric type, so we can tell the function that

those are the levels of the ordinal category and the label of those categories.
Let's see how it works:

```
categoryLevels=c(1,2,3,4,5)
categoryLabels=c("best","good","moderate","bad","worst")
IDXs[,c(2:4)]= lapply(IDXs[,c(2:4)],factor,
                      levels=categoryLevels,
                      labels=categoryLabels,ordered=T)
```

Let's request again a summary for the variables in the data frame (not the
first column):

```
summary(IDXs[-1]) #alternative
```

```
FreedomintheWorld IndexofEconomicFreedom PressFreedomIndex
best      :89       best      : 5        best      :16
good      : 0       good      :33        good      :49
moderate :63       moderate :55        moderate :60
bad       : 0       bad       :62        bad       :51
worst    :57       worst    :24        worst    :18
NA's     : 4       NA's      :34        NA's      :19
```

Notice that the variable `FreedomintheWorld` has two categories with zero
counts: This occurs because that variable has only three categories. Applying
`droplevels(FreedomintheWorld)` will erase the unused categories. Notice
also that the summaries do not give much statistics for these ordinal variables,
so let me share some alternatives.

- All categorical variables can have mode(s):

```
# Find the mode: value that repeats the most...
VARIABLE=IDXs$IndexofEconomicFreedom
names(sort(-table(VARIABLE)))[1]
```
```
[1] "bad"
```

- Ordinal variables have median:

```
VARIABLE=IDXs$FreedomintheWorld
## Option 1
# This only works for numbers, and we have factors:
# median(VARIABLE)
# this works if no ties:
value=median(as.numeric(VARIABLE),na.rm=T)
categoryLabels[value]
```
```
[1] "moderate"
```
```
#confirming:
cumsum(prop.table(table(VARIABLE)))
```
```
     best      good  moderate      bad     worst
0.4258373 0.4258373 0.7272727 0.7272727 1.0000000
```

```
## Option 2:
library(DescTools) #install first!
# also has problems if ties:
median.factor(VARIABLE,na.rm = T)
```
```
[1] moderate
Levels: best < good < moderate < bad < worst
```

Another important fact to consider is that you can draw a box plot with ordinal variables.

It is time to handle categorical data in Python. First, let's get the data for Beautiful Soup:

```
#%%# Collecting table

wiki="http://en.wikipedia.org/wiki/"
link="List_of_freedom_indices"
wikiLink=wiki+link
identification = { "User-Agent" : "Mozilla/5.0"}

from requests import get
wikiPage = get(wikiLink, headers=identification)

from bs4 import BeautifulSoup as BS
wikiSoup = BS(wikiPage.content,"html.parser")
wikiTable = wikiSoup.find("table",{"class":"wikitable sortable"})
```

This time I will not save the data and will only use the data I have, hoping that all the codes I share are helpful when you read this book. Let's go step by step:

1. The following code retrieves the headers. A similar approach was used in our last Python code:

```
#%% Headers

# Scraping Headers
headersHtml=wikiTable.find_all('tr')[0]
headersList=[name.get_text() for name in headersHtml.find_all('th')]

# Cleaning Headers
import regex as re
pattern='\\s+|\\d+|\\[\\]'
nothing=''
headersList=[re.sub(pattern,nothing,x) for x in headersList]
```

2. The following code retrieves the data. A similar approach was used in our last Python code:

```
#%% Data rows (no cleaning)

# Scraping data
```

```
rowsHtml_asList=wikiTable.find_all('tr')[1:]
rowsList=[] # list of cell lists
for row in rowsHtml_asList:
    rowsList.append([cell.get_text() for cell in row.find_all('td')])
```

3. We have headers as a list and data as a list of lists, so we can build a data frame with that:

```
#%% Data frame creation

import pandas as pd

IDXs= pd.DataFrame(data=rowsList, columns=headersList)
```

4. Now let's clean the data in cells. Only the missing value will be replaced; the rest will remain as they are (in R, we kept the number only):

```
#%% Clean data

import numpy as np

badMissing='n/a'
IDXs.replace(badMissing,np.nan,inplace=True)
```

5. We need to format as ordered categorical the columns where the indexes are, labeling them correctly:

```
#%% Format data

# 'apply' acts at row or column level:

#Function to format columns as ordinal
to_Order=lambda x: x.astype("category",ordered=True)

# formatting (all columns but first):
IDXs[headersList[1:]]=IDXs[headersList[1:]].apply(to_Order)
```

Notice that R has a function to carry out what we just did in three steps in Python. Also, pay attention to how useful the function apply is in pandas. We also used extract to get the numbers in each cell; note that this function requires the use of *parentheses* in the regular expression. When the data is cleaned and formatted, you can see a frequency table like this:

```
#%% Explore:

IDXs.iloc[:,1].value_counts(sort=False,dropna=False)
IDXs.iloc[:,2].value_counts(sort=False,dropna=False)
IDXs.iloc[:,3].value_counts(sort=False,dropna=False)
```

We can generate some statistics with the following code:

```
#%% Some statistics on categorical

# describe:
IDXs.describe()
```

```
# mode
value=IDXs.IndexofEconomicFreedom.mode()

# median (using cumulative frequency table)
frequencies=IDXs.iloc[:,2].value_counts(sort=False,normalize=True)
cumulativeTable=np.cumsum(frequencies)

median=0
pos=0
for percent in cumulativeTable:
    if percent < 0.5:
        pos+=1
    else:
        median=percent
        break
# median!!
cumulativeTable.index[pos]
```

Notice that describe will inform which is the mode for every column. I also have a function for that (mode). Computing the median was more difficult, so I needed to write some code to obtain that value from the cumulative frequency.

6.3 Data Transformation

I hope that, by now, you have practiced all the techniques I have shared and that your skills have improved. We have dealt with formatting the data type, but particular methods require that the data have explicit properties. Data transformation enables data to acquire those properties.

Social science data needs more abstraction than engineering data, so the research should be designed to make sense of the number and categories available for analysis. In the next subsections, we will examine different data transformations that may be required.

6.3.1 Basics of Recoding Non-Ordinal Categories

Recoding a categorical variable is needed mainly for two reasons: (1) make tables and graphics more readable and (2) customize the categorical labels for statistical models.

Recoding for Customizing Categories

How results are visualized can determine how they will influence decision makers. Recoding is needed to customize the data to make it readable to your audience. Your data may be clean and in the right type, but the assigned labels of the categories may not convey the information effectively. Let's open a file about some college students who are participating in different sport teams to see how this may be a problem.

```
library(xlsx)
folder=file.path("~","Dropbox","BookData","chapter6")
filename="Sports.xlsx"
fileXLS=file.path(folder,filename)
# Getting what we need:
college = read.xlsx(fileXLS,1,stringsAsFactors=F)
# quick look at what you have
head(college)
```

```
  Student Sport minority weight
1      a1     F        1  68.51
2      a2     B        1  63.30
3      a3     T        1  62.64
4      a4     O        0  61.90
5      a5     B        0  68.50
6      a6     B        0  61.04
```

As you see, the data you got uses just a letter for each sport, and every report you prepare based on this data may need a specific sport name, which you do not have at this moment. Certainly there is a quick way to do the recoding, but we need to make sure it will work well:

- Turn this variable into a factor (remember you read the file avoiding having strings read as factors):

```
college$Sport=factor(college$Sport)
```

- Find out what are the levels of the variable (this is a vector of strings):

```
levels(college$Sport)
```
```
[1] "B" "F" "O" "S" "T"
```

- Change the levels, in the same order:

```
newLabels=c("Basket", "Football","Other","Soccer","Tennis")
college$Sport=factor(college$Sport,
                     labels=newLabels)
```

From the codes above, I believe that the most important information is the order of the original levels. You cannot reorder the categories without that information, because you would not know in what order you would need to prepare the vector of the labels of new levels. Evidently, the original levels are in alphabetic (ascending) order, but you need to know that for sure. Let me now show you how to find out the levels and rename them using Python:

```
#%% RECODING

# Collect data
from pandas import read_excel
from os.path  import join
folder="/Users/JoseManuel/Dropbox/BookData/chapter6"
filename="Sports.xlsx"
fileXLS=join(folder,filename)
college=read_excel(fileXLS)

# Format
college['Sport']=college['Sport'].astype("category")

# Find out levels created
college['Sport'].cat.categories

# Renaming
newLabels=["Basket",  "Football","Other","Soccer","Tennis"]
college['Sport'].cat.rename_categories(newLabels,inplace=True)
```

There is another way to recode the information when you have Boolean values. In this same data file there is a variable indicating whether the student belongs to a minority group or not. You may need some labels instead of numbers for visualization purposes. Let's get them in R[8]:

```
newLabels=c("Minority","Not Minority")
college$minTXT=ifelse(college$minority,newLabels[1],newLabels[2])
college$minTXT=as.factor(college$minTXT)
```

This is an alternative in Python:

```
# mapping of new values from DICTionary
newLabels = {1: "Minority", 0: "Not Minority"}
college['minTXT']=college['minority'].map(newLabels)

# Format
college['minTXT']=college['minorityTXT'].astype("category")
```

As you see in the Python code above, instead of doing a logical comparison as I did in R, I do the recoding simply by *mapping* a dict to the original values. However, that will not be a categorical type until I change the data type. Keep in mind that both codes have created a new variable (the original remains the same), which is sometimes recommended because you may need to make different recodings of the original variable. Notice also that the data is clean, which makes recoding easier.

---

[8] The **car** package in R has more types of coding; see some examples at http://rprogramming .net/recode-data-in-r/.

Recoding and Modeling: The Reference Category

Categorical variables can be used in several statistical modeling techniques. In particular, regression models may use them as independent variables; most modelers use the term *dummy* variable (or "treatment"). For example, if you had a variable `neighborhood zone` with eight zones, you might be interested in the effect of each neighborhood zone on some other variable like `crime`. In this situation, because `neighborhood zone` is categorical, regression models require that you choose a zone as a reference and then see how each of the other zones' effect on crime differs from that of the zone set as reference. In short, with regression models you will discuss dummy variables, and you may need to set the reference or change the default one. In general, the first category is the one chosen as the reference; if you need to choose another category, simply write this code:

```
college$Sport=relevel(college$Sport,ref='Other')
```

From now on, the first category will be "Other". This does not have much importance in most tables or visualizations, but is very important during the modeling stage. When using Python, whenever you have a data frame in pandas and need to make a regression with dummy variables, I recommend you make use of the module **patsy**,[9] which has a function **C** with this syntax: `C(Sports, Treatment(reference="Other"))`

The code above, when used in a regression, could be one of your independent variables, and you will want to see the effect of each neighborhood zone on the dependent variable, when compared to the category `''Other.''`

6.3.2 Conceptual Grouping and Interval Building

Conceptual grouping and interval building are related, the practical difference being that you will produce categories using the former and intervals using the latter. This recoding is mainly needed to present a description of facts and is not generally done at the modeling stages. However, most of the time you need to present data organized in this way to non quantitative audiences.

In practical terms, *conceptual grouping* transforms a numeric type, generally a float type, into a category; in the tradeoff, you sacrifice precision for clarity. In the earlier data about college students there is a numeric variable weight, which could be a very good candidate to be a category. For example, we can

---

[9] If it is not in Anaconda, use **pip** to install it.

create a variable to see if the student has met the maximum weight to compete (considering that weights above 65 are not tolerated). We can use the same code we used before to recode the Boolean values in R:

```
college$elligible=ifelse(college$weight<65,"YES","NO")
college$elligible=as.factor(college$elligible)
```

In Python, we used mapping of a dict onto the original values to recode, but that strategy will not work in this case, so we need a new function:

```
doConceptGroup = lambda x: 'Yes' if x < 65 else 'No'

college['Elligible']=college['weight'].apply(doConceptGroup)
college['Elligible']=college['Elligible'].astype("category")
```

Another alternative way to do conceptual grouping is *flagging*, which simply means creating a variable that informs whether a particular value is in the "neighborhood" of a certain reference value (for example, the mean). If the value is in the neighborhood, the flag is zero, if the value is above, 1; or if the value is below, -1:

```
# FLAG to REFERENCE: signals whether within
#                    reference neighborhood
## determine neighborhood
radius=1.5
reference=mean(college$weight)
leftLimit=reference-radius
rightLimit=reference+radius
originalVal=college$weight
flag_WEIGHT=ifelse(originalVal>rightLimit,1,
              ifelse(originalVal<leftLimit,-1,0))
```

A version in Python is shown below:

```
# FLAG to REFERENCE: signals whether within
#                    reference neighborhood

def flagPython(cell,threshold,reference):
    from pandas import isnull
    from numpy import nan
    radius=threshold # still the mean!
    leftLimit=reference-radius
    rightLimit=reference+radius
    flag=0

    if isnull(cell):
        flag=nan
    if cell < leftLimit:
        flag= -1
```

```
if cell > rightLimit:
    flag=1

return flag

# applying
threshold=1.5
reference=college['weight'].mean()
college['weight'].apply(flagPython,
                args=(threshold,reference))
```

Giving a name to a category is not a simple decision. As you can imagine, deciding what should be labeled as "good" or "very good" is not straightforward and can always be questioned; a difference of one decimal value could make, for example, a country seem less "democratic" than another. The label given to a set of values should be based on a good balance between what is observed and the underlying theory.

Let me focus now on interval building. I will work again with the *Index of Economic Freedom* produced by the Heritage Foundation and the *Wall Street Journal*, but this time I will use the data they provide from their own website,[10] instead of using the wikitable version. Let's upload the file and start by using R:

```
library(xlsx)
folder=file.path("~","Dropbox","BookData","chapter6")
filename="Index2015_data.xls"
fileXLS=file.path(folder,filename)
#
# Initial FILTERS:
lastRow=187   #last row of data
colsToSelect=c(2,4,seq(5,27,2),33) #columns of interest
# Getting what we need:
EcoFree = read.xlsx(fileXLS,sheetName="2014",
                endRow=lastRow,
                stringsAsFactors=F
                )[colsToSelect]
# Renaming some sub-indexes
names(EcoFree)[4]="Score"
names(EcoFree)[8]="GovSpending"
names(EcoFree)[15]="GovSpendingFromGDP"
# Setting NA (new approach)
EcoFree[EcoFree=='N/A']=NA
# Some Formatting (type):
EcoFree[,c(3:15)]=lapply(EcoFree[,c(3:15)],as.numeric)
```

The column Score will be used to set the intervals. We need to know the lowest and highest theoretical value and decide where to cut that range. In R, we simply use the function cut and give the function a vector of breaks, or cut

---

[10] http://www.heritage.org/index/download.

points, which includes the lowest and highest value. This code computes the intervals following the Heritage Foundation's methodology.[11]

```
breakCat=c(0,50,60,70,80,100) # where to cut
countryGroupLevels=c("repressed","mostly unfree",
            "moderately free","mostly free","free")
EcoFree$Categories = cut(EcoFree$Score,
                breaks=breakCat,
                labels=countryGroupLevels,
                include.lowest=T, # include minimum value
                right=T,          # include maximum value
                ordered_result=T) # produce ordered factor
```

The arguments of cut are self-explanatory (right=T is the default, so it is not needed) and offer all the customization you will need when making intervals. You can see the result here:

```
library(plyr)
count(EcoFree,"Categories")
```

```
        Categories freq
1        repressed   26
2    mostly unfree   62
3  moderately free   55
4      mostly free   30
5             free    5
6             <NA>    8
```

The breaks argument can be single number:

```
numBreaks=10
# create ordinal variable
EcoFree$Intervals = cut(EcoFree$Score,
                breaks=numBreaks,
                include.lowest=T,
                right=T,
                ordered_result=T)
# result
count(EcoFree,'Intervals')
```

```
      Intervals freq
1    [1.21,10.1]    1
2    (27.8,36.6]    2
3    (36.6,45.4]    8
4    (45.4,54.3]   39
5    (54.3,63.1]   58
6    (63.1,71.9]   44
7    (71.9,80.7]   22
8    (80.7,89.6]    4
9           <NA>    8
```

[11] http://www.heritage.org/index/book/methodology.

You may remember that in statistics you were taught to compute the number of intervals following some formula (Sturges, Scott, Freedman-Diaconis, and so on). These formulas are already available in R, so there is no need for coding:

```
numBreaks=nclass.Sturges(na.omit(EcoFree$Score))
#
# Other alternatives:
## nclass.scott( ) #Scott's
## nclass.FD( )    #Freedman-Diaconis
EcoFree$Formula = cut(EcoFree$Score,
                      breaks=numBreaks,
                      include.lowest=T,right=T,
                      ordered_result=T)
```

Finally, Figure 6.6 shows the distribution of the index, using each of the computed intervals.

Python has similar options in pandas:

1. Locating the file:

```
from pandas import read_excel, cut
from os.path  import join
folder="/Users/JoseManuel/Dropbox/BookData/chapter6"
filename="Index2015_data.xls"
fileXLS=join(folder,filename)
```

2. Opening the file:

```
# Initial FILTERS:
RowsToSkipFromBottom=6
colsToSelect=[1,3] + range(4,27,2) + [32]# index starts at 0
EcoFree=read_excel(fileXLS,"2014",
                   skip_footer=RowsToSkipFromBottom,
                   na_values="N/A",  #set NaN!
                   parse_cols=colsToSelect,
                   convert_float=False #keep floats!
                   )
```

3. The data is clean and pandas has the data as numbers, so we can make all the intervals as we did in R:

```
# I. Following their methodology
breakCat=[0,50,60,70,80,100]
categories=["repressed","mostly unfree",
            "moderately free","mostly free","free"]
EcoFree["Categories"]=cut(EcoFree["2015 Score"],
                          bins=breakCat,
                          right=True, # NOT NEEDED
                          include_lowest=True,
                          labels=categories)
### Frequency table:
EcoFree["Categories"].value_counts(sort=False,dropna=False)
```

```
# II. Just informing how many intervals
numBreaks=10
EcoFree["Intervals"]=cut(EcoFree["2015 Score"],
                         bins=numBreaks,
                         include_lowest=True)
### Frequency table:
EcoFree["Intervals"].value_counts(sort=False,dropna=False)


# III. Formula
from math import log, ceil
breakStur=lambda n:  ceil(log(len(n),2) + 1)
numBreaks=breakStur(EcoFree["2015 Score"])

EcoFree["Formula"]=cut(EcoFree["2015 Score"],
                       bins=numBreaks,
                       include_lowest=True)
### Frequency table:
EcoFree["Formula"].value_counts(sort=False,dropna=False)
```

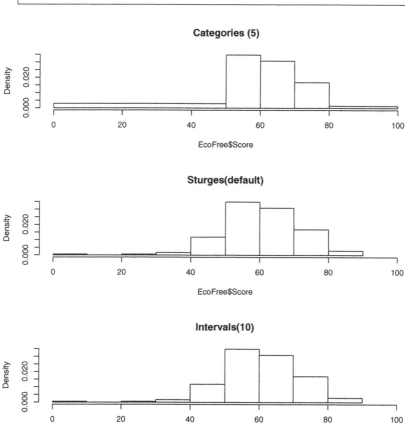

Figure 6.6 Comparison of different interval building techniques.
Source: http://www.heritage.org/index/ranking.

Pandas has a function also named cut, and it has similar arguments (and defaults). Notice that if you need statistical formulas (Sturges, etc.), you have to code them yourself. However, for plotting, matplotlib and numpy have arguments that allow you to select the number of bins based on those formulas.

As an extension of what we just saw, I want to share how to use **cluster analysis** to conceptually group our score and see if the score reflects a close relationship with the clustering output. In general, we use a clustering technique when we are interested in seeing how our cases can form subsets (clusters) based on similarity. How we compute that similarity depends on the measures we have available and the particular technique we use. In our case, we used several measures to compute the index score, and now we will use a clustering technique to determine similarity among the countries. Let me share this simple code in R using the *k-means* technique to find five country groups, this time using the 10 sub-indexes that comprise the composite index:

```
### K-Means
clus = kmeans(na.omit(EcoFree[c(5:14)]), 5)
EcoFree$cluster[
  which(complete.cases(EcoFree[c(5:14)]))] = clus$cluster
```

Interestingly, Figure 6.7 shows that the clusters are not in agreement with the index composite score. Given that the vertical position of the symbols represents the score, you would have expected that the same kinds of symbol were closer to one another, but that is not happening. I do not mean to suggest that using a clustering technique is a better alternative (clustering needs particular formatting too), but I do want to keep reminding you that conceptual grouping is not simple if our research design is not solidly grounded.[12]

6.3.3 Aggregating Data while Changing the Unit of Analysis

There is an important transformation you may need to use when your data needs to be aggregated. Consider the data frame on page 66:

---

[12] In addition, k-means clustering has been used with its default arguments (all numeric). If we were to consider the sub-indexes not as numeric values but as ordinal instead, the dissimilarity matrix should be computed differently (which would allow for other, more complex types of clustering techniques).

**Finding (mis)matches between original score
and k-means clustering**

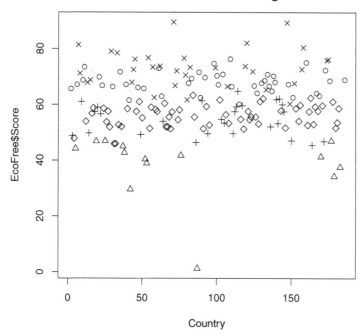

Figure 6.7 Comparing continuous index with k-means clustering. If there was a very close match, you would expect that the symbols of the groups, in EcoFree$cluster, would be horizontally aligned.
Source: http://www.heritage.org/index/ranking.

```
c13c15

          City   region  in2013  in2015
1        Dubai    Asia    9.89   14.26
2    Hong Kong    Asia    8.72    8.66
3     Istanbul  Europe   10.37   12.56
4 Kuala Lumpur    Asia    9.20   11.12
5       London  Europe   15.96   18.82
6     New York America   11.52   12.27
```

In this frame, countries are the unit of analysis, but you may need to analyze continents or regions instead. To change the unit of analysis you will need to apply a function to aggregate the rows of every country in a particular continent. For example, if you are interested in using summaries by a grouping variable, you can use in R the function `tapply()` to create a data frame "GROUPED" by continent like this:

```
#tapply(input column, grouping column,function,parameter)
Group15=tapply(c13c15$in2015, c13c15$region,mean,na.rm=T)
Group13=tapply(c13c15$in2013, c13c15$region,mean,na.rm=T)
GROUPED=as.data.frame(cbind(Group13,Group15))
GROUPED
```

```
          Group13  Group15
America    11.520  12.27000
Asia        9.270  11.34667
Europe     13.165  15.69000
```

This output shows the name of the continents as the indexes.

Certainly, R has alternative ways of achieving the same are using other functions. Applying aggregate() will yield numbers as indexes (as usual):

```
# similar and saving space:
aggregate(c13c15[,c(3,4)],by=list(c13c15[,2]),mean)
```

```
    Group.1  in2013    in2015
1   America  11.520  12.27000
2      Asia   9.270  11.34667
3    Europe  13.165  15.69000
```

Notice that tapply() requires a **vector** not a **list** or a **data frame**. So the two top lines of code will not work in R, but the bottom two will:

```
tapply(c13c15[3], c13c15[2],mean,na.rm=T)
tapply(c13c15[4], c13c15[2],mean,na.rm=T)
# BUT THIS WILL:
tapply(c13c15[,3], c13c15[2],mean,na.rm=T)
tapply(c13c15[,4], c13c15[2],mean,na.rm=T)
```

In the code above, c13c15[4] or c13c15[3] are data frames (of one column), omitting the comma (",") will give you an error. Remember to always check what structure you have.

The analogous code in Python is shown below:

```
#%% similar to tapply in R
myVars=["in2015","in2013"]
c13c15.groupby(['region'],as_index=True)[myVars].mean()
#%% OR:
c13c15.iloc[:,[2,3]].groupby(['region'],as_index=True).mean()
```

Notice the output of these operations in Python gives the names of the cities as indexes (not numbers). If you want the numbers as usual in the index and the grouping categories in a column (series), just set `as_index=False` (if you want the grouping category as the index, you do not need to include `as_index=True` in the code, because that is the default value).

6.3.4 Reversing or Changing monotony

Numeric and ordinal variables have values that can be in ascending or descending order. That monotony has a particular social meaning, because we still need to decide if a higher value is better or worse. For example, in the indexes of freedom we recovered from Wikipedia, increasing values signal a worse situation; that is, the higher the value, the less free a country is. We could argue that the monotony is confusing in that case, because we could expect that the highest value should represent the best situation of the concept under measurement. However, because the three indexes in that website have the same monotony, the interpretation is just a matter of finding the right words to describe them.

However, the last index we just saw was made of several sub-indexes, and if we are not careful we could combine different variables with different monotony in one final score. Situations like this require reversing the values, which is a simple equation:

$$reversed(VAR) = max(VAR) - VAR + min(VAR) \qquad (6.1)$$

The equation may seem simple, but if the variable is ordinal, you still need to make sure the labels are also changed. Let's go back to the IDXs data to reverse the monotony of `FreedomintheWorld`. This is the code in R:

```
# You can change the monotony of an ordinal like this:
VarToReverse=IDXs$FreedomintheWorld
OneVarReversed=factor(VarToReverse,
                      levels=rev(levels(VarToReverse)))
```

If you need to do it in Python, just do this:

```
#%% Changing Monotony function

def changeMonotony(aColumn):
    newOrder= aColumn.cat.categories[::-1]  # reversing levels
    return aColumn.cat.reorder_categories(newOrder,
                                          ordered=True,
                                          inplace=True)

#%% Applying

changeMonotony(IDXs.PressFreedomIndex)
```

6.4 Transformation for Comparability/Integration

You can have clean data that is in the right data type and code, but you then may need to make one column comparable to the other or apply some technique to both. That is not straightforward, because all your variables are not in the same unit of measurement. Intervals help more when working with an individual column, but when you need to go beyond univariate analysis, you may need to transform your data. You should also pay attention to missing values here, because if you want missing values to be considered the highest value, try replacing them with **Inf** (or with **-Inf** if you want them to be considered the lowest values).[13] Let me share some common transformations.

6.4.1 Ranking Variables

This discretizing process that is useful for numeric scores will transform your values into positions. There are some variations to this technique, depending on how you want to manage ties. Run this code to see the differences:

```
library(dplyr)
x = c(99, 60, 75, 88, 88, NA)
row_number(x)   # first 88 gets better ranking
min_rank(x)     # ties share the min position (gap)
dense_rank(x)   # ties share the min position (no gap)
percent_rank(x) # percentile
cume_dist(x)    # rank tell cumulative percent position
```

Because columns are vectors, you can simply apply the function and create a new column with the rank:

```
library(dplyr)
value=EcoFree$GovSpending
EcoFree$GovSpendingRank=dense_rank(EcoFree$GovSpending)
# subset of EcoFree
selection=c('Country.Name','GovSpending','GovSpendingRank')
TEST=EcoFree[,selection]
# see 'ranking':
head(TEST[order(TEST$GovSpendingRank),],10)
```

	Country.Name	GovSpending	GovSpendingRank
42	Cuba	0.0	1
64	Greece	0.0	1
86	Kiribati	0.0	1
87	Korea, North	0.0	1
94	Lesotho	0.0	1
111	Micronesia	0.0	1

---

[13] Think carefully if you want to replace them by zero, because it is a valid number is most indexes.

149	Slovenia	0.0	1
164	Timor-Leste	0.0	1
45	Denmark	1.8	2
58	France	2.5	3

Note that we are considering GovSpending as a variable whose best situation is to be low; thus the best positions are occupied by the lowest values. However, if you needed to show the opposite, you need to alter the monotony of this variable, so that position **1** goes to the greatest value in the score.

Let's do the same in Python:

```
#%%  Renaming
EcoFree.columns.values[7]=u"GovSpending" #Unicode

#%% Ranking and new var:
value=EcoFree.GovSpending
                                      # NOTICE argument 'ascending'
EcoFree['GovSpendingRank']=value.rank(method='dense',ascending=True)

#%% subset:
selection=['Country Name','GovSpending','GovSpendingRank']
TEST=EcoFree[selection]

#%% see ranking
TEST.sort(['GovSpendingRank'], ascending=[1]).head()
```

The code above gave the same result as in R.

6.4.2 Rescaling

Next, let's pay attention to the transformation into Z-scores:

```
# STANDARDIZATION: Z-score replaces value:
EcoFree$GovSpending_Z=as.vector(scale(value))
```

Z-scores are easy to use and understand. It is a common transformation strategy when you need a unitless value by standardization. For their computation, I did not need to explicitly code the formula, but use the function `scale` with its default arguments. This function is also very useful for implementing the following normalizing techniques:

```
# MINMAX Scaling: Values will be in [0,1]
minV=min(value, na.rm=TRUE)
maxV=max(value, na.rm=TRUE)
EcoFree$GovSpending_mM=as.vector(scale(value,
                                       center =minV,
                                       scale = maxV-minV))
```

```
# DISTANCE to REFERENCE Scaling:
## Approach 1: distance as ratio from reference
reference=mean(value,na.rm = TRUE)
EcoFree$GovSpending_Ref1=as.vector(scale(value,
                          center =F,
                          scale = reference))
## Approach 2: distance standardization from reference
EcoFree$GovSpending_Ref2=as.vector(scale(value,
                          center =reference,
                          scale = reference))
```

Notice that in all cases I needed to vectorize the output with `as.vector`, because `scale` returns a matrix.

Pandas does not have these functions, but I can create my own functions to standardize and rescale. Let me share the code in Python:

```
#%% RESCALING

# STANDARDIZATION:
Z = lambda X: (X - X.mean())/X.std(ddof=0)
EcoFree['GovSpending_Z']=Z(value)

# Min-Max scaling

## Let's implement a simple R's scale()
def scalePython(X,center=0,scale=1):
    return (X-center)/scale

## MAX-MIN
c=min(value)
s=value.ptp(0) # ptp computes range: max - min
EcoFree['GovSpending_mM']=scalePython(value,center=c,scale=s)

# DISTANCE to REFERENCE Scaling:
## Approach 1: distance as ratio from reference
s=value.mean()
EcoFree['GovSpending_ref1']=scalePython(value,scale=s)

## Approach 2: distance standardization from reference
EcoFree['GovSpending_ref2']=scalePython(value,s,s)
```

It is good to plot and compare how these indexes are related. Let me show you how to do it in Python (see Figure 6.8), using the package seaborn[14]:

```
import seaborn as sns

DataPlot=EcoFree[['GovSpendingRank','GovSpending_mM','GovSpending_Z']]
sns.pairplot(DataPlot.dropna())
```

[14] You can install it from the Navigator or using conda `install seaborn`.

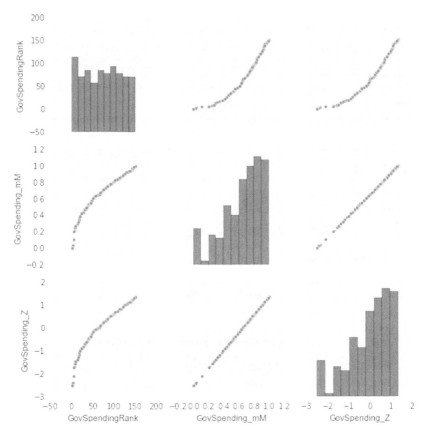

Figure 6.8 Comparing transformations.
Source: http://www.heritage.org/index/ranking.

It is clear that data transformation is something to be careful about. You do not need to transform your data if all your data are in the same units, like a data set of the population of the last 10 censuses in all countries. When units are different, it is clear that you cannot do arithmetic or algebra when you have, for example, water quality and, income per capita. So, you turn to transformation to make different types of data into a common type that would enable the correct use of the algebra or arithmetic needed for the technique. Notice that some of the transformations are difficult and at the same time cause problems for subsequent techniques because they lose information (like *Flag to reference*). As suggested in European Commission et al. (2008), you need some kind of transformation if you want to use principal components analysis (PCA), but not just any kind of transformation. Because the PCA is computed from the covariance matrix, you can expect that simple centering techniques (like MIN-MAX) will not affect it, but more elaborate centering (like standardization) or scaling (like converting from Fahrenheit to Celsius) will have an effect on the covariance matrix of the data. Sometimes, these effects can not be avoided, so make sure to inform those issues in your final reports.

So far, we have collected, cleaned, and formatted data from tables and kept their rectangular shape, because we were working on data frames. Let's see in the last sections of this chapter how to deal with data that represents longitudinal and relational data.

6.5 Formatting Longitudinal Data

There are three longitudinal structures that we consider in this section: the panel structure, the time series, and survival or event-history data (or EHA, as presented in Box-Steffensmeier and Jones (2004)).

6.5.1 Formatting Time-Series Data

The second example of this chapter about the dollar-euro exchange rate, we got data in a time-series format. Typically, the dates are in the first column on the left, and the variables varying at each time point are in the columns to the right. We created a data frame in that format on exchange rates between the euro and the U.S. dollar, named `ratesEuroDollar` in R. Let's take a look at what we got after the cleaning and formatting:

```
summary(ratesEuroDollar)
```

```
        date                dollarRate
Min.    :2000-01-03   Min.    :0.8252
1st Qu.:2003-12-18   1st Qu.:1.1221
Median :2007-12-04   Median :1.2754
Mean    :2007-12-06   Mean    :1.2289
3rd Qu.:2011-11-18   3rd Qu.:1.3527
Max.    :2015-11-30   Max.    :1.5990
                     NA's     :61
```

```
str(ratesEuroDollar)
```

```
'data.frame':   4133 obs. of  2 variables:
 $ date      : Date, format: "2015-11-30" "2015-11-27" ...
 $ dollarRate: num  1.06 1.06 1.06 1.06 1.07 ...
```

As we know, the first column is a date, but this data is not yet ready for time-series analysis in R. For that we need to convert this data frame into a time-series object. There are many packages in R that can make that conversion.[15] I will use the **xts** package, created by Ryan and Ulrich (2014):

```
#install.packages("xts")
library(xts)
values=ratesEuroDollar$dollarRate
index=ratesEuroDollar$date
about='Daily rates Euro/Dollar from European Bank'
TSratesEurDol=xts(values,index, descr=about)
```

We can see with the next commands that we have something different from a classic data frame:

```
class(TSratesEurDol)
```

```
[1] "xts" "zoo"
```

You may remember that there are days with no information, so it would be convenient to have a mean per month:

```
MTSratesEurDol=apply.monthly(TSratesEurDol, mean,na.rm=T)
```

With this new data, we can make a forecast for the next 10 months with complete cases. The result can be seen in Figure 6.9.

```
#install.packages("forecast")
library(forecast)
plot(forecast(MTSratesEurDol, h=10))
```

The same result can be obtained easily in Python, because the settings in pandas allow us to get the data in a time-series format. You can practice these commands:

```
#%% Time series

# Set column as index:
ratesEuroDollar.set_index('date',inplace=True)
# Select Year 2007
ratesEuroDollar["2007"]
# Series by Month average:
ratesEuroDollar.resample('M').mean()
# Plot monthly average:
ratesEuroDollar.resample('M').mean().plot()
```

---

[15] In https://cran.r-project.org/web/views/TimeSeries.html you can find the current offering.

Forecasts from ETS(M,N,N)

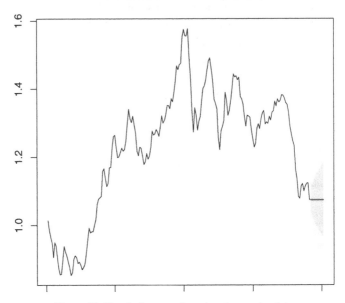

Figure 6.9 Simple forecast plot using time-series data.

If you are eager to apply all your knowledge on time series, you are now all set.

6.5.2 Formatting Panel Data

Panel data does not need to be longitudinal: What matters is the shape of the data. Our data frames so far offer what is called a "wide format" of data, but sometimes the technique you want to use needs the data in a "long format." Let me get in R a wide format using the data from the Human Development Index we discussed on page 139, but this time I will use another sheet (`Table 2`), which presents historic information.

```
library(xlsx)
folder=file.path("~","Dropbox","BookData","chapter6")
filename="2015_statistical_annex_tables_all.xls"
fileHDI=file.path(folder,filename)
# Initial FILTERS:
firstRow=7    #SKIP PRESENTATION
lastRow=207   #OMIT FOOTNOTES
colsToSelect=c(2,seq(3,15,2))  #columns of interest: OMIT CALLS
# Getting what we need:
PanelHDI = read.xlsx(fileHDI,"Table 2",startRow=firstRow,endRow=lastRow,
```

```
                stringsAsFactors=F, header=T)[colsToSelect]
names(PanelHDI)  # what vars do we have?
```

```
[1] "NA..1"  "X1990"  "X2000"  "X2010"  "X2011"  "X2012"  "X2013"  "X2014"
```

```
    Country       X1990              X2000              X2010              X2011              X2012              X2013
1    Norway 0.849367673322206 0.916869844202246 0.939844408684883  0.94069678456633 0.942292684540323 0.94232198340324 0
2 Australia 0.865475508814518 0.897513636613355 0.927409977912633 0.92965629355537 0.932190241478753 0.933389190628233 0.!
3 Switzerland 0.830818066036327 0.887927007745966 0.924370413174531 0.92455954170824 0.926960150429181 0.92831194106279 0.!
4   Denmark 0.798723448774635 0.861817008525798 0.908387714666287 0.92048836143966 0.921083738435812 0.922809360089480.!
5 Netherlands 0.829240422088652 0.876810172590143 0.909236032164183 0.919071387047012 0.92045406815646 0.920442319440992 0.!
6   Germany 0.800912566404262 0.855195380752095 0.906466666261025 0.910603875898982 0.914762983484051 0.915162282896167 0.!
```

Figure 6.10 Panel data in a wide format.

As you see, the names are not what we expected. The first one should be the country name. The other columns are not in that bad shape, and we can work with them, but we need to get rid of the subtitles, this time using complete.cases:

```
names(PanelHDI)[1]="Country"  #renaming column
PanelHDI = PanelHDI[complete.cases(PanelHDI),]  # bye subtitles.
rownames(PanelHDI)=NULL  # resetting index (good after erasing rows)
```

Notice that I did not set the string ``..'' as NA before applying complete.cases. If I had done so, the command above would have erased countries with missing values in some years. Now, I can do that to have my clean panel data:

```
PanelHDI[PanelHDI==".."] = NA
```

Remember that, on page 143, I used the command replace in lapply to set missing values. That piece of code was useful in the general case when you have several strings as missing values; the code above works only for ONE string. Therefore do need lapply again to set all variables as numeric:

```
PanelHDI[,2:8]=lapply(PanelHDI[,2:8],as.numeric)
```

The clean panel data is ready, as shown in Figure 6.10. As you see it is longitudinal and has a wide format.

Then, when you need the long format,you can code this:

```
LongPanelHDI=reshape(PanelHDI,
    varying = list(2:8), # row values to be transposed
    v.names = "HDI", #name of column for 'varying'
```

```
timevar = "YEAR", # Old column name, now as a cell (a label).
idvar= "Country", # Unit of analysis, appearing more than once now.
times = names(PanelHDI[,2:8]), # values of 'timevar'
direction = "long")
## Sorting by country
LongPanelHDI=LongPanelHDI[order(LongPanelHDI$Country),]
rownames(LongPanelHDI)=NULL ## Resetting row names
head(LongPanelHDI,12) # And here you are:
```

```
      Country   YEAR         HDI
1  Afghanistan  X1990  0.2966808
2  Afghanistan  X2000  0.3342629
3  Afghanistan  X2010  0.4477216
4  Afghanistan  X2011  0.4556178
5  Afghanistan  X2012  0.4630188
6  Afghanistan  X2013  0.4639229
7  Afghanistan  X2014  0.4652643
8      Albania  X1990  0.6242103
9      Albania  X2000  0.6564023
10     Albania  X2010  0.7224895
11     Albania  X2011  0.7280141
12     Albania  X2012  0.7294338
```

The **reshape** command gives you the options you need to reformat your data frame. But please take a while to understand the arguments. In Figure 6.10 you have the variables in wide format where each column indicates the variation of HDI across time per country, so those variable **positions** are the ones that I wrote first: varying = list(2:8). What you are measuring in those positions (columns) is the HDI, so use v.names = "HDI" to indicate that to R. You can give names to what those columns in a wide format represent: A good name is "Year", so I wrote timevar = "YEAR". In Figure 6.10 it is clear that country is the unit of analysis (it is not a "measure"), so I wrote idvar= "Country" (you can have more than one value in idvar). You can also customize the categories of the values. Because I wanted to keep the column names I wrote times = names(PanelHDI[,2:8]) so that the categories in Year have the same names as the original columns; this argument allows you to rename them, if you want. In the last argument, I only indicated the direction of change. I made some extra arrangements to my new panel in long format, so that it is ordered by the country name and with index names reset.[16]

Of course you can work in the opposite direction, from long to wide:

```
WidePanelHDI = reshape(LongPanelHDI,
    timevar = "YEAR",
    idvar = "Country",
    direction = "wide")
```

---

[16] If you apply complete.cases to the long format, you will delete all the rows with an NA, liberating much memory space.

Let's see how it works in Python. First, get and clean the data:

```
#%% Getting Data
from pandas import read_excel
from os.path  import join
folder='/Users/JoseManuel/Dropbox/BookData/chapter6'
filename="2015_statistical_annex_tables_all.xls"
fileXLS=join(folder,filename)

# Initial FILTERS:
f=6  # first row to get
l=38 # do not consider these many rows from bottom-up
cols=[1] + range(2,14,2) # columns to select
PanelHDI=read_excel(fileXLS,"Table 2",skiprows=f,skip_footer=1,
                    parse_cols=cols)

#%% Cleaning
import numpy as np
PanelHDI.rename(columns={'Unnamed: 0':'Country'}, inplace=True)#rename
PanelHDI.dropna(inplace=True) # bye subtitles:
PanelHDI.replace('..', np.nan, regex=False,inplace=True) # Set NAs
PanelHDI.reset_index(drop=True,inplace=True) # Reset index
```

Next, I will do the formatting of the data frame into a long format. I only
need the pandas function melt. Therefore, to get the same result we obtained
in R, I need less arguments. Notice I include as comments the respective R
arguments.

```
#%% Wide to long:
from pandas import melt
LongPanelHDI=melt(PanelHDI,
                  value_name='HDI',    # v.names
                  id_vars=['Country'], # idvar
                  var_name='Year')     # timevar
# some arrangements:
toSort=["Country"]; Order=[True] ## Sorting:
LongPanelHDI.sort_values(toSort,ascending=Order,inplace=True)
LongPanelHDI.dropna(inplace=True) # bye rows with NAs
LongPanelHDI.reset_index(drop=True,inplace=True) ## resetting indexes
```

In the code above, I also include the arrangements needed to get a clean format, as I did in R. Finally, let me share the inverse process (from long to wide
format):

```
#%% from Long to Wide (dirty result)
WidePanelHDI=LongPanelHDI.pivot(index="Country",
                                columns="Year",
                                values="HDI")
```

You have *almost* what you need. See Figure 6.11 to realize that the output of
the function pivot created elements not present in R:

```
WidePanelHDI.head()
```

Year	1990	2000	2010	2011	2012	2013
Country						
Afghanistan	0.296681	0.334263	0.447722	0.455618	0.463019	0.463923
Albania	0.624210	0.656402	0.722489	0.728014	0.729434	0.732245
Algeria	0.574486	0.640132	0.725421	0.730241	0.731827	0.733622
Andorra	NaN	NaN	0.822628	0.821324	0.843578	0.843505
Angola	NaN	0.389657	0.508625	0.521132	0.524199	0.529679

Figure 6.11 Some issues in wide-format output in Python.

To get the best result, we need to erase the columns' name, because it is Year instead of the actual year digits. We also need to reset the indexes (you see countries as indexes), but without dropping the index names because the countries are serving as those indexes. If we do not drop them, the indexes (country names) will be a new column:

```
# Resetting column names
WidePanelHDI.columns.name=None
# Resetting index and recovering Country as column
WidePanelHDI.reset_index(drop=False,inplace=True)
```

6.5.3 Formatting Survival Data

Survival data has become very important in social and policy studies, where it is also known as event history analysis; see Box-Steffensmeier and Jones (2004) or Allison (2014) for further details. In particular Studies, It is important for studying duration. track, for example, an individual situation for a period of time, and survival data indicate what is the state of the situation when tracking ends. Sometimes, we cannot tell whether a situation we are observing ever changes. At other times we do not know what is the initial state of the situation we are observing.

Survival data analysis enables researchers to explore possible explanations for the duration of a particular situation. For instance, I created a data set about recidivism that indicates the following information: the personal attributes of the person under study, the date this person was released, the last time the status of this person was recorded, and whether that person returned to jail or not. If the person was reimprisoned, the day he or she returned is precisely the last day this person was observed. A person cannot be observed for other reasons (perhaps the person died or moved away, and so on).

Survival analysis can be conducted using many techniques in R and Python, but all of them require that you format the data in a particular way. Let's start with R:

```
# Getting the Data:
folder=file.path("~","Dropbox","BookData","chapter6")
fileCSV=file.path(folder,"BackToJail.csv")
survDat=read.csv(fileCSV, stringsAsFactors=F)
str(survDat)
```

```
'data.frame':    200 obs. of  7 variables:
 $ ID          : int  1 2 3 4 5 6 7 8 9 10 ...
 $ sex         : int  1 1 0 0 1 1 1 0 1 0 ...
 $ depAtRel    : int  0 0 0 1 0 1 1 1 0 0 ...
 $ educAtRel   : int  3 3 3 1 3 2 3 2 1 1 ...
 $ ReleaseDate: chr  "5/1/98" "3/6/90" "4/13/92" "2/18/92" ...
 $ lastFollow  : chr  "5/10/10" "6/29/10" "10/31/11" "8/27/11" ...
 $ JailAgain   : int  0 1 0 1 1 0 0 0 0 0 ...
```

The data from my file has the right values, but the dates and the factors need
to be correctly formatted:

```
# capturing dates from string:
survDat[,c(5,6)]=lapply(survDat[,c(5,6)],
                        strptime,"%m/%d/%y")
# setting captured format as Dates:
survDat[,c(5,6)]=lapply(survDat[,c(5,6)],as.Date)
survDat[,c(2,3,7)]=lapply(survDat[,c(2,3,7)],as.factor)
survDat[,4]=as.ordered(survDat[,4])
str(survDat)
```

```
'data.frame':    200 obs. of  7 variables:
 $ ID          : int  1 2 3 4 5 6 7 8 9 10 ...
 $ sex         : Factor w/ 2 levels "0","1": 2 2 1 1 2 2 2 1 2 1 ...
 $ depAtRel    : Factor w/ 2 levels "0","1": 1 1 1 2 1 2 2 2 1 1 ...
 $ educAtRel   : Ord.factor w/ 3 levels "1"<"2"<"3": 3 3 3 1 3 2 3 2 1 1 ...
 $ ReleaseDate: Date, format: "1998-05-01" "1990-03-06" ...
 $ lastFollow  : Date, format: "2010-05-10" "2010-06-29" ...
 $ JailAgain   : Factor w/ 2 levels "0","1": 1 2 1 2 2 1 1 1 1 1 ...
```

With the two dates, we need to compute duration. Let's compute duration
in days:

```
survDat$duration=as.numeric(survDat[,6]-survDat[,5])
```

We have now all the elements to make a survival object and use it for survival
analysis:

```
library(survival)
survDat$obj=Surv(survDat$duration,
                 survDat$JailAgain==1)
survObj.fit = survfit(obj ~ sex,
                      data = survDat)
survObj.fit
```

```
Call: survfit(formula = obj ~ sex, data = survDat)

        n events median 0.95LCL 0.95UCL
sex=0 100     48   6924    6482    7413
sex=1 100     49   6979    6661    7420
```

Making your data ready in Python requires the installation of a new module called **lifelines** by Davidson-Pilon (2015), which works with pandas data frames.[17] The steps are pretty straightforward. Let's get the data:

```
#%% Get Data:
import os
from pandas import read_csv

folderData=os.path.join("~","Dropbox","BookData","chapter6")
fileCSV=os.path.join(folderData,"BackToJail.csv")
survDat=read_csv(fileCSV,
                 parse_dates = [4,5]) #dates in these columns!
```

We only have a pandas data frame here, so we need to use the dates to compute duration as before:

```
#%% Compute Duration
from lifelines.utils import datetimes_to_durations

start_times=survDat["ReleaseDate"]
end_times=survDat["lastFollow"]
T, E = datetimes_to_durations(start_times, end_times)
survDat["T"]=T #T has the duration
# E will not be used for Events:
# survDat["JailAgain"]
```

Notice that the function datetimes_to_durations gives two results: the duration "T" and the events "E", which the function computes from the data. In our case, we have already "E" in "JailAgain." The function computes "E" in the cases where you do not have the second date ("lastFollow"), so it will consider that they are right-censored. This last piece of code simply computes survival curves based on the Kaplan-Meier estimator (please run it if you are knowledgeable about survival analysis; otherwise just omit the code).

```
from lifelines import KaplanMeierFitter

kmf = KaplanMeierFitter() # kmf has the filter to use Kaplan-Meier
groups = survDat['sex']   # We will plot 2 groups
ix = (groups == 1) # flags
#plotting
```

---

[17] Install it in your environment using pip install lifelines.

```
kmf.fit(survDat["T"][~ix],survDat["JailAgain"][~ix],label='female')
ax = kmf.plot()
kmf.fit(survDat["T"][ix], survDat["JailAgain"][ix],label='male')
kmf.plot(ax=ax)
```

	Home	Insert	Page Layout
E3563	▲▼		*fx*

	A	B	C
1	to	from	weight
2	D08726376	D09070449	13
3	D08726376	D31159670	1
4	D08726376	D02655217	1
5	D08726376	D07537643	5
6	D08726376	D22258392	10
7	D08726376	D06422354	1
8	D08726376	D23853839	1
9	D08726376	D06023956	17

Figure 6.12 Basic list of edges.

6.6 Formatting Network Data Sets

Network data is becoming pervasive in social and policy research. Let me show you how to transform different data formats into a social network object.

6.6.1 Networks from Edge Lists

Figure 6.12 shows a format known as an edge list. Each row in the figure describes a link or edge between two people, in this case legislators. If a bill has more cosponsors, there will be another row with two legislators; one can repeat, but not both at the same time. Of course, it is possible that a pair of legislators repeat, and that is the purpose of the column `weight`, which, in this case, indicates how many times a pair of legislators have sponsored a law together.

R has two interesting packages to work with networks: **igraph** or **statnet**, and I will show you both. Let me upload the file first:

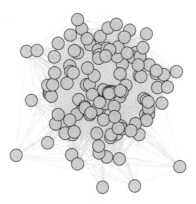

Figure 6.13 A network plot from an edge list.

```
folder=file.path("~","Dropbox","BookData","chapter6")
fileCSV=file.path(folder,"cosponsorshipEdges.csv")
edgeList=read.csv(fileCSV,stringsAsFactors=F)
```

And to give these data a network format, we use either of the packages mentioned:

```
#install.packages("statnet")
library(statnet)
billNet=network(edgeList,matrix.type="edgelist",directed=FALSE)
#install.packages("igraph")
library(igraph)
billNet=graph.data.frame(edgeList,directed=FALSE)
```

That is all the formatting needed.[18] Now you have a network that can be plotted using the code below (see Figure 6.13).

```
plot.igraph(billNet,layout=layout_with_kk,vertex.label=NA)
# The 'layout' is the Kamada-Kawai,there are many more!
# For statnet: gplot(billNet)
```

In Python, it is also very easy to create a network by combining pandas and **Networkx**:

```
#%% Get Data:
import os
from pandas import read_csv
```

---

[18] The function graph.data.frame can have as an input another data frame with the attributes of the nodes (need to use: vertices='' ...'').

```
folderData=os.path.join("~","Dropbox","BookData","chapter7")
fileCSV=os.path.join(folderData,"cosponsorshipEdges.csv")
edgeList=read_csv(fileCSV)

#%% Formatting into a network
import networkx as net

originNode='to'; targetNode='from'
attributesToInclude=['weight']
billNet=net.from_pandas_dataframe(edgeList,originNode,targetNode,
                                  attributesToInclude)
# plot using: net.draw(billNet)
```

	A	B	C	D	E	F	G	H	I	J	K	L
1	Names	Romero	Grana	Miro Quesada	Moreyra	Fort	De La Puente	Wiese	Onrubia	Brescia	Nicolini	Montero
2	Romero	0	1	1	1	1	1	0	1	1	1	0
3	Grana	1	0	1	0	1	1	1	0	0	0	1
4	Miro Quesada	1	1	0	0	1	1	1	0	0	0	1
5	Moreyra	1	0	0	0	1	1	1	1	1	0	1
6	Fort	1	1	1	1	0	1	0	1	1	1	0
7	De La Puente	1	1	1	1	1	0	1	0	0	0	1
8	Wiese	0	1	1	1	0	1	0	0	0	0	1
9	Onrubia	1	0	0	1	1	0	0	0	1	1	0
10	Brescia	1	0	0	1	1	0	0	1	0	0	0
11	Nicolini	1	0	0	0	1	0	0	1	0	0	0
12	Montero	0	1	1	1	0	1	1	0	0	0	0

Figure 6.14 An adjacency matrix.

6.6.2 Networks from an Adjacency Matrix

Another network format is the adjacency matrix, whose format you can see in Figure 6.14. In this case, the nodes are in the headers and in the row names, and the matrix tells when two nodes are connected by writing a number in the corresponding intersection. These data come from an study carried out by Figueroa (2008), where the nodes represent a member of the most important companies in Peru; if a link exists, it means that these two people are members of the board of the same company.

As always, let's get the data:

```
library(xlsx)
folder=file.path("~","Dropbox","BookData","chapter6")
fileXLS=file.path(folder,"dataFigueroa.xlsx")
dataMatrix=read.xlsx(fileXLS,sheetName="matrix",
                     check.names = F,row.names=1)  # VERY IMPORTANT
```

In spreadsheets, row indexes or row names are consecutive numbers. That is also the default a data frame. But now, we need a matrix. Think of a matrix like an extension of a vector: All its elements are of ONE kind. The first column of this spreadsheet has strings, but since our data frame was created above with the argument row.names=1, that first column will be the name of the row.

So now all the elements are numbers (disregard the header names). However, you still have a data frame. To turn your data frame into a matrix just type

```
adjMatrix=as.matrix(dataMatrix)
```

We need to confirm that this is a squared matrix. For that, we simply run

```
# dimesions:
dim(adjMatrix)
```

```
[1] 37 37
```

The results confirm we have what we need. Now, we can make the network with the two different packages we have:

- Using `igraph`:

```
# version with igraph
# library(igraph) # install it first!
Igraph_eliteNet=graph.adjacency(adjMatrix,
                                mode="undirected",
                                weighted=NULL)
```

- Using `statnet`:

```
# version with statnet
# library(statnet) # install it first!
Statnet_eliteNet=network(adjMatrix,
                         matrix.type="adjacency",
                         directed=FALSE)
```

Once you have the network objects, you can continue your network analysis work.

Similar steps should be followed in Python. We first collect the data, making sure that the first column is the index (here it is "0" position). I also compute the dimensions of the data (see page 54) to make sure I have a squared matrix.

```
#%% Get Data:
import os
from pandas import read_excel

folderData=os.path.join("~","Dropbox","BookData","chapter6")
fileXLS=os.path.join(folderData,"dataFigueroa.xlsx")
dataMatrix=read_excel(fileXLS,index_col=0)

dimensions=dataMatrix.shape
```

To make the network simply run the following:

```
#%% Formatting into a network
import networkx as net

Py_elite = net.Graph(dataMatrix.values) #.values creates matrix
# see what you have: eliteNet.nodes(data=True)
```

If you take a look with the suggested command, you will see this:

eliteNet.nodes(data=True)

```
[(0, {}),
 (1, {}),
 (2, {}),
 (3, {}),
 (4, {}),
 (5, {}),
 (6, {}),
 (7, {}),
 (8, {}),
 (9, {}),
 (10, {}),
 (11, {}),
 (12, {}),
 ( 13    {})
```

This command shows you the name of each node and its attributes. We do not have attributes, but I want to have the names of the businesspeople instead of numbers. This requires that I relabel the network nodes:

```
#%% relabeling

currentNodeLabels=range(dimensions[0])
newNodeLabels=list(dataMatrix)
mapping=zip(currentNodeLabels, newNodeLabels)

net.relabel_nodes(Py_elite,
                  dict(mapping),   # has to be a dictionary
                  copy=False)      # This makes the changes 'in place'
```

Relabeling the nodes requires that you supply both the original names and the new ones. Both lists have to be combined as a dictionary to get the expected changes. The key command to combine is zip, because it created the mapping,

as shown in Figure 6.15. Notice that the mapping is later converted into a
dictionary (relabel_nodes requires a dict).

```
currentNodeLabels          newNodeLabels          zip(currentNodeLabels, newNodeLabels)

[0,                        ['Romero',             [(0, 'Romero'),
 1,                         'Grana',               (1, 'Grana'),
 2,                         'Miro Quesada',        (2, 'Miro Quesada'),
 3,                         'Moreyra',             (3, 'Moreyra'),
 4,                         'Fort',        →       (4, 'Fort'),
 5,                         'De La Puente',        (5, 'De La Puente'),
 6,                         'Wiese',               (6, 'Wiese'),
 7,                         'Onrubia',             (7, 'Onrubia'),
 8,                         'Brescia',             (8, 'Brescia'),
 9,                         'Nicolini',            (9, 'Nicolini'),
```

Figure 6.15 Zipping lists in Python. The command zip is very useful in preparing
these mappings.

6.6.3 Networks from an Adjacency List

An interesting structure for networks is the adjacency list, where the first node
to the left is connected to all the nodes to its right in the same row. Figure 6.16
shows a basic example of an adjacency list, which shows border conflict among
countries.

To work with that data in R, we need to format it carefully because neither
igraph nor Statnet easily reads adjacency lists directly (they have functions
that also need previous reshaping to read this structure). Let's get the data first:

```
library(xlsx)
folder=file.path("~","Dropbox","BookData","chapter6")
filename="warsAdjListX.xlsx"
fileXLS=file.path(folder,filename)
# Getting what we need:
dataAdjList = read.xlsx(fileXLS,1,
                        startRow=3,
                        stringsAsFactors=F,
                        header =F)
```

Let's take a look at what we have now:

```
head(dataAdjList)
```

```
          X1          X2       X3           X4
1      Turkey       Syria     <NA>         <NA>
2  Bangladesh       India     <NA>         <NA>
3     Eritrea    Ethiopia Djibouti         <NA>
4       Sudan South Sudan     <NA>         <NA>
5     Lebanon      Israel     <NA>         <NA>
6     Mongolia   Manchukuo    Japan Soviet Union
```

```
● ● ●                        warsAdjList
# war among countries
# from https://en.wikipedia.org/wiki/List_of_border_conflicts
Turkey,Syria
Bangladesh,India
Eritrea,Ethiopia,Djibouti
Sudan,South Sudan
Lebanon,Israel
Mongolia,Manchukuo,Japan,Soviet Union
Ethiopia,Somalia
Slovakia,Hungary
Peru,Bolivia,Ecuador,Chile
Laos,Thailand
Bolivia,Paraguay,Chile
Burkina Faso,Mali
Manchukuo,Japan,Soviet Union
Iran,Iraq
Japan,Soviet Union
China,Vietnam,India,Soviet Union
Thailand,Cambodia
Mauritania,Senegal
North Korea,South Korea
Pakistan,India
Angola,South Africa
Mexico,United States
```

Figure 6.16 An adjacency list. This indicates that, for instance, in the third row, Eritrea had a conflict with Ethiopia and Djibouti, but it does not mean that Ethiopia and Djibouti were also at war. If they had been at war, there should be another row specifying that.
Source: https://en.wikipedia.org/wiki/List_of_border_conflicts.

This data is in Excel. I saved it in Excel beause adjacency lists are easily read from Excel or CSV, but are more difficult in "txt", exactly the opposite as in Python. This data frame needs first to be reshaped into an **edge list**. This formatting, as we saw previously, will do the trick:

```
EdgeList_butDirty= reshape(dataAdjList,
                        varying = list(2:4),  # like panel!
                        idvar= "X1",          # fixed
                        direction = "long")
# what do we have?
head(EdgeList_butDirty)
```

	X1	time	X2
Turkey.1	Turkey	1	Syria
Bangladesh.1	Bangladesh	1	India
Eritrea.1	Eritrea	1	Ethiopia
Sudan.1	Sudan	1	South Sudan
Lebanon.1	Lebanon	1	Israel
Mongolia.1	Mongolia	1	Manchukuo

Now we have an edge list from the adjacency list. The latter has been treated as panel data, so that columns 2 to 4 are repeated measures of the first column. However, the result is not yet clean. Let's get rid of the NA in the second column and keep the columns named X1 and X2 (first and third):

```
EdgeList=EdgeList_butDirty[!is.na(EdgeList_butDirty$X2),][c(1,3)]
```

Having an edge list, you can simply apply the previous commands from subsection 6.6.1:

```
warNet=graph.data.frame(EdgeList)# for igraph:
```

This time, Python will make it really easy when using this file as a "txt":

```
#%% Prepare link
import os
folderData="/Users/JoseManuel/Dropbox/BookData/chapter7"
fileTXT=os.path.join(folderData,"warsAdjList.txt")

#%%
import networkx as net
warNet=net.read_adjlist(fileTXT,delimiter=',')
```

6.7 A Comment on Complex Survey Design Data

Survey data may come from complex designs through processes where it was collected in several steps using clusters and strata. In particular, the data from ANES is complex, but we only used it to show how to import SPSS files into R or Python, without describing its complicated design. These data have columns that carry information on the complex design of the sampling units, the strata, the sampling weights, and size corrections. Survey experts can compute the correct functions using those columns to get population estimate, but if you are not an expert you will need specific packages in R or Python that can give you support. Python has a package *pysurvey*, but it does not offer the support for the kind of data presented in this section; in fact, it is under discussion whether such a package is needed or if pandas should include that support.[19] However, R does offer the package **survey**, which offers the support needed.[20]

---

[19] Visit https://github.com/pandas-dev/pandas/issues/10030 to see if this decision has been made.
[20] Visit http://r-survey.r-forge.r-project.org/survey/ for tutorials about data tables.

It is important to consider when your research requires a complex design. There is a current discussion among economists on the estimation of causal effects. I recommend you read the report by Solon et al. (2013) to have a clear idea of this discussion.

The next chapter presents the final step, integrating and storing data, which is not as easy as it seems.

7

Integrating and Storing Data

In general, when you collect, clean, and format data, you are working with independent files, but most of the time your analytic work needs to combine files from different sources to answer the questions you define in your research design. It is rarely the case that your research question depends on *one* particular data set or on several files from *one* source. Integration is the process of combining your data to produce the file you need. The material on storage focuses on how to code for data retrieval, updating, and sharing; topics that go beyond simply saving your files for later use.

7.1 Integrating Data

7.1.1 Preparing the Integration: Cleaning the Keys

To be able to integrate different data sets, you need one column that serves as a key to merge the data. Sometimes, you may even need two columns. That *key column* is the common column in every data set to be integrated. The headers do not have to be the same (no need for that), but the contents do. For example, if you have two data files of cities from different countries, the key could be the city name. If one file has more cities than the other, it is not a problem, as long as the cities that appear on both files are written using the same spelling. For this example, I will combine some known data sets from different sources to show the issues you face when integrating data.

- Human Development Index (HDI)[1]
- Freedom of the World Index (WORLD)[2]

---

[1] http://hdr.undp.org/sites/default/files/2015_statistical_annex_tables_all.xls.
[2] https://freedomhouse.org/sites/default/files/Individual Country Ratings and Status, 1973-2015 (FINAL).xls.

226

- Economic Freedom Index (ECO)[3]
- Freedom of the Press (PRESS)[4]
- A table with the country names and their ISO and FIPS (CODES)[5] from America's Open Geocode (http://www.opengeocode.org/) database[6]

The unit of analysis is the country; the column with the country names can be used as the key, but I prefer some kind of country code, so the ISO or FIPS codes are the best option to ease the merging. Notice that I will use the official link to the data this time (the ones provided in the previous footnotes) to avoid scrapping (and mistakes in Wikipedia information). Let's start by getting the ISO and FIPS codes.

To get the codes you can use this link (which I have written in parts because of its length):

```
subLink1 = "http://ec2-54-201-183-195."
subLink2="us-west-2.compute.amazonaws.com"
subLink12=paste(subLink1,subLink2,sep="")
subLink3="cow/cow.csv"
myFile=file.path(subLink12,subLink3)
```

But, to be sure you can replicate my example, use the file in the folder of this chapter (cow.csv).

```
folderData=file.path("~","Dropbox","BookData","chapter7")
myFile=file.path(folderData,"cow.csv")
CODES = read.csv(myFile,
                 stringsAsFactors=FALSE,
                 na.strings=NULL,
                 blank.lines.skip = F,
                 sep = ",")
```

Note that, because I am dealing with ISO codes that are combinations of letters, I set na.strings=NULL, so that the ISO2 for Namibia ("NA") will not be interpreted as a missing value.[7] This file has 77 columns; let me select the columns needed:

```
CODES=CODES[,c(1,2,3,6,68,71,72)] #selecting
```

I do not need all the rows. This is a comprehensive file, so I am going to use the column Currency.Symbol (renamed later as "sys"), which indicates

---

[3] http://www.heritage.org/index/excel/2015/index2015_data.xls.
[4] http://fr.rsf.org/IMG/csv/2015wpfi.csv.
[5] Federal Information Processing Standards (FIPS) codes are intended for general use throughout the U.S. government.
[6] http://ec2-54-201-183-195.us-west-2.compute.amazonaws.com/cow/cow.csv.
[7] By default, "NA" and "blanks" are transformed as missing values.

in what system the name of the country has been written. In this case, I need the English version (en-iso):

```
CODES=CODES[CODES$Currency.Symbol=="en-iso",] #filtering
```

I selected the ISO system because it has a code for almost every territory. I also want to keep the variants of ISO codes, so I rename them as "iso2," "iso3," and "niso3." I kept the FIPS codes as well, but we may not use them, because they are not available for every territory. This code carries out what I want:

```
titles=c("iso2","iso3","niso3","fips",
         "sys","name1","name2")
colnames(CODES)=titles #renaming
CODES$sys=NULL          # deleting column
row.names(CODES)=NULL   # resetting indexes
```

This is what we have now:

```
head(CODES)
```

```
  iso2 iso3 niso3 fips        name1          name2
1   AF  AFG     4   AF  Afghanistan    Afghanistan
2   AL  ALB     8   AL      Albania        Albania
3   DZ  DZA    12   AG      Algeria        Algeria
4   AS  ASM    16   AQ American Samoa American Samoa
5   AD  AND    20   AN      Andorra        Andorra
6   AO  AGO    24   AO       Angola         Angola
```

7.1.2 Merging, Appending, and Fuzzy Matching

I present now an example that requires every function we have seen before. In general, most examples of merging are very easy, but because I am dealing with real data this example will make you work harder. You may need to run the codes in small chunks to test what they are doing, but by now you should be able to do that.

The first data we will work with is the HDI. That file is originally in Excel, and if you want to collect it using the link, I recommend using the package *gdata*, which needs extra installation if you are using Windows.[8] This should work for that:

---

[8] If you are using **Windows**, please install **PERL** following the instructions given at: https://cran .r-project.org/web/packages/gdata/INSTALL.

```
library(gdata)
web='http://hdr.undp.org/sites/default/files'
fileweb='2015_statistical_annex_tables_all.xls'
fileHDI=file.path(web,fileweb)
# read.xls from package gdata
HDI=read.xls(fileHDI,sheet = "Table 1",
        skip=9,header=F,encoding="latin1", #French (ISO)
        blank.lines.skip=F,stringsAsFactors=F)[c(2,3)]
```

However, I will use the file in this folder to ensure you can follow me:

```
library(xlsx)   # back to this library!
#
folder=file.path("~","Dropbox","BookData","chapter7")
filename="2015_statistical_annex_tables_all.xls"
fileHDI=file.path(folder,filename)
HDI=read.xlsx(fileHDI,
            sheetName ="Table 1",
            encoding="latin1", # for French names
            stringsAsFactors=F)[c(2,3)]
```

The data frame HDI has some issues. The most serious one is that it lacks ISO or FIPS codes. Their absence will force us to merge this file using the country names.

A minor problem is that this data has extra rows. Earlier to address this problem, I put values in the arguments to filter those rows; now I will show you how to do it without using that argument. First let me find the first country:

```
head(HDI[,1],8)
```

```
[1] "Table 1: Human Development Index and its components "
[2] NA
[3] NA
[4] "Country"
[5] NA
[6] "VERY HIGH HUMAN DEVELOPMENT"
[7] "Norway"
[8] "Australia"
```

Then, I get rid of the unused rows from the top:

```
HDI=HDI[-c(1:6),]
```

Now, let me find the position of the last country. Make sure to reset the index numbers, because the previous deletion did not take care of that.

```
row.names(HDI)=NULL # resetting index number
head(tail(HDI,72)) # finding the 'head' of the 'tail' requested
```

		NA..1	NA..2
197	San Marino		..
198	Somalia		..
199	Tuvalu		..
200	<NA>		<NA>
201	Human development groups		<NA>
202	Very high human development	0.896389904013282

You see that Tuvalu is the last country with index 199. If we had not reset the index number, you would see a different number. Then, I use that position to keep the rows I need:

```
HDI=HDI[c(1:199),] # 199 was the position of Tuvalu
```

I can rename the columns with a more descriptive header:

```
names(HDI)=c("Country", "hdi")
```

Let's find the row without the HDI score (empty cells have been read as NA):

```
HDI[!complete.cases(HDI$hdi),]
```

		Country	hdi
50	HIGH HUMAN DEVELOPMENT		<NA>
107	MEDIUM HUMAN DEVELOPMENT		<NA>
147	LOW HUMAN DEVELOPMENT		<NA>
192	OTHER COUNTRIES OR TERRITORIES		<NA>

You know that those rows are section names (not country names), so I subset HDI without those ones:

```
HDI=HDI[complete.cases(HDI$hdi),]
row.names(HDI)=NULL # reset index, you took away rows!
```

We have the symbol .. as the missing value for the index but because the merging process will create missing values, I am going to put "message unavailable" instead of NA. This is not strictly necessary, but I just want to reinforce the use of grep to obtain positions:

```
# change the string for NAs:
positionsNA = grep("..",HDI$hdi, fixed=T)
HDI$hdi[positionsNA]="unavailable" # my message!
```

Before doing the merging, it is good to know the size of both data frames to be merged:

```
nrow(CODES)≥nrow(HDI) #249>195
```

```
[1] TRUE
```

I verified their sizes, because I do not want to end up with different amounts of rows in the data frames.

We now use the function `merge()`, which can merge only TWO data frames whose order of input matters. The first one will be considered "*x*" and the second "*y*." The arguments by.x and by.y request that you indicate what are the key columns for each data frame. You want to include also all.x and all.y and set them as true; with those options you will see the countries that appear in both data frames, and also the rows from each data frame that could not be matched. This merge will create missing values, which help you find the differences:

```
HDIdirty=merge(HDI,CODES, #data frames
               by.x="Country",by.y="name1", # key columns
               all.x = T,all.y=T)
```

Whenever you do merging with these or similar arguments (in R, Python, or any other program), you can expect the following:

- HDIdirty, the current result, has *some* columns from HDI and CODES without missing values. These are some of the **matched** rows and columns:

```
head(HDIdirty[!is.na(HDIdirty$iso2)&!is.na(HDIdirty$hdi),][-7])
```

	Country	hdi	iso2	iso3	niso3	fips
1	Afghanistan	0.465264260207532	AF	AFG	4	AF
3	Albania	0.732765802641622	AL	ALB	8	AL
4	Algeria	0.735623767134645	DZ	DZA	12	AG
6	Andorra	0.844641908378314	AD	AND	20	AN
7	Angola	0.531591421824396	AO	AGO	24	AO
10	Antigua and Barbuda	0.783367264384529	AG	ATG	28	AC

- The column Country in HDIdirty will keep the rows that were not matched from HDI with its value hdi, but will have missing values in the other columns coming from CODES. This is the effect of requesting all.x. You can see this with this code:

```
# Showing some rows and columns!
HDIdirty[is.na(HDIdirty$iso2),][-7]
```

```
> HDIdirty[is.na(HDIdirty$iso2),][c(1:6)]
                                      Country       hdi iso2 iso3 niso3 fips
27              Bolivia (Plurinational State of) 0.661830764207645 <NA> <NA>   NA <NA>
39                              CÃ´te d'Ivoire 0.462221996949664 <NA> <NA>   NA <NA>
40                                  Cabo Verde 0.646240272542626 <NA> <NA>   NA <NA>
55           Congo (Democratic Republic of the)  0.43313535394693 <NA> <NA>   NA <NA>
105                          Hong Kong, China (SAR) 0.909951869585351 <NA> <NA>   NA <NA>
110                      Iran (Islamic Republic of) 0.765590711027114 <NA> <NA>   NA <NA>
124        Korea (Democratic People's Rep. of)       unavailable <NA> <NA>   NA <NA>
125                          Korea (Republic of) 0.89833413494607 <NA> <NA>   NA <NA>
153              Micronesia (Federated States of) 0.639590168781703 <NA> <NA>   NA <NA>
155                      Moldova (Republic of) 0.693302690570274 <NA> <NA>   NA <NA>
230              Tanzania (United Republic of) 0.521214355954627 <NA> <NA>   NA <NA>
233 The former Yugoslav Republic of Macedonia 0.747252859936566 <NA> <NA>   NA <NA>
253        Venezuela (Bolivarian Republic of) 0.762252400296525 <NA> <NA>   NA <NA>
```

Figure 7.1 Unmatched values from merging HDI and CODES.

The result is shown in Figure 7.1 (without the last column: name2). Notice the presence of parentheses with repetitive strings inside. That will become important soon when I discuss *normalizing text*.

- HDIdirty will also have the rows from CODES that were not matched with HDI. These country names appear in the last column (name2). These rows will have NA in the hdi. This is the result of requesting all.y. Let's see the first, second, and last column, and the last four rows of this subset:

```
#showing some rows and columns...
tail(HDIdirty[is.na(HDIdirty$hdi),][,c(1,2,7)],4)

                      Country   hdi             name2
256  Virgin Islands, British  <NA>  British Virgin Islands
257      Virgin Islands, U.S.  <NA>      U.S. Virgin Islands
258        Wallis and Futuna  <NA>        Wallis and Futuna

259          Western Sahara  <NA>          Western Sahara
```

Notice that it was very important that I wrote 'unavailable' in hdi before, because I did not want that row to be in this last subset.

Now, we need to pay attention to how to complete the merging; we cannot leave things the way they are now. That is when **fuzzy matching** comes into play. This technique determines how similar two strings are, so I will implement it to find the most similar spellings among the country names from the two original data frames. R has a function agrep that implements the distance between strings proposed by Levenshtein (1966). For that, I need to save three kinds of results from the merging done earlier:

```
# good ones without last column
matched=HDIdirty[!is.na(HDIdirty$iso2)&!is.na(HDIdirty$hdi),][-7]
# the ones without codes, without last column
unmatched=HDIdirty[is.na(HDIdirty$iso2),][-7]
# the ones without hdi score, without last column
where=HDIdirty[is.na(HDIdirty$hdi),][-c(1,2)]
```

I will apply fuzzy matching to those subdata frames, but let me show you how the function `agrep` works:

```
# 1. This is a country that could not match a code:
unmatchedString=unmatched[11,1]
# 1. These are the unassigned codes:
whereToLookFor=where$name2
# 3. This is how you get the 'possible' index position:
agrep(unmatchedString,whereToLookFor,max.distance=0.2)
```

```
integer(0)
```

The result above tells me that, with that distance (0.2), no match was found. So, let me try again with a larger value:

```
agrep(unmatchedString,whereToLookFor,max.distance=0.7)
```

```
[1]  7 10 15 29 32 35 36 38 41 42 52 56 59 61 62 63
```

This result was even less helpful (too many matches). Let's try a smaller value:

```
agrep(unmatchedString,whereToLookFor,max.distance=0.35)
```

```
[1] 59
```

Changing the distance gave me ONE match:

```
unmatchedString
```

```
[1] "Tanzania (United Republic of)"
```

And `agrep` proposes the position 59, which returns this value when applied to `where`:

```
where$name2[59]
```

```
[1] "United Republic of Tanzania"
```

You see that the idea is simple, but the implementation can be complicated. You
want to find one good match, but sometimes you do not get it. For example, this
country name

```
unmatched[10,1]
```

```
[1] "Moldova (Republic of)"
```

gets this result in where using the same distance that proved helpful last time:

```
where$name2[agrep(unmatched[10,1],whereToLookFor,0.35)]
```

```
[1] "Islamic Republic of Iran"
[2] "Democratic People's Republic of Korea"
[3] "The Former Yugoslav Republic of Macedonia"
[4] "United Republic of Tanzania"
```

As you see, not only did I get many matches but they all are wrong. Here, you
need to reflect on how the Levenshtein's algorithm can work better in the way
agrep implements it in R:

- If we want the fuzzy matching to be efficient and effective, similar phrases
  need to have their words in the same order. In this example, the words
  are not in the same order: The order of the names of the countries in
  unmatched (for example: 'Tanzania (United Republic of)') is different from the order of the names of the countries in where (for instance:
  'United Republic of Tanzania'). The first step is to swap the texts
  when we split by commas or parentheses. I will make a function for that:

```
# swapping:
swap=function(aColumn,symbol=','){ # default is ','
  newCells=c() # new column
  for (cell in aColumn){
    # split gives a LIST, then you get first element
    oldStrings=strsplit(cell,symbol,fixed = T)[[1]]
    # if splitting gave you more than one element:
    if (length(oldStrings)>1){
      # swap the elements
      newStrings=paste0(oldStrings[2],oldStrings[1])
      newCells=c(newCells,newStrings)
    }else{
      # if split returned one string
      # just add that string (unmodified)
```

```
        newCells=c(newCells,oldStrings)
      }
    }
    newCells
  }
```

We can apply that function to the country names in unmatched. First, I use the default ',' and then the parentheses:

```
unmatched$Country=swap(unmatched$Country) # using default.
unmatched$Country=swap(unmatched$Country,symbol='(')
```

- **Normalizing** is a way of simplifying the operations on the text. In this case, I need to replace the phrase Republic of with nothing; that will leave in the cell a shortened country name. Normalizing is not cleaning, because the phrase we will delete is not wrong, but is a strategy to reduce the number of modifications the algorithm needs to make to find the match.

```
require(stringi)
pattern="Republic of|Rep. of|\\)|SAR"  # to be replaced
# no more pattern:
unmatched$Country=stri_replace_all(unmatched$Country, '',
                                   regex=pattern)
where$name2=stri_replace_all(where$name2, '', regex=pattern)
# cleaning trailing and leading spaces
unmatched$Country=stri_trim(unmatched$Country)
where$name2=stri_trim(where$name2)
```

We are now in a better situation to create an efficient application of the agrep function:

1. We need to take every country name from unmatched and get the matches from where.
2. If you get MORE than one match, accept none of them, and get the next country name from unmatched.
3. If you get ONE match keep it. Add that match to a new data frame (rematched).
4. Delete every match added to rematched from unmatched and where.
5. If unmatched is not empty, increase the distance allowed. If it is empty, finish.
6. If you reached the maximum distance allowed, finish.
7. Prepare the data frame (rematched) to be returned. Also return the unmatched and where data frame.

This code below could be the implementation that follows closely the strategy explained above, in a different order, as a function:

```
fuzzyMerge=function(Unmatched,Where,
                    keyUnmatched='Country',keyWhere='name2',
                    maxD=0.4,increment=0.05){
  Rematched=c()
  # Do the fuzzy using this distance
  for (d in seq(0,maxD,increment)) {  # FOR START
    #
    # Finish if Unmatched is empty
    if (nrow(Unmatched)==0) {           # IF START
      break}                           # IF END
    #
    for (i in 1:nrow(Unmatched)) {   # NESTED FOR START
      # Visit cell in Unmatched
      cellUnmatched=Unmatched[i,keyUnmatched]
      # Where to look for matches
      possibleMatches=Where[,keyWhere]
      # Get matches
      position=agrep(cellUnmatched,possibleMatches,d)
      # If you get ONE match:
      if (length(position)==1){        # sub IF START
        # create new row with right information
        newrow=c(Unmatched[i,c(1,2)],Where[position,c(1:4)])
        # append newrow to rematched
        Rematched=rbind(Rematched,newrow)

        # shrink the two data frames
        Where=Where[-position,]
        Unmatched=Unmatched[-i,]
      }                                # sub IF END
    }                                  # NESTED FOR END
  }                                    # FOR END
  #
  # Last message
  if (nrow(Unmatched)>0){
    print ("still some rows unmatched")
  } else{
    print ("All matches achieved!!")
  }
  #
  # Formatting
  Rematched=as.data.frame(Rematched)
  row.names(Rematched)=NULL
  #
  # returning: a list of data frames
  return (list(rematched=Rematched,
               where=Where,
               unmatched=Unmatched))}
```

Our function is ready. Notice that this function could accept six arguments. The first two are the data frames you will input, and the next two are the key column names of those data frames. The last two are the numeric arguments for the matching algorithm that will be controlled by the loops; that is, to control **for (d in seq(0,maxD,increment))**. The code follows closely the explanation detailed above, but note that this is the first time we return a list that contains data frames. Let me show you what to do with that.

```
# applying function
results=fuzzyMerge(unmatched,where)
```

```
[1] "All matches achieved!!"
```

According to the message, the code found all the matches. You now need to see
the results:

```
# head of rematched:
head(results$rematched)
```

```
                            Country           hdi iso2 iso3 niso3 fips
1                           Moldova 0.693302690570274  MD  MDA   498   MD
2   Plurinational State ofBolivia 0.661830764207645  BO  BOL    68   BL
3           Democratic theCongo 0.43313535394693  CD  COD   180   CG
4              Islamic Iran 0.765590711027114  IR  IRN   364   IR
5   Federated States ofMicronesia 0.639590168781703  FM  FSM   583   FM
6 The former Yugoslav  Macedonia 0.747252859936566  MK  MKD   807   MK
```

Then results$unmatched must be empty, and results$where has the countries that are not present in the HDI data frame.

Now, you need to do **horizontal appending**; that is, append the contents of
"rematched" to the bottom of "matched." You can horizontally append data if
those structures share the same column names and in the same order.

```
names(results$rematched)==names(matched)
```

```
[1] TRUE TRUE TRUE TRUE TRUE TRUE
```

According to the last test, it is safe to do the appending:

```
matched=rbind(matched,results$rematched)     #APPENDING
rownames(matched)=NULL                         #cleaning indexes
```

Is matched similar to the HDI data frame?

```
nrow(HDI)==nrow(matched)
```

```
[1] TRUE
```

And just in case:

```
# are there repeated countries? If they are, this is FALSE
length(unique(matched$Country))==nrow(matched)
```

```
[1] TRUE
```

To finish, replace HDI, delete matched, and set the "unavailable" as NA:

```
HDI=matched
HDI[HDI$hdi=='unavailable',]$hdi=NA
matched=NULL
```

The newest HDI will have some countries with different spellings, because the rematched was made by swapping and normalizing. However, the main goal was to get the ISO codes into the data frame. The country name is not a good key in this case: The ISO is more reliable.[9]

We can repeat the same workflow for the other data sets. Let's work with the Freedom of the Press Index:

```
folder=file.path("~","Dropbox","BookData","chapter7")
filename="2015wpfi.csv"
filePress=file.path(folder,filename)
colsToSelect=c(2:4)
PRESS=read.csv(filePress,
               sep = ";", # different separator!
               dec=",",   # for decimal flag!
               stringsAsFactors = F)[colsToSelect]
# what do we have:
head(PRESS)
```

```
   ISO  EN_country Sco15
1  FIN      Finland   7.5
2  NOR       Norway   7.8
3  DNK      Denmark   8.2
4  NLD  Netherlands   9.2
5  SWE       Sweden   9.5
6  NZL  New Zealand  10.1
```

Note that this file has ISO codes (ISO3), so merging could be less troublesome. Also note that the command for importing the file needs to indicate that this particular file uses ";" instead of "," to separate the values. The CSV files can have that delimiter when some of the values need to use commas. In this case the file uses the comma for the decimals. For that reason, I also set dec="," to indicate that the comma was used as the decimal symbol. I do not find the headers to be correct for my work, so I change them:

```
names(PRESS)=c("iso3","Country","press")
```

The merging process can start now:

```
PRESSdirty=merge(PRESS,CODES,
                 by="iso3", # no real need for this!
                 all.x = T)
```

---

[9] However, the Python implementation will keep the names unchanged.

If an **iso3** code is present in PRESS and in CODES, all the rows from CODES will be added to PRESSdirty, when an **iso3** in PRESS is not present in CODES the argument all. x=T will keep the rows from PRESS that did not find a match in the resulting merge PRESSdirty, simply putting an NA in the "iso3" column; but if all.x = F you will not see. We can verify if some country in PRESS did not get the codes from CODES, simply by checking when one of the columns from CODES is missing. Let's use iso2:

```
PRESSdirty[is.na(PRESSdirty$iso2),]
```

```
      iso3        Country press iso2 niso3 fips name1 name2
89    KOS          Kosovo    31 <NA>    NA <NA> <NA> <NA>
118  NCYP  Cyprus North      28 <NA>    NA <NA> <NA> <NA>
```

As you see, two countries are not present. Officially, Kosovo has the same ISO as Serbia, and Cyprus North the same as Cyprus at the country level.[10] So, we just keep the merge we found, without the last two columns, originally from CODES:

```
PRESS=PRESSdirty[-c(7,8)]
```

Now, PRESS has the other ISO and FIPS codes.

We have two more data sets. Let me get those two data files:

- Index of World Freedom:

```
# Reading this file takes a while, be patient!
library(xlsx)
folder=file.path("~","Dropbox","BookData","chapter7")
filename="worldfreedom2015.xls"
fileWORLD=file.path(folder,filename)
# Initial FILTERS:
firstRow=8    #first row of data
colsToSelect=c(1,127) #columns of interest
# Getting what we need:
WORLD = read.xlsx(fileWORLD,1,
                  startRow=firstRow,
                  stringsAsFactors=F,
                  header=F)[colsToSelect]
#renaming
titles=c("Country", "free")
names(WORLD)=titles
WORLD=WORLD[1:205,]
```

- Index of Economic Freedom (ECO):

```
filename='index2015_data.xls'
fileECO=file.path(folder,filename) # same folder
```

---

[10] You can search for the ISO codes at https://www.iso.org/.

```
colsToSelect=c(2,7)
ECO=read.xlsx(fileECO,1,
        stringsAsFactors=F)[colsToSelect]
#renaming
titles=c("Country", "eco")
names(ECO)=titles
ECO=ECO[1:186,]
```

None of the files has ISO or FIPS codes, so I will need to use country names. That operation requires a merging process similar to the one we followed with HDI.

Let me start with with ECO:

```
# Merging:
ECOdirty=merge(ECO,CODES,by.x ="Country", by.y="name1",
        all.x=T,all.y = T)
```

Then, get the three sub-data frames to apply the fuzzy matching:

```
matched=ECOdirty[!is.na(ECOdirty$iso2)&!is.na(ECOdirty$eco),][-7]
unmatched=ECOdirty[is.na(ECOdirty$iso2),][-7]
where=ECOdirty[is.na(ECOdirty$eco),][-c(1,2)]
```

The unmatched data can be seen in Figure 7.2.

The order and spellings of the names are less problematic, so I will neither do swapping nor normalization. Let's apply our function:

```
results=fuzzyMerge(unmatched,where,maxD = 0.25)
```

```
[1] "still some rows unmatched"
```

The rows that could not be matched are

```
results$unmatched
```

	Country	eco	iso2	iso3	niso3	fips
38	Burma	46.9098719334824	<NA>	<NA>	NA	<NA>
56	Congo, Republic of	42.6977361475045	<NA>	<NA>	NA	<NA>
127	Korea, North	1.3	<NA>	<NA>	NA	<NA>
129	Korea, South	71.5390860663547	<NA>	<NA>	NA	<NA>
130	Kosovo	N/A	<NA>	<NA>	NA	<NA>
132	Kyrgyz Republic	61.3479161045883	<NA>	<NA>	NA	<NA>
134	Lao P.D.R.	51.3770806898766	<NA>	<NA>	NA	<NA>
223	Slovak Republic	67.2418491316855	<NA>	<NA>	NA	<NA>

We have to decide what to do now, because you may spend more time in programming than in doing the last changes manually. Use these considerations to make your decision how to proceed:

	Country	eco	iso2	iso3	niso3	fips
27	Bolivia	46.8	<NA>	<NA>	NA	<NA>
38	Burma	46.9	<NA>	<NA>	NA	<NA>
40	Cabo Verde	66.4	<NA>	<NA>	NA	<NA>
55	Congo, Democratic Republic of the Congo	45.0	<NA>	<NA>	NA	<NA>
56	Congo, Republic of	42.7	<NA>	<NA>	NA	<NA>
60	Côte d'Ivoire	58.5	<NA>	<NA>	NA	<NA>
107	Hong Kong SAR	89.6	<NA>	<NA>	NA	<NA>
112	Iran	41.8	<NA>	<NA>	NA	<NA>
127	Korea, North	1.3	<NA>	<NA>	NA	<NA>
129	Korea, South	71.5	<NA>	<NA>	NA	<NA>
130	Kosovo	N/A	<NA>	<NA>	NA	<NA>
132	Kyrgyz Republic	61.3	<NA>	<NA>	NA	<NA>
134	Lao P.D.R.	51.4	<NA>	<NA>	NA	<NA>
145	Macau	70.3	<NA>	<NA>	NA	<NA>
146	Macedonia	67.1	<NA>	<NA>	NA	<NA>
160	Micronesia	49.6	<NA>	<NA>	NA	<NA>
162	Moldova	57.5	<NA>	<NA>	NA	<NA>
200	Russia	52.1	<NA>	<NA>	NA	<NA>
210	Saint. Lucia	70.2	<NA>	<NA>	NA	<NA>
211	Saint. Vincent and the Grenadines	68.0	<NA>	<NA>	NA	<NA>
215	São Tomé and Príncipe	53.3	<NA>	<NA>	NA	<NA>
223	Slovak Republic	67.2	<NA>	<NA>	NA	<NA>
239	Syria	N/A	<NA>	<NA>	NA	<NA>
241	Taiwan	75.1	<NA>	<NA>	NA	<NA>
244	Tanzania	57.5	<NA>	<NA>	NA	<NA>
266	Venezuela	34.3	<NA>	<NA>	NA	<NA>
269	Vietnam	51.7	<NA>	<NA>	NA	<NA>

Figure 7.2 Unmatched values for Index of Economic Freedom.

- You have eight countries remaining.
- No code could match "Burma" or "Kosovo" in the codes data, because the former is currently named "Myanmar" and the latter is not in that list.
- No code could match the Koreas, because the official name in the CODES data frame does not include the words "North" or "South" so swapping could only recover Congo. Could you code for four countries?

As you see, it is difficult to find a unique way to do merges. So let's work manually, but trying to use the same strategy.[11] First, let me prepare the data frames with the clean rows I have:

```
names(matched)==names(results$rematched)
```

```
[1] TRUE TRUE TRUE TRUE TRUE TRUE
```

---

[11] I will create a function to do this in Python.

```
matched=rbind(matched,results$rematched)
row.names(matched)=NULL
```

We also need to replace our old `where` and `rematched` data frames:

```
where=results$where
unmatched=results$unmatched
```

And the manual cleaning would be as follows:

```
# 1. Find the index of the country in 'where'
index=grep("Myanmar",where$name2,fixed = T)
# 2. Replace missing data in 'unmatched' with info from 'where':
unmatched[1,c(3:6)]=where[index,c(1:4)]
# 3. Shrink 'where'
where=where[-index,]
```

This is the result in `unmatched`:

```
                 Country          eco iso2 iso3 niso3 fips
38                 Burma 46.9098719334824   MM  MMR   104   BM
56   Congo, Republic of 42.6977361475045 <NA> <NA>    NA <NA>
127         Korea, North              1.3 <NA> <NA>    NA <NA>
129         Korea, South 71.5390860663547 <NA> <NA>    NA <NA>
130               Kosovo              N/A <NA> <NA>    NA <NA>
132      Kyrgyz Republic 61.3479161045883 <NA> <NA>    NA <NA>
134            Lao P.D.R. 51.3770806898766 <NA> <NA>    NA <NA>

223      Slovak Republic 67.2418491316855 <NA> <NA>    NA <NA>
```

Because the steps are the same, we could do the following:

```
index=grep("Congo",where$name2,fixed = T)
unmatched[2,c(3:6)]=where[index,c(1:4)]
where=where[-index,]
# Using regex, then 'fixed' is FALSE:
# string where 'Democratic' appears before then 'Korea'
# with anything in between those words '.*'.
index=grep("Democratic.*Korea",where$name2,fixed = F)
unmatched[3,c(3:6)]=where[index,c(1:4)]
where=where[-index,]
#
index=grep("Korea",where$name2,fixed = T)
unmatched[4,c(3:6)]=where[index,c(1:4)]
where=where[-index,]
# NO KOSOVO, jump to row 6
index=grep("Kyrgyz",where$name2,fixed = T)
unmatched[6,c(3:6)]=where[index,c(1:4)]
where=where[-index,]
#
index=grep("Lao ",where$name2,fixed = T)
unmatched[7,c(3:6)]=where[index,c(1:4)]
where=where[-index,]
```

```
#
index=grep("Slovak",where$name2,fixed = T)
unmatched[8,c(3:6)]=where[index,c(1:4)]
where=where[-index,]
```

And finally, we update the ECO data frame:

```
ECO=rbind(matched,unmatched)  # append
ECO[ECO=='N/A']=NA            # set NAs
rownames(ECO)=NULL            # reset indexes
```

Let's pay attention to the "Freedom in the World" data (WORLD). Our first step is doing the merging between WORLD and CODES:

```
WRDdirty=merge(WORLD,CODES,by.x ="Country", by.y="name1",
               all.x=T,all.y = T)
```

Now, as we did before, we need to subset WRDdirty to get the subdata frames that will be used during fuzzy matching:

```
matched=WRDdirty[!is.na(WRDdirty$iso2)&!is.na(WRDdirty$free),][-7]
unmatched=WRDdirty[is.na(WRDdirty$iso2),][-7]
where=WRDdirty[is.na(WRDdirty$free),][-c(1,2)]
```

In Figure 7.3, you can see that several scores use ".." as a missing value for that year (2015). These belong to countries that no longer exist.

Then, let's save the nonexistent countries and erase them from unmatched:

```
#saving
oldies=unmatched[unmatched$free=='..',]
#unmatched without old names for countries.
unmatched=unmatched[unmatched$free!='..',]
```

Let's use a max distance of 0.4 (the default in the function)[12] for our function:

```
results=fuzzyMerge(unmatched,where)
```

```
[1] "still some rows unmatched"
```

---

[12] I got most matches using 0.25; using, 0.4 Gambia was matched.

```
> unmatched
                        Country free iso2 iso3 niso3 fips
10                Antigua & Barbuda    F <NA> <NA>    NA <NA>
28                          Bolivia   PF <NA> <NA>    NA <NA>
32               Bosnia-Herzegovina   PF <NA> <NA>    NA <NA>
37                           Brunei   NF <NA> <NA>    NA <NA>
41                            Burma   NF <NA> <NA>    NA <NA>
57              Congo (Brazzaville)   NF <NA> <NA>    NA <NA>
58                Congo (Kinshasa)    NF <NA> <NA>    NA <NA>
62                  Cote d'Ivoire    PF <NA> <NA>    NA <NA>
69                   Czechoslovakia   .. <NA> <NA>    NA <NA>
74                      East Timor   PF <NA> <NA>    NA <NA>
92                      Gambia, The   NF <NA> <NA>    NA <NA>
95                      Germany, E.   .. <NA> <NA>    NA <NA>
96                      Germany, W.   .. <NA> <NA>    NA <NA>
118                            Iran   NF <NA> <NA>    NA <NA>
134                          Kosovo   PF <NA> <NA>    NA <NA>
138                            Laos   NF <NA> <NA>    NA <NA>
148                       Macedonia   PF <NA> <NA>    NA <NA>
162                      Micronesia    F <NA> <NA>    NA <NA>
164                         Moldova   PF <NA> <NA>    NA <NA>
184                     North Korea   NF <NA> <NA>    NA <NA>
203                          Russia   NF <NA> <NA>    NA <NA>
212       Saint Vincent & Grenadines   F <NA> <NA>    NA <NA>
216          Sao Tome & Principe       F <NA> <NA>    NA <NA>
231                     South Korea    F <NA> <NA>    NA <NA>
241                           Syria   NF <NA> <NA>    NA <NA>
243                          Taiwan    F <NA> <NA>    NA <NA>
246                        Tanzania   PF <NA> <NA>    NA <NA>
253              Trinidad & Tobago     F <NA> <NA>    NA <NA>
267                            USSR   .. <NA> <NA>    NA <NA>
270                       Venezuela   PF <NA> <NA>    NA <NA>
273                         Vietnam   NF <NA> <NA>    NA <NA>
274                     Vietnam, N.   .. <NA> <NA>    NA <NA>
275                     Vietnam, S.   .. <NA> <NA>    NA <NA>
281                       Yemen, N.   .. <NA> <NA>    NA <NA>
282                       Yemen, S.   .. <NA> <NA>    NA <NA>
283                      Yugoslavia   .. <NA> <NA>    NA <NA>
284 Yugoslavia (Serbia & Montenegro)  .. <NA> <NA>    NA <NA>
```

Figure 7.3 Unmatched values from merge of WORLD and CODES.

These are the values unmatched:

```
results$unmatched
```

```
                  Country free iso2  iso3  niso3 fips
41                  Burma    NF <NA>  <NA>    NA <NA>
57   Congo (Brazzaville)    NF <NA>  <NA>    NA <NA>
58     Congo (Kinshasa)    NF <NA>  <NA>    NA <NA>
74            East Timor    PF <NA>  <NA>    NA <NA>
134              Kosovo    PF <NA>  <NA>    NA <NA>
184          North Korea    NF <NA>  <NA>    NA <NA>
231          South Korea     F <NA>  <NA>    NA <NA>
```

The unmatched results are similar to the ones we obtained in the previous data set, so we could use the same "manual" strategy:

```
# updating;
unmatched=results$unmatched
where=results$where
rematched=results$rematched
index=grep("Myanmar",where$name2,fixed = T)
unmatched[1,c(3:6)]=where[index,c(1:4)]
where=where[-index,]
#
index=grep("Democratic.*Congo",where$name2,fixed = F)
unmatched[3,c(3:6)]=where[index,c(1:4)]
where=where[-index,]
#
index=grep("Congo",where$name2,fixed = T)
unmatched[2,c(3:6)]=where[index,c(1:4)]
where=where[-index,]
#
index=grep("Timor",where$name2,fixed = T)
unmatched[4,c(3:6)]=where[index,c(1:4)]
where=where[-index,]
#
index=grep("Democratic.*Korea",where$name2,fixed = F)
unmatched[6,c(3:6)]=where[index,c(1:4)]
where=where[-index,]
#
index=grep("Korea",where$name2,fixed = T)
unmatched[7,c(3:6)]=where[index,c(1:4)]
where=where[-index,]
```

The above code updated the unmatched data frame, so this is how it looks:

```
                  Country free iso2  iso3  niso3 fips
41                  Burma    NF   MM   MMR   104   BM
57   Congo (Brazzaville)    NF   CG   COG   178   CF
58     Congo (Kinshasa)    NF   CD   COD   180   CG
74            East Timor    PF   TL   TLS   626   TT
134              Kosovo    PF <NA>  <NA>    NA <NA>
184          North Korea    NF   KP   PRK   408   KN
231          South Korea     F   KR   KOR   410   KS
```

246   7 Integrating and Storing Data

The unmatched data frame is as complete as possible, so we can do our last
steps to merge WORLD with the ISO and FIPS codes:

```
# 1. Append 'matched','rematched','unmatched' into 'matched'
matched=rbind(matched,rematched,unmatched)
# 2. Confirm 'matched' is equal to 'WORLD'
nrow(matched)==nrow(WORLD)
```

```
[1] FALSE
```

From this result, you know something is missing: It is the oldies, the data
frame with unused country names. Then do the following:

```
# 3. Append 'oldies' and 'matched':
MatchedAndOldies=rbind(matched,oldies)
# do step 2 again:
nrow(MatchedAndOldies)==nrow(WORLD)
```

```
[1] TRUE
```

```
# 4. replace WORLD
WORLD=MatchedAndOldies
# 5. Update NA:
WORLD[WORLD=='..']=NA
```

It is important that you understand very well everything we have done here
before turning to the Python version. I will follow closely the same approach,
while sharing some other coding strategies.

The first variation in my Python code is how I organize the reading of the
data. As you know, we have five data sets, so my plan here is to read all of them
at the same time, considering they have some elements in common. These are
the steps to read them simultaneously:

1. To prepare the links to every file:

```
#%% Setting Up links
import os

folderData=os.path.join("~","Dropbox","BookData","chapter7")

filenameHDI="2015_statistical_annex_tables_all.xls"
filenameWORLD="worldfreedom2015.xls"
filenameECO="index2015_data.xls"
filenamePRESS="2015wpfi.csv"
filenameCODES="cow.csv"

HLink=os.path.join(folderData,filenameHDI)
WLink=os.path.join(folderData,filenameWORLD)
ELink=os.path.join(folderData,filenameECO)
```

```
PLink=os.path.join(folderData,filenamePRESS)
CLink=os.path.join(folderData,filenameCODES)
```

2. As you know, every file needs some arguments when read, and the name of the argument depends on the function you use. The data we need has different rows at the start and end, and not all the columns are needed. Therefore I will organize those arguments in dictionaries:

```
#%% Organizing input ARGS (arguments)

ARGS=[
("xls",({"io":HLink, "header":None, "skiprows":9,
         "skip_footer":68,"parse_cols":[1,2],
         "convert_float":False,"names":["Country", "hdi"]},
        {"io":WLink,"header":None,"skiprows":7,
         "skip_footer":32,"parse_cols":[0,126],
         "convert_float":False,"names":["Country", "world"]},
        {"io":ELink,"sheetname":0, "header":0,
         "keep_default_na":False,
         "skiprows":0, "skip_footer":6, "parse_cols":[1,6],
         "convert_float":False,"names":["Country", "eco"]})
 ),
("csv",({"filepath_or_buffer": PLink, "sep":";",
         "na_values":None, "usecols":range(1,4),
         "na_filter":False, "decimal":",","header":0,
         "encoding":"latin-1",
         "names":["iso3","Country","press"]},
        {"filepath_or_buffer": CLink,
         "na_values":None, "usecols":[0,1,2,5,67,70],
         "na_filter":False,"header":0,
         "encoding":"utf-8",
         "names":["iso2","iso3","niso3","fips",
         "sys","Country"]})
 )
]
```

Pay attention to the list ARGS:

- It is a list with two tuples (I could have lists instead).
- Each tuple has two elements. Every first element indicates the type of file (an Excel spreadsheet or a CSV file), so the program decides what function has to be applied.
- The second element of the tuple is a tuple of dictionaries. Each dictionary has the link to the file we want to read and the values for the arguments.

3. To actually get the data from the files, you can write:

```
#%% Getting data as a list of pandas' Data Frames

from pandas import read_csv, read_excel

D=[] #Here you will have the data frames.
for aTuple in ARGS:
    if aTuple[0]=="xls":
        # '**arg' inputs all argument in aTuple[1] (dict)
        D=[read_excel(**arg) for arg in aTuple[1]]
```

```
    else:
        D.extend([read_csv(**arg) for arg in aTuple[1]])
```

In the code above, I visit the tuples in the list ARGS. At every tuple, I read aTuple[0], the first tuple element, to see what kind of file I have. I need a particular function to read the file if it is a CSV. The arguments for the function are in aTuple[1], the second tuple element. Note that when you send all the arguments in a dict, you have to use **arg.[13] Every data file read is saved in the list **D**. Remember that in R, the CODES header for the country name was name1; this time I am opening that file (see the last one in the CSV group) using the header Country for country name.

I have the data frames in a list. Some cleaning is needed in two of the data frames in the list. The HDI has section names that need to be deleted, and the CODES needs to change header names and reset the indexes:

```
#%% Cleaning particular data frames:

# HDI:
D[0].dropna(inplace=True) #Bye subtitles (list-wise deletion)

# CODES
D[4]=D[4][D[4].sys=="en-iso"]   # Subsetting
D[4].drop("sys", axis=1, inplace=True) # deleting column 'sys'
D[4].reset_index(inplace=True, drop=True) # resetting indexes
## drop=True avoids that reset index keeps the old index!
```

The data frames with the indexes will interact with the data frame CODES, which is the last one in the list (D[4]). In this code I am merging and saving the results in a list:

```
#%% INITIAL MERGING

from pandas import merge

Merges=[] # This list will have ALL the merges

sub=[0,1,2,3]

for i in sub:
    if i<3: # ALL but PRESS
        Merges.extend([merge(D[i],D[4],how="outer",indicator=True)])
    else:   # PRESS will merge differently
        Merges.extend([merge(D[i],D[4],
                            left_on='iso3', right_on='iso3',
                            how="left",indicator=True)])
```

---

[13] You will see later that I will create some functions with several arguments, some of which have default values. In those cases, you must remember that ALL arguments with default values should always be at the end of the arguments definition in the function.

Merges[1]

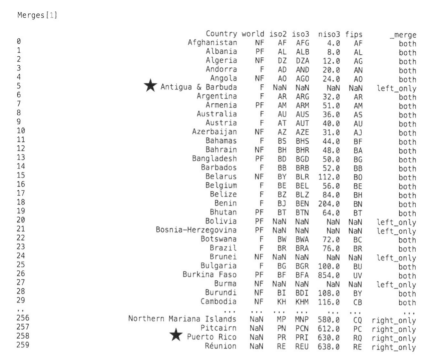

	Country	world	iso2	iso3	niso3	fips	_merge
0	Afghanistan	NF	AF	AFG	4.0	AF	both
1	Albania	PF	AL	ALB	8.0	AL	both
2	Algeria	NF	DZ	DZA	12.0	AG	both
3	Andorra	F	AD	AND	20.0	AN	both
4	Angola	NF	AO	AGO	24.0	AO	both
5	★ Antigua & Barbuda	F	NaN	NaN	NaN	NaN	left_only
6	Argentina	F	AR	ARG	32.0	AR	both
7	Armenia	PF	AM	ARM	51.0	AM	both
8	Australia	F	AU	AUS	36.0	AS	both
9	Austria	F	AT	AUT	40.0	AU	both
10	Azerbaijan	NF	AZ	AZE	31.0	AJ	both
11	Bahamas	F	BS	BHS	44.0	BF	both
12	Bahrain	NF	BH	BHR	48.0	BA	both
13	Bangladesh	PF	BD	BGD	50.0	BG	both
14	Barbados	F	BB	BRB	52.0	BB	both
15	Belarus	NF	BY	BLR	112.0	BO	both
16	Belgium	F	BE	BEL	56.0	BE	both
17	Belize	F	BZ	BLZ	84.0	BH	both
18	Benin	F	BJ	BEN	204.0	BN	both
19	Bhutan	PF	BT	BTN	64.0	BT	both
20	Bolivia	PF	NaN	NaN	NaN	NaN	left_only
21	Bosnia-Herzegovina	PF	NaN	NaN	NaN	NaN	left_only
22	Botswana	F	BW	BWA	72.0	BC	both
23	Brazil	F	BR	BRA	76.0	BR	both
24	Brunei	NF	NaN	NaN	NaN	NaN	left_only
25	Bulgaria	F	BG	BGR	100.0	BU	both
26	Burkina Faso	PF	BF	BFA	854.0	UV	both
27	Burma	NF	NaN	NaN	NaN	NaN	left_only
28	Burundi	NF	BI	BDI	108.0	BY	both
29	Cambodia	NF	KH	KHM	116.0	CB	both
..	...	...	...	...	...	...	...
256	Northern Mariana Islands	NaN	MP	MNP	580.0	CQ	right_only
257	Pitcairn	NaN	PN	PCN	612.0	PC	right_only
258	★ Puerto Rico	NaN	PR	PRI	630.0	RQ	right_only
259	Réunion	NaN	RE	REU	638.0	RE	right_only

Figure 7.4 Structure of the merge result in Python. Notice the last column, which is used to subset each merging result. I have put a start to some rows to highlight the differences.

Notice I am merging the PRESS data frame with different arguments:

- Using the option outer for the argument how gives the same result we got from R when both all.x and all.y were set as true.
- The use of left in that same argument has the effect of setting all.x as true in R.
- An important difference is the parameter indicator, which will create an additional column. That additional column tells you
  - if the row is the result of a perfect match, labeled as **both** in that cell;
  - if the value shown was only present in the first data frame (where the score is) using left_only;
  - if it was present only in the second data frame (where the ISO and FIPS codes are) using right_only.

The effect of these arguments is shown in Figure 7.4 for the merge between freedom in the world and the ISO and FIPS codes.

The extra column created during merging in the previous step (_merge as shown in Figure 7.4) will be useful when creating the sub-data frames. Here, I create a list for every type of subset using that column:

```
#%% Subsetting before fuzzy merging

Matched=[] # List that will hold all FULL MATCHES
Matched.extend(m[m._merge=="both"] for m in Merges)

UNmatched=[] # List that will hold COUNTRIES, with names unmatched
UNmatched.extend(u[u._merge=="left_only"] for u in Merges)

Where=[] #List will have the CODES yet to be assigned
Where.extend(w[w._merge=="right_only"] for w in Merges)
```

I need a couple of helper functions to use the fuzzy matching function effectively. My *first helper function* takes care of normalizing the strings by deleting common words. Notice the function receives one argument, the string, and that the words to be replaced by *nothing* are inside the function in a list. In a different case, you may need to change that list (or put it as an argument):

```
#%% Helper function for Normalizing

def WordReplacer(stringIn):
    '''stringIn is the text of a cell
        and if the words in 'listByeWords' are present there,
        the matches will replaced by ''.
    '''
    import re
    listByeWords=["Republic of", "State of", "Island",
                  "of","Islands","Republic","Rep.",
                  "Federation","Saint","the", "The","\\(","\\)"]
    ToSubstitute="("+"|".join(listByeWords)+")"
    p = re.compile(ToSubstitute)
    stringOut=p.sub('', stringIn)

    return stringOut
```

This is the first time I am writing an extensive comment at the beginning using ' ' '. These are your instructions for the user, who only needs to type print WordReplacer.__doc__ to recover that information (after it is actually run).

During the process of fuzzy matching some matches are accepted and others are not. The function below is in action when a match is accepted. This *second helper function* is in charge of building the new row from the fuzzy matching process. It takes some cells from the unmatched data (unmatched: country name and its score) and the others from the unassigned codes data frame

(Where: iso3,iso2 niso3, fips); this last data frame will also bring the _merge cell created in the initial merging process. The function receives several arguments that are produced during the fuzzy matching process:

1. countryUnmatched is the country that has no codes when it is inputted in the function. The function will add the ISO and FIPS codes to it.
2. measure is the name of the score of the country (ECO, PRESS, etc.); this is in the unmatched data.
3. countryW_Norm is the column of country names in the CODES data frame, but after normalization (deletion of common strings). It has the same amount of rows as the original, and, most important, the same position numbers for the rows. Those positions are critical, because I will use the positions in the normalized column to retrieve the columns I need from the non-normalized column (the original).
4. fuzzyMatch is the name of the country selected from countryW_Norm that approximately matches countryUnmatched.

The other arguments require less explanation, and they will keep appearing (unmatched, where, and their keys: keyU and keyW). With this information, I know how to build the row by parts. This is how you build the first part:

1. Get the row from unmatched where countryUnmatched is.
2. Get the position of the row you got in the previous step.
3. Use the position you now have to select the cells you need from unmatched. You do not need all the cells, only those up to the column measure.
4. Transform the cells you obtained into a list (very important).

The second part follows the same mechanism, but using the information from the unassigned codes data frame. The rematched data frame will later be made out of each of these rows. I can combine those parts in a row simply by using the addition symbol (+):

```
#%% Helper function for preparing the new fuzzy-matched row

def UpdateRows(countryUnmatched,measure,countriesW_Norm,fuzzyMatch,
        unmatched,where, keyU,keyW='iso2'):
    ''' This functions creates a row to be added at the
        rematched data frame during the fuzzy merging process.
        The new row is the concatenating of two parts from
        'unmatched' and 'where'.
        Returns the new row, and two indexes:
        position_rowFromU is the position in unmatched (U)
        position_rowFromW is the position in CODES (W)
    '''
    # step1
```

```
rowFromU=unmatched[unmatched[keyU]==countryUnmatched]
# step2
position_rowFromU=rowFromU.index[0]
# step 3 and 4
part_U=list(unmatched.loc[position_rowFromU,:measure])

rowFromW=countriesW_Norm[countriesW_Norm==fuzzyMatch]
position_rowFromW=rowFromW.index[0]
part_W=list(where.loc[position_rowFromW,keyW:])

return [part_U + part_W,position_rowFromU,position_rowFromW]
```

Here, I have the main function. The first thing you need to do is installing two external libraries in your environment: fuzzywuzzy and python-Levenshtein; you need to use **pip** for both cases. The previous helper functions are used inside the program, which also reduces the number of lines of code. Similar to what we did in R, I vary the limit, but in a descending way. Then, I follow these steps:

1. A country is selected from the unmatched data frame (U).
2. The selected country (countryUnmatched) is normalized (countryU_Norm).
3. The whole column with the country names from the unassigned codes (W) is also normalized (countriesW_Norm). This data frame is inside a for-loop, and it will be modified within the loop when a match is found, so this column may be smaller at the start of every iteration.
4. The fuzzy function will be applied to both normalized objects, giving you a suggestion. The suggestion comes with two values: the suggested match from countriesW_Norm and *similarity* measure.
5. Assign the suggestions to different objects.
6. If the similarity measure is greater than the current limit, you will proceed to prepare the new row (here we will use our helper UpdateRows).
7. The new row will be saved with the previous new rows.
8. The new row will be deleted (dropped) from the data frames that were used to build it.
9. This process will continue until the limit is met. Then, all the new rows will be turned into a data frame that will have the same headers (structure) as the unmatched data frame.
10. The new data frame created in the previous step will be added to the one with all the good matches (matched). This is the Rematched data frame.
11. This code finally sends a message, letting you know whether all columns were matched or not.

```
#%% Function Fuzzy

def fuzzyMerge(measure,matched,unmatched,where,
               keyU='Country',keyW='Country',limit=90):
    '''
        fuzzyMerge(measure,matched,unmatched,where,
               keyU='Country',keyW='Country',limit=90)
        Input the measure (index header: hdi, world, etc).
        You have to input 3 data frames).
        The first one (M) has all the good matches
        The second one (U) is the countries without code.
        The third one (W) is the unassigned codes.
        'keyU' and 'keyW' are the columns for merging;
        alter the defaults as needed.
        Alter the value of "limit" as needed.
        The function returns 3 data frames:
        - Rematched: with all good new matches
        - U: countries without codes
        - W: codes unassigned
    '''

    from fuzzywuzzy.process import extractOne as fuzzy
    from pandas import DataFrame as DF
    U=unmatched.copy(deep=True)
    W=where.copy(deep=True)
    newRows=[]

    # main process
    for currentlimit in range(100,limit+1,-1):
        # step 1
        for countryUnmatched in U[keyU]:
            # step 2
            countryU_Norm= WordReplacer(countryUnmatched)
            # step 3
            countriesW_Norm=W[keyW].apply(WordReplacer)
            # step 4
            fuzzySuggestion=fuzzy(countryU_Norm,countriesW_Norm)
            # step 5
            similarity = fuzzySuggestion[1]
            fuzzyMatch = fuzzySuggestion[0]

            if similarity >= currentlimit:
                # step 6
                updateArgs=[countryUnmatched,measure,countriesW_Norm,
                            fuzzyMatch,U,W,keyU]
                row,indexU,indexW=UpdateRows(*updateArgs)
                # step 7
                newRows.append(row)
                # step 8
                W.drop(indexW,inplace=True)
                U.drop(indexU,inplace=True)

        # step 9
        fuzzyMatches=DF(newRows,columns=list(U.columns.values))
        # step 10
        Rematched=matched.append(fuzzyMatches,ignore_index=True)
        # step 11
        if len(U)>0: print "still unmatched columns"
        else: print "all columns match"

    return Rematched,U,W
```

Note that I am using a list (updateArgs) to input the parameters in step 6. Whenever I input a list, I use one star (dictionaries use two).[14]

We know these data, and that will help us anticipate certain problems, because our fuzzy merging may not work perfectly because of some particularities of the data. We know that some country names are spelled in ways that will give bad matches; we also know that some names are not used any more so their actual indexes are missing and their ISO codes are not available; and so on. In contrast to what I did in R, I have written a Python function to deal with these issues.[15] This function will read your data frames and look for the patterns you give (a regex pattern) in a *queue* of replacements; the country names in the queue must keep the order they have in the unmatched results, although the pattern needs no particular order.

```
#%% Cleanser function

def ManualClean(rematched,unmatched,measure,queue,
                pattern,notExisting,omit='..',keyU='Country'):

    from pandas import concat

    # '_merge' is a category, change it to string
    unmatched['_merge']=unmatched['_merge'].astype(basestring)

    # when you find the pattern, change '_merge' with new name
    place=0
    badNames=unmatched[unmatched[keyU].str.contains(pattern)]
    for i in badNames.index:
        unmatched.loc[i,'_merge']=queue[place]
        place+=1

    # collect the rows that cannot be merged (impossibles)
    try: #maybe no oldies
        oldies=unmatched[unmatched[measure].str.contains(omit,
                                                regex=False)]
    except:
        oldies=None
    try: #maybe no notInCodes
        notInCodes=unmatched[unmatched[keyU].str.contains(notExisting)]
    except:
        notInCodes=None
    try: #maybe neither
        impossibles=concat([oldies,notInCodes])
    except:
        impossibles=None

    # delete those 'impossibles' from unmatched
    unmatched=unmatched[~unmatched.index.isin(impossibles.index)]
    # append those 'impossibles' to rematched
```

---

[14] Notice that with dictionaries, you write the name of the argument and the value; however, in this case, when using a list of arguments, you need to impute the values in the same order as the arguments were defined in the function header.

[15] This function is not helpful if you need to do this procedure for lots of cases.

```
rematched=concat([rematched,impossibles])

return rematched,unmatched
```

There are several `try-except` structures. I need to use them because the operations under `try` may not be needed.

It is now time to apply all these functions and get the data frames we need. Let's start doing fuzzy merging with HDI, which should rematch all the rows:

```
#%% first and only try
measure='hdi'
r,u,w=fuzzyMerge(measure, Matched[0],UNmatched[0],Where[0],limit=78)
#%% just create HDI
HDI=r
```

Remember that the ECO and the WORLD data had some issues, so, the fuzzy function will not be successful. Let's see the Freedom in the World data first:

```
#%% first try
measure='world'
r1,u1,w1=fuzzyMerge(measure,Matched[1],UNmatched[1],Where[1],limit=91)
```

The message tells us what we expected. If we try reducing the `limit` we may be inducing errors, because of the way some countries are written. So, let's apply the `ManualClean` function:

```
#%% need for cleaning
argsWorld={'rematched':r1,
           'unmatched':u1,
           'measure':measure,
           'queue':['Myanmar',"Congo, the Democratic",
                    "Korea, Democratic People","Korea"],
           'pattern':'urma|outh|orth|Kinshasa',
           'notExisting':'osovo'}

r1,u1=ManualClean(**argsWorld)
```

You need to use the output to try rematching again. But be careful, because the changes have been applied to the _merge column; you first need to make the changes using that column:

```
#%% second try
r2,u2,w2=fuzzyMerge(measure,r1,u1,w1,keyU='_merge',limit=90)
```

You still need to apply it again, with a lower limit; this time you will get the all
the matches, so we can safely create the next data frame:

```
#%% third try
r3,u3,w3=fuzzyMerge(measure,r2,u2,w2,limit=65)
#%% saving result in new object
WORLD=r3
```

For the ECO data frame you will do the same as above:

```
#%% First try
measure='eco'
r1,u1,w1=fuzzyMerge(measure,Matched[2],UNmatched[2],Where[2],limit=95)
#%% cleaning
argsEco={'rematched':r1,'unmatched':u1,'measure':measure,
         'queue':['Myanmar',"Korea, Democratic People","Korea"],
         'pattern':'urma|outh|orth','notExisting':'osovo'}
r1,u1=ManualClean(**argsEco)
#%% Second try with changes:
r2,u2,w2=fuzzyMerge(measure,r1,u1,w1,keyU='_merge',limit=90)
#%% Last try:
r3,u3,w3=fuzzyMerge(measure,r2,u2,w2,limit=75)
#%% Saving result
ECO=r3
```

The PRESS data frame required none of these functions:

```
#%% Working with PRESS
PRESS=Matched[3].append(UNmatched[3],ignore_index=True)
```

And finally, I will set up the missing values where needed:

```
#%% Set missing data

import numpy as np
HDI.replace("..",np.nan,regex=False,inplace=True)
WORLD.replace("..",np.nan,regex=False,inplace=True)
ECO.replace("N/A",np.nan,regex=False,inplace=True)
```

7.2 Integrating Network Data

Merging data frames is one thing; merging network data is a different, more
complicated task, which fortunately has good support in Python and R.

7.2.1 Adding Attributes to the Network from a File

Let me open the data for the network we saw in Section 6.6.2 on page 219 (this data is now in Excel):

```
library(xlsx)
folder=file.path("~","Dropbox","BookData","chapter7")
fileXLS=file.path(folder,"dataFigueroa.xlsx")
dataMatrix=read.xlsx(fileXLS,sheetName="matrix",
                     check.names = F,row.names=1)
adjMatrix=as.matrix(dataMatrix)
library(igraph)  # version with igraph
I_elite=graph.adjacency(adjMatrix,mode="undirected")
library(statnet) # version with igraph
S_elite=network(adjMatrix,matrix.type="adjacency",directed=F)
```

We have the data in both packages, but we do not have any information on the nodes. However, in the same spreadsheet, I have a worksheet named "attributes," which tells me whether the network represents a multinational firm. You can "merge" that data frame with the network like this:

```
dataAttr=read.xlsx(fileXLS,sheetName="attributes")
# matching gives positions in Igraph
positionsI = match(V(I_elite)$name, dataAttr$Nodes)
set_vertex_attr(graph = I_elite, name = 'multi',
                value = dataAttr$multi[positionsI])
# matching gives positions in statnet
positionsS = match(S_elite%v%"vertex.names", dataAttr$Nodes)
set.vertex.attribute(S_elite, attrname = 'multi',
                     value = dataAttr$multi[positionsS])
```

Our merge here used the function match, which returns the positions of the rows Nodes and name (or 'vertex.names' in the case or *statnet*) that are in common. A simple plot can show that some nodes are different from others (see Figure 7.5):

```
gplot(S_elite,usearrows = F,vertex.col=S_elite %v% "multi")
# for igraph:
plot.igraph(I_elite,vertex.label=NA,vertex.color=V(I_elite)$multi)
```

It takes some more steps to add the attribute in Python. Networkx uses dictionaries to keep the information on the nodes, which makes for fast manipulation. If you run the instruction PeliteNet.nodes(data=True) after the Python code on page 221, you will see what is in your nodes; in this case, only the node name is present (see Figure 7.6):

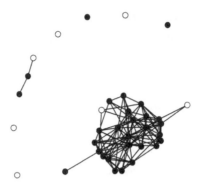

Figure 7.5 A network plot from an adjacency matrix. Notice that an attribute has been used to color the nodes.

So we need to fill that dictionary, being careful that the attribute belongs to the node. For example, this code `Py_elite.node['Galsky']` tells you what the node has. If you request to see `Py_elite.node['Galsky']['multi']` you will get an error, because that attribute does not exist. With the following code, we visit every node and create the attribute (after opening the file):

```
#%% Opening file with attributes
dataAttr=read_excel(fileXLS,sheetname="attributes",index_col=0)

#%% visit each node and add attribute
for person in Py_elite.nodes():
    # attribute 'multi' of this person=this value with 'person' in row
    Py_elite.node[person]['multi']=dataAttr.loc[person,'multinational']
```

If you want to see a similar plot to Figure 7.5, you can use the code in Figure 7.7:

```
[('Woodman Pollit', {}),
 ('Wong Lu', {}),
 ('Bustamante', {}),
 ('Raffo', {}),
 ('Arias Davila', {}),
 ('Ikeda', {}),
 ('Custer', {}),
 ('Berckemeyer', {}),
 ('Cilloniz', {}),
 ('Rizo Patron', {}),
```

Figure 7.6 Contents of nodes in Python. Notice the empty dictionaries.

```
color_map = {1:'k', 0:'w'} #BLACk and wHITE
col=[color_map[Py_elite.node[node]['multi']] for node in Py_elite]
net.draw(Py_elite,node_color=col)
```

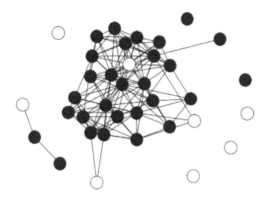

Figure 7.7 Plotting a network with color by attribute in Python.

7.2.2 Adding Attributes to a Network while Scraping

The data used in subsection 6.6.3 on page 222 was originally produced from scraping the web; we used the same table in previous chapters. I am sharing now the scraping code in Python. The first step is known:

```
#%% Get data from web:
wikiLink='http://en.wikipedia.org/wiki/List_of_border_wars'
identification = { 'User-Agent' : 'Mozilla/5.0'}
from requests import get
wikiPage = get(wikiLink, headers=identification)
from bs4 import BeautifulSoup as BS
wikiPage = BS(wikiPage.content,'html.parser')
wikiTables = wikiPage.findAll('table', {'class': 'sortable wikitable'})
```

The key element is in this next section of code. In earlier chapters, I wanted to build a data frame, but here I want to create a network. As you may have guessed, the network of this data will be made out of the war connections among countries. That is, if there is an edge between two countries, it is because they were involved in the same war (not necessarily enemies). So, this code focuses only on the countries connected by war and forgets the rest (you could have added some information to the network from the information I am not using). This time I am using the name of each country to get to its webpage in

Wikipedia; once on its webpage I will recover the country's latitude and longitude, as a pair of attributes for the node. Notice the use of *itertools*, whose function `combinations` allows me to create pairs of countries.

```python
import networkx as net
import re

warNet=net.Graph()   # creating empty network

from itertools import combinations # 'combinations' is used below

for eachTable in wikiTables: # Do this for each table
    allRows=eachTable.find_all("tr") # all the rows in the table
    for eachRow in allRows[1:]: # omit first row

        allCells = eachRow.find_all("td") # Get all the cells
        countryInfo=allCells[3].find_all('a')

        # List of country names in the current cell:
        names=[txt.get_text() for txt in countryInfo]
        # Cleaning country names:
        CHINAS='PRC|^.*China'
        names=[re.sub(CHINAS, 'China',name) for name in names]

        # Getting the link to each country webpage
        # You will get an incomplete URL, so 'base' is needed:
        base='http://en.wikipedia.org' # to complete url
        links=[base + url.get('href') for url in countryInfo]
        # Cleaning country links:
        USSR='Soviet_Union'
        links=[re.sub(USSR, 'Russia',link) for link in links]

        coords=[]   # list to store (lat, lon)

        # For every link collected
        for link in links:
            url=BS(get(link).content,'html.parser')
            # get coordinates
            coordinates=url.find_all("span",{'class':'geo'})[0]
            # split and unpack the coordinates
            lat,lon=coordinates.get_text().split('; ')
            # adding the coordinates to list
            coords.append((float(lat),float(lon)))

        # pair up countries with its coordinates:
        countryInfo=zip(names,coords)

        #populating graph

        for name,(lat,lon)in countryInfo:
            warNet.add_node(name, lat=lat,lon=lon) ## adding nodes
        for pair in combinations (names,2):
            warNet.add_edge(*pair) ## creating edges
```

If you want to make a plot using the longitude and latitude of each country, this is the code:

```
#%% Plotting
X=net.get_node_attributes(warNet,'lon')
Y=net.get_node_attributes(warNet,'lat')
countryNames=warNet.nodes()
posNet=dict((C,(X[C],Y[C])) for C in countryNames)
net.draw(warNet,pos=posNet,with_labels=True)
```

Let's turn now our attention to storing our work.

7.3 Storing Your Work

By now you may be thinking it is strange that we have not saved all the data we have produced. Even though I shared the original files, you definitively want to save the clean and formatted data that you have produced with the coding.

Storing your work is not done for the sole purpose of archiving but also to allow you the possibility of retrieving your own material to revise, improve, and advance your work. Storing also enables you to share your work, because you may also require participation of colleagues or assistants. With that in mind, I will discuss the storing process using the tools I recommended you install in Chapter 2, particularly subsection 2.3 on page 22. In that subsection, I only asked you to create an account if you needed one.

Let's first save the files in our machines and see how to save and recover the data. For this exercise, I use the indexes of freedom obtained from Wikipedia, which were collected, clean, and formatted in Section 6.2 on page 185. Let me share again that code in R (a smaller version):

```
#COLLECTING
library(XML);library(RCurl);library(stringi)
wikiLink = "https://en.wikipedia.org/wiki/List_of_freedom_indices"
wikiPage = getURL(wikiLink)
wikiTables = readHTMLTable(wikiPage,encoding="UTF-8",
                          stringsAsFactors=F)
IDXs=wikiTables[[3]]
#CLEANING
pattern='\\s+|\\d+|\\[|\\]'; nothing=''
names(IDXs)=gsub(pattern,nothing,names(IDXs))
ExtractConvert_toNum=function(x) {
   library(stringi)
   pattern = "\\d+"
   numberExtracted=stri_extract_first_regex(x,pattern)
   return (as.numeric(numberExtracted))}
IDXs[,c(2:4)]=lapply(IDXs[,c(2:4)],ExtractConvert_toNum)
#FORMATTING
categoryLabels=c("best","good","moderate","bad","worst")
categoryLevels=c(1,2,3,4,5)
IDXs[,c(2:4)]= lapply(IDXs[,c(2:4)],factor,
levels=categoryLevels, labels=categoryLabels,ordered=T)
```

So, as shown above, you have finally obtained your clean data set with categorical data. Now, you can save it simply by writing

```
# SAVING for R:
savefolder=file.path("~","Dropbox","myData")
savefilenameR="freedomR.rds"
toSaveR=file.path(savefolder,savefilenameR)
saveRDS(IDXs,toSaveR)
# SAVING as CSV:
savefilenameCSV="freedomC.csv"
toSaveCSV=file.path(savefolder,savefilenameCSV)
write.csv(IDXs,toSaveCSV,na="",row.names=F) # saving!
# SAVING for Excel:
library(xlsx)
# notice path!
savefolder=file.path("/Users","JoseManuel","Dropbox","myData")
savefilenameEXCEL="freedomX.xlsx"
toSaveEXCEL=file.path(savefolder,savefilenameEXCEL)
write.xlsx(IDXs,toSaveEXCEL,showNA=F,row.names=F) # saving!
```

One important thing to notice is that I am producing CSV and XLSX files with empty cells where there were NAs; this will prevent another software program from receiving the "NA" symbol from R. I also ensured that neither the CSV nor the Excel version saved the index number in each row (`rownames`). Of course, if the indexes are not simple numbers but important names, you should not do that.

The code above immediately creates those files in the folder you indicated; you can use the command `list.files` together with `file.info` to see the contents of a particular folder and the size of each one (you can also see that by visiting you computer too):

```
# requesting only the first column...
file.info(list.files(savefolder, full.names=TRUE))[1]
```

```
                                                    size
/Users/JoseManuel/Dropbox/myData/freedomC.csv       7430
/Users/JoseManuel/Dropbox/myData/freedomR.rds       2167
/Users/JoseManuel/Dropbox/myData/freedomX.xlsx      8564
```

Saving seems easy, but you need to consider some facts:

- R will not send you a warning if you are rewriting a previous file.
- You must be sure in what folder you are saving your work.
- Different types of files have different sizes, but size is just one consideration. The native R data type is the smallest but if you are planing to send your work to a non-R user that would be a poor choice. A CSV file can be opened by most programs, so that is the best choice here.

Let me open the files again:

```
# OPENING from CSV:
IDXcsv=read.csv(toSaveCSV,na.strings=c("","NA"))
# OPENING from Excel:
library(xlsx)
IDXxls=read.xlsx(toSaveEXCEL,1)
# # OPENING from R:
IDXr=readRDS(toSaveR)
```

Now, it would be good to see how the variables came back:

```
# Original (in memory now):
str(IDXs,width = 50, strict.width = "cut")
```

```
'data.frame':  213 obs. of  4 variables:
 $ Country                 : chr  "Abkhazia" "Afg"..
 $ FreedomintheWorld       : Ord.factor w/ 5 leve"..
 $ IndexofEconomicFreedom: Ord.factor w/ 5 leve"..
 $ PressFreedomIndex       : Ord.factor w/ 5 leve"..
```

```
# collected:
str(IDXcsv,width = 50, strict.width = "cut")
```

```
'data.frame':  213 obs. of  4 variables:
 $ Country                 : Factor w/ 213 levels"..
 $ FreedomintheWorld       : Factor w/ 3 levels  ""..
 $ IndexofEconomicFreedom: Factor w/ 5 levels  ""..
 $ PressFreedomIndex       : Factor w/ 5 levels  ""..
```

```
str(IDXxls,width = 50, strict.width = "cut")
```

```
'data.frame':  213 obs. of  4 variables:
 $ Country                 : Factor w/ 213 levels"..
 $ FreedomintheWorld       : Factor w/ 3 levels  ""..
 $ IndexofEconomicFreedom: Factor w/ 5 levels  ""..
 $ PressFreedomIndex       : Factor w/ 5 levels  ""..
```

```
str(IDXr,width = 50, strict.width = "cut")
```

```
'data.frame':  213 obs. of  4 variables:
 $ Country                 : chr  "Abkhazia" "Afg"..
 $ FreedomintheWorld       : Ord.factor w/ 5 leve"..
 $ IndexofEconomicFreedom: Ord.factor w/ 5 leve"..
 $ PressFreedomIndex       : Ord.factor w/ 5 leve"..
```

As you see, only the file in the R format retained the formatting you gave to the ordinal variables. With these considerations, let's see what works best using our third-party tools.

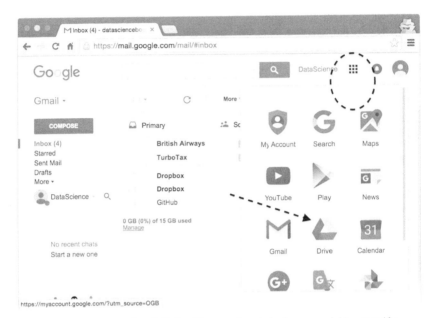

Figure 7.8 Finding Google Drive. The apps icon is in the upper right corner (the dotted oval is around it), and the Google Drive icon is below (an arrow is pointing toward it).

7.4 Storing and Google Drive

7.4.1 R and Google Sheets

Working with Google Drive is actually very fun. It allows you to create different kinds of documents, but the ones we are interested in are the Google Sheets, which are spreadsheets with the basic functionality of Excel, but in the "cloud" of Google.[16] For the purposes of this book, we need to learn how to interact with Google Drive to be able to read and update our files, even if they are not in our machines. The first thing you need to do is go into your Gmail account and click on the *Google Apps* icon to select the *Drive* icon. This is shown in Figure 7.8.

Once you select Google Drive, you will see a page similar to the one shown in Figure 7.9. There we need to create a new folder, which I will call "Gdata."

After creating the folder, you should go to settings (see Figure 7.10).

---

[16] You may want later to take a look at this tutorial on Google Sheets: https://www.youtube.com/watch?v=QTgvX5MLPC8.

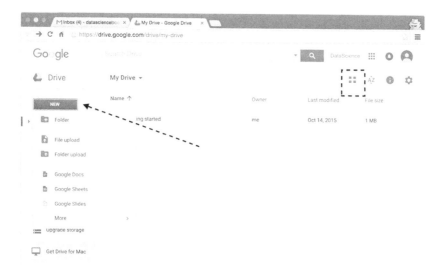

Figure 7.9 The Google Drive environment. This is the *list* view, and you can toggle to the *grid* view by clicking the icon signaled with a dotted rectangle. To start working, click on the icon signaled with the arrow and select "folder."

When you select the option "settings," you should see the options shown in Figure 7.11. Make sure the option **Convert uploads** is checked. After that, select "Done," and go into the Gdata folder. This setting will turn your CSV or Excel files, into Google Sheets as soon as you upload them.

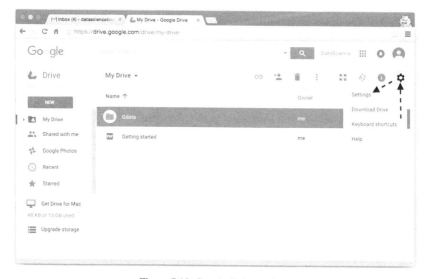

Figure 7.10 Google Drive settings.

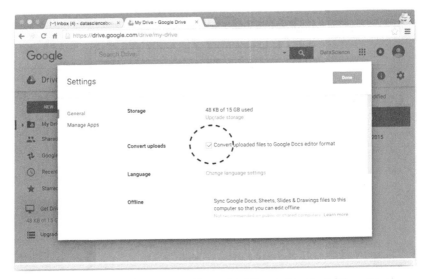

Figure 7.11 Google Drive convert files option. You need to check this option to
enable the Excel file and the CSV file to be converted into the Google format.

In the "Gdata" folder, you will see in the middle of the webpage the message
"Drop files here." Just practice putting some files from your computer as shown
in Figure 7.12.

As expected, the XLS and CSV files have been converted automatically into
Google Sheets. Figure 7.13 shows you that our files are now in the folder. At the
bottom of the figure is confirmation that the two files were converted. Notice
that the R file could not be converted.

Now that you know the files from the computer are in Google Drive, let me
share the steps to manipulate them.

1. Install and load the following packages. This time I will use `devtools`, a
   package that allows you to install the *development* version (most recent but
   not still available in the repositories that RStudio uses to search for packages.

```
devtools::install_github("jennybc/googlesheets")
library(googlesheets)
```

The package `googlesheets` might require these other packages, so install
and load them (just in case):

```
library(dplyr)
library(httpuv)
library(readr)
```

Figure 7.12 Converting data frames into Google Sheets. Not all files can be converted.

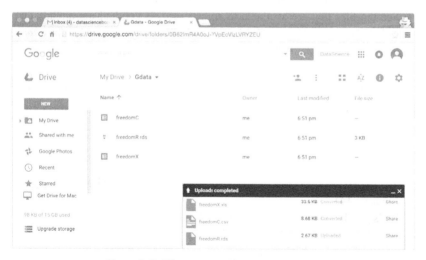

Figure 7.13 Files converted into Google Sheets.

```
> FreedomMetadata = gs_title("freedomC")
Sheet successfully identifed: "freedomC"
> FreedomMetadata
                     Spreadsheet title: freedomC
                    Spreadsheet author: datasciencebook
        Date of googlesheets registration: 2016-01-17 23:16:58 GMT
        Date of last spreadsheet update: 2016-01-17 22:30:05 GMT
                              visibility: private
                             permissions: rw
                                 version: new

Contains 1 worksheets:
(Title): (Nominal worksheet extent as rows x columns)
freedomC: 217 x 9

Key: 1R4yFBvlul0Ndgxi_QjUkn20051X-SUJFikl3Vc1QCEo
Browser URL: https://docs.google.com/spreadsheets/d/1R4yFBvlul0Ndgxi_QjUkn20051X-SUJFikl3Vc1QCEo/
```

Figure 7.14 Info for a Google Sheet. You might see different results.

2. Authorize *googlesheets* to access Google. Run the code below, which will take you to your internet browser; just follow the instructions.

```
gs_auth(new_user = TRUE)
```

You need to use the argument *new_user = TRUE* only once, so if you write now

```
gs_auth()
```

you will not be asked for that information again.

3. See the files that are available to be accessed. If you had not already converted the CSV or Excel files into Google Sheets, you would not see those file names here (the R data file will not be shown properly for that reason):

```
gs_ls()
```

4. Use the the name of the file you want exactly as it appears in the "sheet_title" column:

```
freedomInfo = gs_title("freedomC.csv")
```

gs_title gets no data, but reports some information about the file (see Figure 7.14).

5. Let's get the data frame we saved originally as a CSV file:

```
FreedomData = gs_read(freedomInfo,ws = 1) # first sheet
```

Now we have the data. You can confirm that as usual:

```
str(FreedomData)
```

6. Finally, we can alter the data frame and update the sheet in Google Drive:

```
# 1. Create a new column:
FreedomData$Weird=apply(FreedomData[,2:4],1,max, na.rm=T)
# 2. Send this column as FreedomData[5]
freedomInfo=gs_edit_cells(freedomInfo,
                          ws = 1,
                          anchor='E1',
                          input=FreedomData[5],
                          trim = T,
                          col_names = T)
```

Notice the use of anchor. You need to use FreedomData[5] instead of FreedomData$Weird, and you must update the position of the first cell with these values in the argument anchor. If you want to omit the use of anchor, you need to update the whole data frame, like this:

```
# 2. Update the whole file:
freedomInfo=gs_edit_cells(freedomInfo,
                          ws = 1,
                          input=FreedomData,
                          trim = T,
                          col_names = T)
```

7.4.2 Python and Google Sheets

Python has two packages that deal with Google spreadsheets: **gspread**[17] and **df2gspread**.[18] They both need to be installed in your environment using pip. Each of them has detailed instructions on how to use them, and each requires that you follow a particular process to obtain permission from Google to interact with it. This situation can bring some complications, and you need to be aware of the sudden and frequent changes that Google implements to grant access. So, for the case of Python, I recommend that you follow their instructions when you are reading this book. It is important to consider, for both Python and R, that the way Google offers interactivity with its tools may vary over time. In fact, I have installed this package several times and twice my code had some issues after working well.[19] So, what works today may not work at all tomorrow. Sometimes, the package version changes, sometimes the policy changes, and at other times other features may change. That is why, if you are going to use Google Drive as a way to save your data and you want it to be available anytime, it is good to have Google Drive installed on your computer.

---

[17] https://github.com/burnash/gspread.   [18] https://github.com/maybelinot/df2gspread.
[19] I have kept the example in R because the code worked well; even when I needed to reinstall the package googlesheets again, the code remained the same.

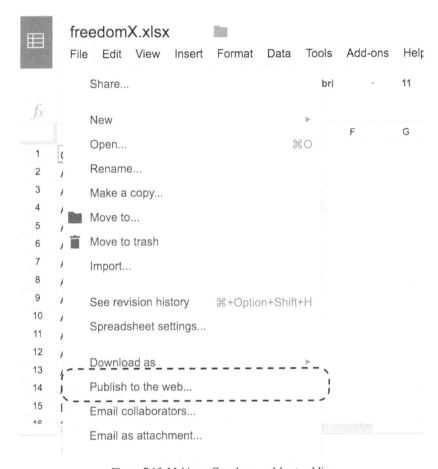

Figure 7.15 Making a Google spreadsheet public.

However, if you still have a strong need to interact with some data from Google Drive[20] but do not want to install it on your computer, you can get a link to read that data as a CSV file. This is done in two simple steps. First, open the Google spreadsheet, and select the option to make it public on the web, as shown in Figure 7.15.

The next step requires that you choose how to make it public. Google will give you several options (HTML, CSV, etc); and after you choose one, Google will offer you a link that you can treat as a file name to be used in pandas. That link can be shared, making your spreadsheet accessible by anyone who has the

---

[20] Some people use Google Forms and may want to analyze the data as it populates the spreadsheet with the answers.

Publish to the web

This document is not published to the web.

Make your content visible to anyone by publishing it to the web. You can link to or embed your document. Learn more

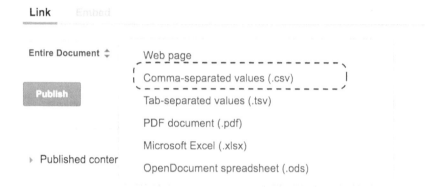

Link   Embed

Entire Document ⇕   Web page

                         Comma-separated values (.csv)

Publish   Tab-separated values (.tsv)

                         PDF document (.pdf)

                         Microsoft Excel (.xlsx)

▸ Published conter   OpenDocument spreadsheet (.ods)

Figure 7.16 Making a Google spreadsheet public as a CSV.

link. However, you cannot alter the contents using the link; it just allows you to read the data. Then, any alteration you make to the data requires that you save your file locally and upload it into Google Drive (or just drop it if you are using the app). In our case, we will choose to make it available as a CSV file, as shown in Figure 7.16.

Use the link you get in **pd.read_csv(link)** to obtain the data in pandas.

7.5 Storing and Dropbox

I am a user of Dropbox. All our files are stored there, have been there, and I have shared a link for you to get them into your own Dropbox file. Just as with Google Drive, you can install Dropbox on your computer and create a folder for your work, knowing that the Dropbox app will synchronize its contents in the web interface. So, while Google Drive seems to hypnotize you to do everything in Google (notice the apps offered), Dropbox simply is a great file-sharing system.

Let's pretend you are using a machine on which you cannot install Dropbox. However, you want to interact with your data, which is in a file in SPSS in a Dropbox folder, as shown in Figure 7.17.

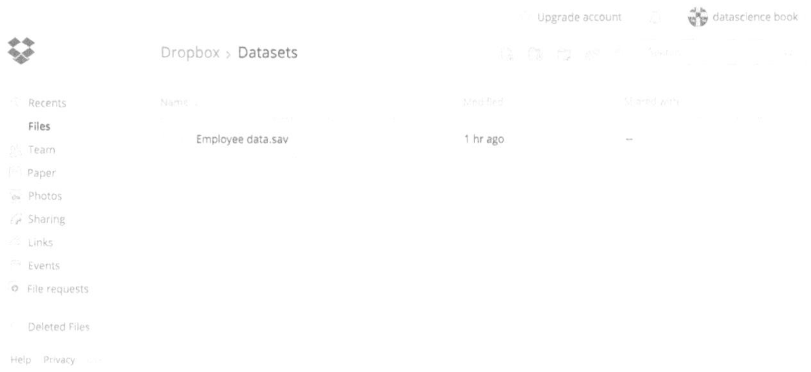

Figure 7.17 Dropbox contents before interacting with them. This is a particular folder named "Datasets."

Again, if you are not on your machine, it would be nice to have a code to access that file. As in the case of Google Drive, I am assuming this file is clean and formatted, but you need it to prepare some analytics. Let's try it in R first.

7.5.1 R and Dropbox

Let's make this work in R first, using *rdrop2* by Ram (2015). Simply follow the directions in the rdrop2 repository in GitHub (please read it the instructions posgted on GitHub[21]), while using our own example.

- Install the package:

```
#Install and enable the package
install.packages('rdrop2')
library(rdrop2)
```

- As in the step 2 on page 268, when you request authorization, you will be taken to a webpage. Use this first:

```
drop_auth()
```

As before, you may not need to go to the browser again if you just use one machine.
- Now, confirm it is working. Simply request what you have in the Dropbox folder Datasets:

```
drop_dir("Datasets")
```

---

[21] https://github.com/karthik/rdrop2.

If you omit the name of the folder, you will get the content at the root of Dropbox.[22]

- You see that in the "Datasets" folder you have a familiar file: "Employee data.sav." Let me get it into my machine:

```
# Destination in local computer:
where=file.path("~","Documents","myWorkingData")
destination=file.path(where,"employeedata.sav")
# Downloading the file in the local computer
drop_get("/Datasets/Employee data.sav",
         local_file =destination,
         overwrite = TRUE)
```

It is extremely important that you know where you are sending the file you are downloading from Dropbox. I have a folder named "myWorkingData" (destination has the path) where I want to send this data; you should have have a folder like this too. Also note that I am allowing overwriting, because I think you may need to call this file many times.

You can certainly open the file in R, manipulate it, and send it back to Dropbox. In this case, you can simply convert the file into a CSV file:

```
# Reading the file as a data frame:
library(Hmisc)
employeeData=spss.get(destination, datevars=c('bdate'))
# Saving your data frame as CSV:
csvFile="employeeData.csv"
write.csv(employeeData,
          file.path(where,csvFile),row.names=F)
# Sending the CSV into Dropbox
drop_upload(file.path(where,csvFile), dest="Datasets")
```

Be sure to indicate where you are sending this file; in my case, I set the argument dest to Datasets. This is a very important step. After running this last piece of R code, you will see that Dropbox has your new data set (see Figure 7.18).

Keep in mind that you are doing all of this not only because you want to access your data anywhere from any machine but also because you are collaborating on some project and need other people to work with the data. If you are sharing, consider carefully when you should allow someone else to update the data contents.

---

[22] In Google Drive, if you try to upload a file a to a folder, everything will go to the root folder. It may have changed, but the googlesheets package could not save a file in a particular folder, only in the root folder, at the time I was preparing the book.

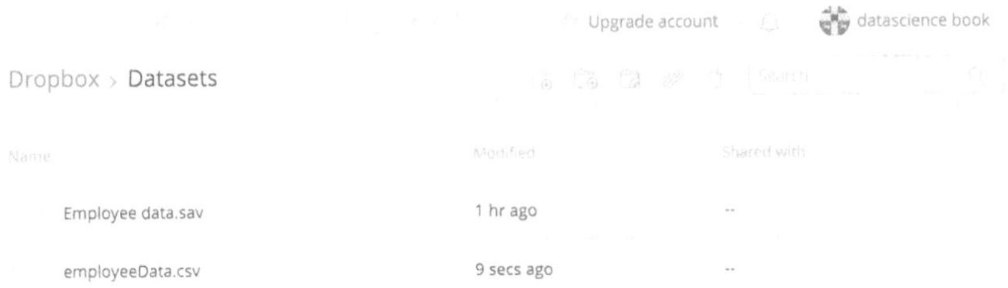

Figure 7.18 Dropbox contents after interacting with R. Now you have a copy of
the file in SPSS in CSV type.

7.5.2 Python and Dropbox

Python can interact with Dropbox using the package **dropbox**. If you want to
follow this example, you need to visit:

https://github.com/dropbox/dropbox-sdk-python

There you will see many steps, but just need to pay attention to these two:

- Create an **app**.
- Obtain an **access token**.

You need to tell Dropbox you have an *app*lication that will interact with your
account; then Dropbox will give you a long code (the **access token**) that you
will use in your Python code. The link provided above will give you the most
updated instructions.

If you have your token, you may install the package in your environment
using *pip*:

```
pip install dropbox
```

After that, you are ready. For this example, follow these steps:

1. Activate the library and get access to your Dropbox:

```
import dropbox
client = dropbox.Dropbox(access_token)
```

2. Get a file from Dropbox into pandas:

```
metaData,raw= client.files_download('/Datasets/employeeData.csv')

from pandas import read_csv
from StringIO import StringIO

employee_asDF=read_csv(StringIO(raw.content))
```

Notice that the command `files_download` actually returns metadata and the data in a raw format that is not directly readable by pandas. That is why I use the command `StringIO` to convert it to a readable format (like a CSV). The object `employee_asDF` is a data frame, which you can use as before.

Always check what version Dropbox is using for its API so you can use the correct commands.

7.6 Storing and GitHub

For a non-expert, Google Drive and Dropbox may seem the same or at least very similar. However, both require that you have a dedicated folder in your computer, which may force you to purchase more storage space if your work demands more than is granted for free. So in principle, this could be a great advantage for GitHub. It offers you unlimited space (as many folders as you want, but the files cannot be larger than 50 Mb; if they are bigger, you can use a different service[23]). The other important advantage is that you get to decide where to create the folder in your computer. My final example in this book will take you on a hands-on tour on GitHub; as always, there will be two parallel cases: R markdown file from RStudio and a Python notebook from Jupiter (IPython).

Before doing any coding, be sure that you have already created your GitHub account and installed the GitHub client in your computer, as I requested in Section 2.3 on page 22. Remember that the GitHub client will not create any folder as does Google Drive or Dropbox; it will be taking care of synchronizing your files. I like GitHub because it motivates you to plan a project and all the contents of your project will be stored in a repository (or repo). So let's **create repositories**.

7.6.1 Creating a GitHub "Repo"

These are the step to create a repo:

1. Go to https://github.com/login and sign in. When you are there, you may see many messages. Just go to your profile, which is shown in Figure 7.19. You can edit your profile now, adding your picture, logo, or email for people to contact you, if you have not already done it. But it is not necessary to update it now.

---

[23] https://github.com/blog/1986-announcing-git-large-file-storage-lfs.

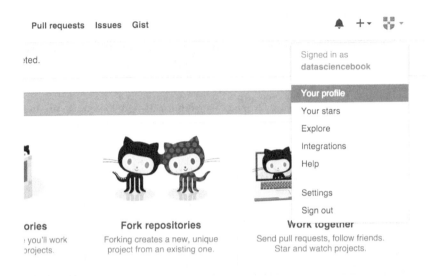

Pull requests   Issues   Gist

Signed in as
datasciencebook

Your profile

Your stars

Explore

Integrations

Help

Settings

Sign out

ories   Fork repositories   Work together
you'll work   Forking creates a new, unique   Send pull requests, follow friends.
projects.   project from an existing one.   Star and watch projects.

Figure 7.19 Creating a git repository (I): going to your profile.

2. Go to your profile page. First select the tab `repositories` and after that click on the green button `New`. This will take you to another window to create the repository. Where first, I will name my repo "dataprojR" (this will have my R codes), which has to be public[24]; second, I will write a short description, and third, I will create a default README file. This is shown in Figure 7.20. If all that information has been entered, click on `Create repository`, at the bottom of the page.

By now you should have done the same; feel free to name your repo as you wish.

We now have our new repo (for our R project). Note I have omitted discussing the *license*. Some people develop software in GitHub and make it available for free, but the conditions of the use depend on the kind of license you set at this time. If you plan to develop a shareable product, you should consider reading the licenses available there.

7.6.2 Hosting a Webpage in GitHub

A very nice feature in GitHub is that it can help you show your project as a webpage. And that is the direction we are going to take now.

---

[24] You need to pay to have private repos. However, for academic use, you need to apply to get private repos at: https://education.github.com/discount_requests/new

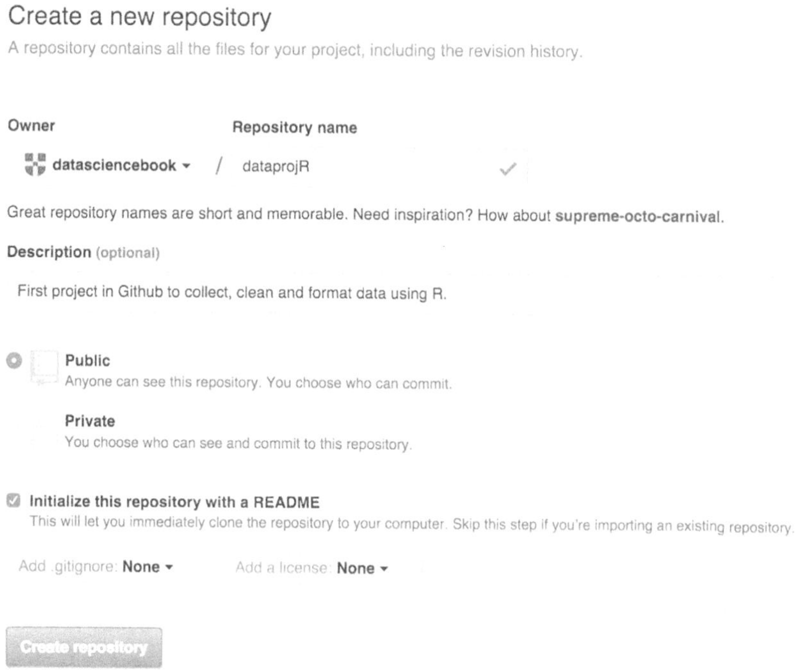

Create a new repository

A repository contains all the files for your project, including the revision history.

Owner   Repository name

⬛ datasciencebook ▾   /   dataprojR   ✓

Great repository names are short and memorable. Need inspiration? How about **supreme-octo-carnival**.

Description (optional)

First project in Github to collect, clean and format data using R.

○   Public
     Anyone can see this repository. You choose who can commit.

     Private
     You choose who can see and commit to this repository.

☑ **Initialize this repository with a README**
    This will let you immediately clone the repository to your computer. Skip this step if you're importing an existing repository.

Add .gitignore: **None** ▾   Add a license: **None** ▾

Create repository

Figure 7.20 Creating a git repository (II). Registering the repo name and creating it.

To prepare your repo to host your project website, do the following, as shown in Figure 7.21:

1. Click on the Branches button.
2. Type gh-pages.
3. Create the branch.

Now, you want to set the gh-pages as the default branch. Follow these steps, as shown in Figure 7.22:

1. Go to the Settings tab.
2. Choose the option Branches on the side menu.
3. Click the drop-down menu at Default branch. The current branch is "master."
4. Choose gh-pages from the drop-down menu.
5. Click Update to finish (you will get a message 'Changing your default branch can have unintended consequences that can affect new pull requests and clones').

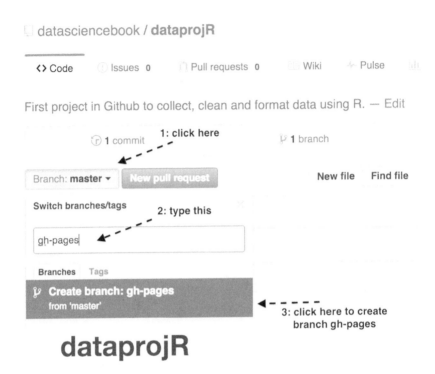

Figure 7.21 Creating a branch in GitHub. Here is where your project files will remain.

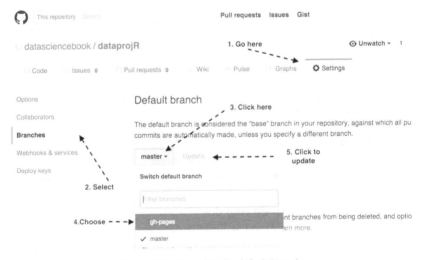

Figure 7.22 Changing the default branch.

Now simply confirm the update and continue. You are almost done. And remember that you will need to do this process just once.

As I mentioned before, you can put the repo in your computer to always have a synchronized version locally and on GitHub. You do not need to put it any place in particular (as with Dropbox or Google Drive). I only recommend that you not put the local version of the repo in your Dropbox folder. If you want, you can create a folder to store all your repos. In my case, I will create a local folder for all my repos and name it `githubREPOS`.

The act of putting the repo in your local machine is called **cloning** in GitHub. Cloning means that you are downloading not only the repo to your machine but also other features invisible to you that the **GitHub desktop** program will use. Do not clone if you have not installed the desktop app.[25] To clone, you have to be in the webpage of your repo in GitHub and do the following:

1. Click the green button saying `Clone or download`.
2. Select the option `Open in desktop`.
3. You may receive a message asking for permission to launch the desktop app; just accept. You then will choose where to put the clone of your repo; in my case, I will clone the repo in the folder "githubREPOS."

The first two steps are shown in Figure 7.23.

After the cloning, I have a folder with the name of the repo inside it: "githubREPOS." My GitHub desktop is running and shows me it has the repo (every repo you create will appear there), as in Figure 7.24.

If you are new to GitHub, you will only see one repo. In my case, I have other repos, and they are shown there as well. It does not matter where those repos are. In my case, not every repo is in the folder I created for this example (githubREPOS). Whenever you make a change to a file in your repo or add new content to it, the desktop app will tell you that there are *uncommitted changes*. When you make a change, click on the top tab shown in Figure 7.24 (currently saying "no uncommitted changes") to see if you want to commit and synchronize.

7.6.3 R and GitHub

Whatever we do in our RStudio project (codes, files, figure, etc.) has to also be in the repo we just created. Then, we need to set the repo as our working

---

[25] Remember the app is here: https://desktop.github.com/

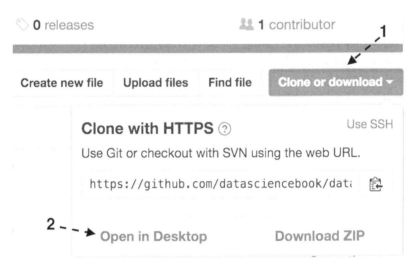

Figure 7.23 Cloning a repo.

directory in RStudio. For that, simply go to the *files, plots and packages* window (shown in Figure 2.2 on page 14), and from there navigate to the repo folder (use the "three dots" to do that). The window should show that only the README file is there. Set it as the working directory using the setting icon. This setting and the desired status are shown in Figure 7.25.

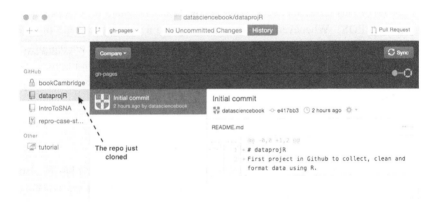

Figure 7.24 Repo in the GitHub desktop. Notice that I have other repos in the machine I am using.

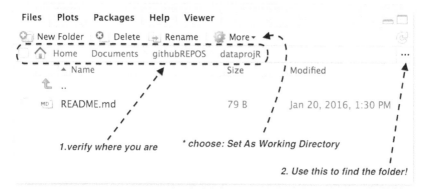

Figure 7.25 Repo folder in GitHub. You have to be inside the repo folder, and it has to be set as the working directory.

Our project has only the README file. To populate that folder (altering the repo), let me save in it the indexes we cleaned and formatted on page 256 (in Python):

```python
names=["HDI","WORLD","ECO","PRESS"]
IDXs=[HDI, WORLD, ECO, PRESS]

import os

folderSave=os.path.join('~','Documents','githubREPOS','dataprojR')

for IDX,name in zip(IDXs,names):
    fileName=name + ".csv"
    currentFile=os.path.join(folderSave,fileName)
```

After you run the code above, you will see that in RStudio you have those files, but most important, the GitHub desktop app will detect the change, as shown in Figure 7.26.

The GitHub desktop window now shows you the additions to the repo in your machine, but these files are not in GitHub yet. To send them online, there are two steps: committing and synchronizing. To commit, you simply have to write what your commit is about. I write **sending csv**. You can optionally write a longer description in the box below. After you are done writing these statements, press **Commit to gh-pages**. The files will disappear from the uncommitted files window when committing is done. Synchronizing will send to GitHub only what you committed. If for some reason you make a change in a file and

Figure 7.26 Detecting local changes in the GitHub desktop. Click the upper tab (next to "History" tab) on the GitHub window to see this image (see the dotted oval on top).

you unselect that file in the uncommitted changes window, then the changes in the file will stay on your machine but not on GitHub. When ready to commit, press **Sync** in the top right of the desktop app window. If you go to GitHub webpage, the files will now be there.[26]

Let's do some setup in R. First, make sure you have the package **knitr** installed in R; if it is not yet installed, do it now. Then, in the upper menu of RStudio, select Tools, and from its drop-down menu choose Global Options. RStudio will show a window to change RStudio Global options. Do not worry; these changes will do no harm to anything you have done

---

[26] Reload your GitHub page if you do not see them.

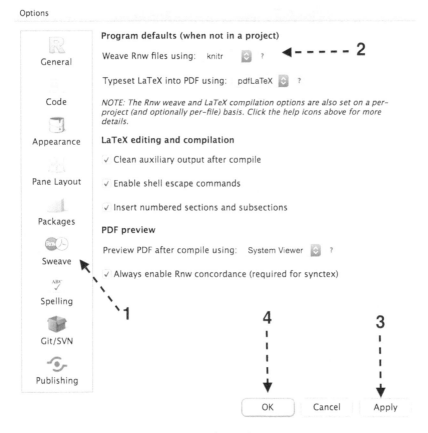

Figure 7.27 Setting up the R project. This setup is internal to the project. It makes no changes to GitHub.

so far. Then, for `knitr` to work, select `Sweave` from the menu to the left, and make sure the option `Weave Rnw files using` is set to `knitr`. Then, simply apply the changes and press `OK`. These options are shown in Figure 7.27.

I can create my new file in R, a **R Markdown**(Rmd) file type. In RStudio you can create one of these files simply by choosing that option in the `New File` icon. Use Figure 7.28 as a reference.

After you create a new markdown file, RStudio will ask you for the title of the file and the name of the author. Figure 7.29 displays what I write in that window.

RStudio will create the file, but you will see it is not empty: It includes the title and your name (my initials in this case), and some example code. Before

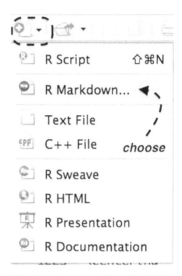

Figure 7.28 Creating a markdown file in RStudio (I).

doing anything, save this file by using the *save icon*. Most importantly, **name it "index."** As you can see in Figure 7.30, I am saving this file in the repo folder in my machine. If you go to your GitHub desktop, you will see that this file is waiting to be committed; I will NOT do that yet.

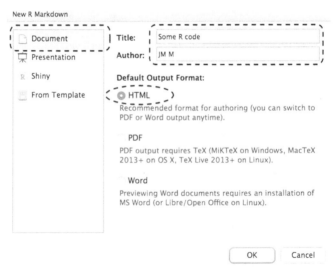

Figure 7.29 Creating a markdown file in RStudio (II). This shows the basic configuration of the Rmd file. Make sure you select HTML.

Figure 7.30 Saving an Rmd file as a webpage.

Take a look at the **index.Rmd** file we just created. Be aware that this file has two types of contents:

- Markdown content
- R code (*chunks*)

Figure 7.31 shows what I wrote in the RStudio Rmd file. The R codes are organized into chunks and need those symbols to show the beginning and the end of a chunk. Whatever is outside the R chunks is markdown. For example an "*" before and after a sentence or word will give *italic* format. But using "**" before and after will give **bold** text. When you want to see the output of your file, press "knit HTML" (as shown in Figure 7.31).

Notice that the letter **r** is not optional in the chunks header: It has to be there. In the header, after the comma, you can include several options to customize how the R code will be interpreted.[27] Keep in mind that pressing Knit HTML not only shows the output in markdown but will also create an HTML file. All of these results will be saved in the cloned repo in your machine if you have set the repo folder as the default directory as previously requested.

---

[27] You may want to search for knitr tutorials later.

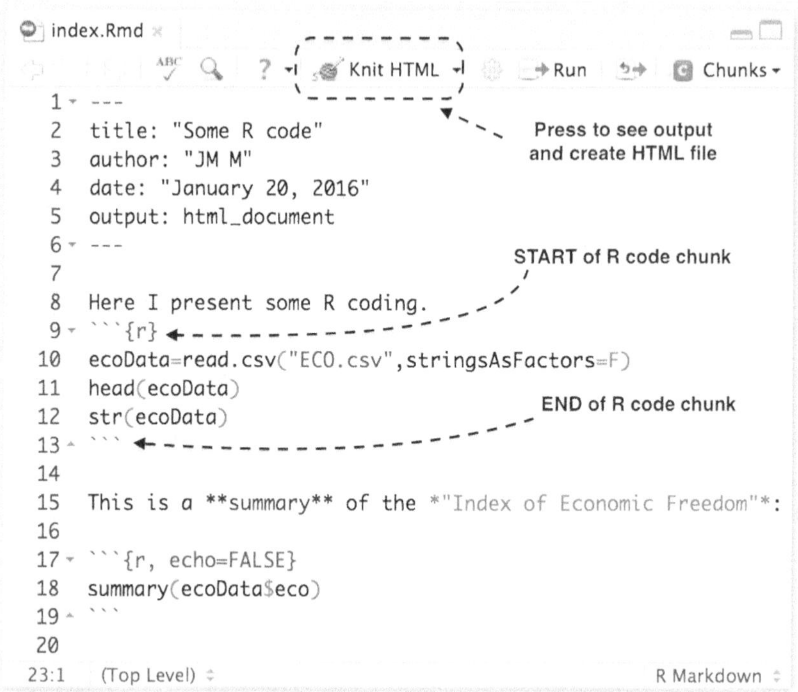

Figure 7.31 Structure of an Rmd code.

The output is shown in Figure 7.32. Notice the following:

- The command head is executed, and the command and the result are shown.
- The command str is executed, and the command and the result are shown.
- The command summary is executed, BUT only the result is shown; the command is not shown in the output.You can see it is the result of writing echo=false between the curly braces.

In Figure 7.31 you see that the header sizes vary depending on whether it is a main title or a lower level subtitle. You also see the differences among the markdown text I wrote (white background by default); the R code is in the visible chunks (gray background), and the results are in different font types. All of these defaults can be customized, and you can even color the syntax of the code in the chunks.[28]

The GitHub desktop should have detected all these modifications. Since the last time you committed, you created the index file in markdown (Rmd) and

---

[28] Visit: http://yihui.name/knitr/options/ for more details.

Some R code

JM M

January 20, 2016

Here I present som R coding.

```
ecoData=read.csv("ECO.csv",stringsAsFactors=F)
head(ecoData)
```

```
##        Country       eco fips iso2 iso3 niso3
## 1 Afghanistan        NA   AF   AF  AFG     4
## 2      Albania 65.65003   AL   AL  ALB     8
## 3      Algeria 48.88186   AG   DZ  DZA    12
## 4       Angola 47.88580   AO   AO  AGO    24
## 5    Argentina 44.13892   AR   AR  ARG    32
## 6      Armenia 67.12509   AM   AM  ARM    51
```

```
str(ecoData)
```

```
## 'data.frame':    183 obs. of  6 variables:
## $ Country: chr  "Afghanistan" "Albania" "Algeria" "Angola" ...
## $ eco    : num  NA 65.7 48.9 47.9 44.1 ...
## $ fips   : chr  "AF" "AL" "AG" "AO" ...
## $ iso2   : chr  "AF" "AL" "DZ" "AO" ...
## $ iso3   : chr  "AFG" "ALB" "DZA" "AGO" ...
## $ niso3  : num  4 8 12 24 32 51 36 40 31 44 ...
```

This is a **summary** of the *"Index of Economic Freedom"*:

```
##    Min. 1st Qu.  Median    Mean 3rd Qu.    Max.  NA's
##   29.64   53.70   60.12   60.80   67.88   89.55     8
```

Figure 7.32 Basic output in HTML. This output is produced from the markdown file using RStudio. Notice that the markdown file has the instructions to render this output.

also generated the HTML version of it. When you take a look at the GitHub desktop app you will see those two files in the list of uncommitted ones. Take a look at Figure 7.33, and you will also see that I name this commit "easy coding done" and the description will be the same. Because you have not altered a byte in any of the previously committed files in your local folder, you will not see them, and that earlier version is still in GitHub. Before pressing sync,

Figure 7.33 Committing the first codes. Notice that only two files are detected (Rmd and html). These files are being committed to the gh-pages branch.

remember that you are committing your changes to a particular *branch* in your repo. In general, you commit to the *master* branch (like the root folder), but we created a branch gh-pages, which is currently activated in the desktop app window (see the upper part of Figure 7.33 with the dotted oval). You can synchronize now. Keep in mind that you do not need to synchronize every time you make a change in one file. You can wait as long as you want, but the idea is that you commit and synchronize when you want to commit a particular and relevant change that deserves a *description*.

You can now go to your browser and see the new commits in GitHub (you may need to refresh the page of the repo so GitHub shows you the recent commits).

When you committed to gh-pages, GitHub will recognize the **index.html** and publish it. Now you have a webpage showing your results. Certainly you need to know what is the address of that webpage (*URL*). The URL will be found following the next steps, shown in Figure 7.34:

- You need to be at your repo page in GitHub.
- Go to the settings tab.
- Scroll down and find the section GitHub Pages. You will find the URL in that section.

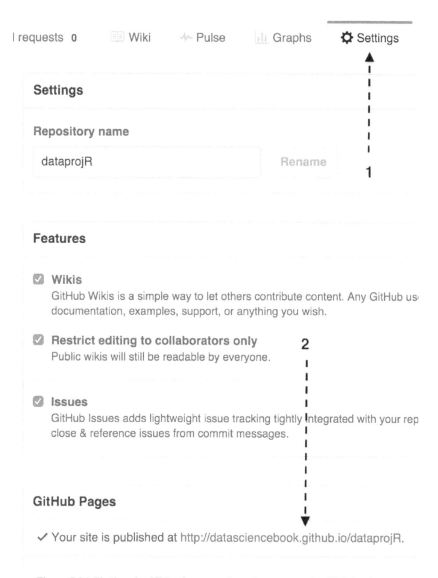

Figure 7.34 Finding the URL of your project. As you see, the URL is always **username**.github.io/**repository name/**.

Now your GitHub repo not only hosts your data and your code but also has published your work. You can disseminate that URL in the way you want it. Remember that all repos in GitHub are public, so by knowing the URL people can access your code. If you pay or qualify to get a private repo, the repo will be hidden, but the webpage will still be visible by anybody with the link.

```
22 ▾ ## How is the Economic Freedom distributed in the world?
23
24   I will add the data from the Index of Economic freedom as another
     attribute of the countries in the map of the world. The map was
     downloaded from [this link](http://thematicmapping.org). These are the
     steps I followed.
25
26 ▾ ### Merge the data of my CSV with the DBF using a common field:
27   This is not a common merge. You need to do the merge, keeping all the
     values of the map, and keeping in the same order. So a **sorter**
     variable is added to re order the map data before saving.
28 ▾ ```{r,warning=FALSE,message=FALSE,cache=TRUE}
29   library(foreign)
30   DBF=file.path("map","TM_WORLD_BORDERS-0.3.dbf")
31   mapData=read.dbf(DBF)
32   names(mapData)
33   ecoData=ecoData[,c(5,2)] # just the iso3 and eco value
34   ecoData=ecoData[complete.cases(ecoData),] # no NAs
35   mapData$sorter <- as.numeric(rownames(mapData)) # extra var to re order
36   mapData=merge(mapData,ecoData,by.x="ISO3", by.y="iso3",all.x = T)
37   mapData=mapData[order(mapData$sorter),] # reordering
38   rownames(mapData)=NULL
39   write.dbf(mapData,DBF) #saving updated file
40 ▾ ```
41
```

Figure 7.35 More complex code in R Markdown (I).

In our final example in R we will merge data from the world map used earlier with the Index of Economic Freedom. You will need to copy the whole folder of the map data into our repo folder.[29] Let me describe the code shown in Figure 7.35, where you will find some interesting details with respect to markdown and the R code chunks:

- Notice the use of markdown to denote the size of the titles, using '#'s in lines 22 and 26. Using one '#' gives the biggest font size.
- Note how to include hyperlinks while you are writing (line 24, third line).
- See the options for the code chunks. When `warnings` and `messages` are set as FALSE (lower or upper case will work) you will not see them in the output. First run your code with warnings and messages allowed and then evaluate if they are important so you can decide if you should discard them.
- Another important option here is `cache`. Note that I am reading a file and updating it (the dbf). When you knit your Rmd file, you run everything again by default, so you will be creating more columns to the dbf file. Setting **cache = TRUE** avoids running a chunk again.

---

[29] I do not need to copy the folder, but just have to reference the files.

```
42 ▾  ### Time to plot the Index:
43    Now we can plot, the <b style='color:green'>greener</b> the better, the
      <b style='color:red'>redder</b> the worse. Black is missing value.
44
45 ▾  ```{r,warning=FALSE,message=FALSE,fig.width=12,fig.height=6}
46    library(maptools)
47    SHP=file.path("map","TM_WORLD_BORDERS-0.3.shp")
48    worldmap=readShapeSpatial(SHP)
49    library(ggplot2)
50    worldmapGG <- fortify(worldmap, region = "ISO3")
51    map= ggplot(data = worldmap@data,
52                aes(map_id = ISO3)) +
53        geom_map(aes(fill = worldmap@data$eco),
54                 map = worldmapGG) +
55        expand_limits(x = worldmap@data$LON,
56                      y = worldmap@data$LAT) +
57        scale_fill_continuous(low='red', high='green',
58                              na.value = "white") +
59        guides(fill=FALSE) #no AREA legend
60
61    map
62 ▾  ```
63
```

Figure 7.36 More complex code in R Markdown (II).

The code, which continues in Figure 7.36, will produce the plot of the index. It is a simple plot, but this code is useful for many applications. Again you see a title of level 2 in line 42, but the most important element is the change of the font color in line 43. In the options of the chunk code I included some parameters to control the width and height of the plot to be produced.

After coding these two parts, you will realize that many changes have been made in your repo folder. Notice also that you have a couple of folders that were created automatically. In fact, these are folders created by the cache argument of the chunks.[30]

It is time to finish this mini-project, so let's save the markdown and go to the GitHub desktop to commit the last changes. I will name this last commit, "eco map done" and the description will be the same. After synchronizing, everything will be in GitHub online. You will see that your webpage will update immediately, because you replace your index.html when you *knit* the Rmd file.

Now that you have this basic knowledge of GitHub, you may be interested in learning more. For example, if you want to know the history of the index.Rmd go to your GitHub account online. Click on the name of the file and you will be

---

[30] For small projects, it may not be necessary to use the cache argument.

Figure 7.37 Getting the link to a data file in GitHub.

taken to a page that offers you the **Raw** and **History** buttons. When you click on the latter you should see that there are two versions of that file in GitHub. It is because we made two commits, and in each commit that file changed. It is different for the ECO.csv file; if you see its history, you will see only one version, because even though we made two commits, this file never changed after it was first synchronized. Spend some time in the history page of your files to become familiar with the options you have.

When you click a file to visit its history, you also see the **Raw** button, which will give you a shareable link to your file. As with Dropbox or Google Drive, you can simply share a link to the data and R can read it immediately, but you do NOT need an API. For instance, the ECO.csv already in GitHub has a link that can be shared to download it:

https://github.com/datasciencebook/dataprojR/raw/gh-pages/ECO.csv

To get that link, click on the file and get the link from the **Raw** button by right-clicking it. Figure 7.37 shows this little detail.

You can get that any link to your data in this way. For example, the code below uses an SPSS file in GitHub:

```
library(Hmisc)
link1="https://github.com/datasciencebook"
link2="/dataprojR/raw/gh-pages/employeedata.sav"
filelink=file.path(link1,link2)
employee = spss.get(filelink,datevars=c('bdate'))
head(employee)
```

Figure 7.38 New GitHub repo for Python. The repo is shown in the list of repos on the right.

There are many other things that GitHub offers. I recommend taking a look at its sharing process, which is presented with the concepts *forking*, *pulling*, and *pushing*. Let's turn to Python now.

7.6.4 Python and GitHub

My code in Python will not create a webpage; it will create a *notebook*, a common way in the Python community to publish online. As before, I will create a new repo called "dataprojPy" (you can review how we created a repo following steps 1 and 2 [Figures 7.19 and 7.20] on page 275). The description I will use is Demo on hosting my work using Python. I will check the same options as in Figure 7.20, and my repo will be created. However, I will NOT create the gh-pages branch this time. If you have done the same steps, just clone this repo. GitHub will allow me to choose where to put the repo, and I will put it inside my "githubREPOS" folder, where the other repo is. You will see that the GitHub desktop app has added this new repo to its list, which is shown in Figure 7.38. Remember that it is not strictly necessary that your two repos are in the same folder; wherever you save that cloned repo, GitHub desktop will detect it.

To create this *notebook*, I will use **Jupyter**, not *Spyder*. You do not need to close *Spyder* to work with Jupyter, and neither is it necessary to close RStudio. Simply go to the window of the Anaconda Navigator, the one shown in Figure 3.4 on page 28. When you are there, select the icon *Jupyter* (see Figure 7.39).

When you *launch Jupyter*, two things will happen. First, the console will pop up and then your browser will show you a webpage. The webpage is not in the

Figure 7.39 Jupyter icon that you need to click to create the notebook.

internet; it is locally in your computer. The title of the webpage is Jupyter. Both of these events are shown in Figure 7.40.

You can navigate Jupyter's local webpage. Just click on the folder names until you get to the repo folder just created. You need to be inside your repo folder to create the notebook. Just as in RStudio, you are going to put everything you need in this new project in that folder: the notebook, the data, images, etc. So, create the notebook in your repo folder as indicated in Figure 7.41.

Figure 7.40 Jupyter and Console events. The console, to the right, tells you Jupyter is working.

Figure 7.41 Creating a new Jupyter notebook. First navigate to the repo folder, click on New, and then choose Python 2.

A notebook will work as our Rmd file; that is, it will have two elements: markdown and code. But in contrast to Rmd files, markdowns and codes have to be written inside a notebook *cell*. The notebook opens with a cell ready for you to code in. If you want to first write some text (no coding) you need to tell Jupyter that the cell will contain markdown and not code. Figure 7.42 shows the new notebook I just created. I have not done anything there yet, so when you create your first notebook, you will see the same screen. You can first write the name of the file and then select what kind of content your cell will have.

The notebook will always open in another browser window, so you can always take a look at what files are in the repo if you go to the browser window shown in Figure 7.41.

Let's fill some cells with content. I will save this notebook as "**networks**," to remind myself that we will be working with the data on networks we built from the Wikipedia page on wars between countries that we used before. I will use some markdown in the first cell to give my notebook a title and a subtitle. When you are done writing your content, press the "play" button in the upper menu, which runs the current cell (you can achieve the same by pressing *SHIFT* and *ENTER* in the keyboard). The result of this first step is shown in Figure 7.43.

Figure 7.42 Elements of a new notebook. The most important element here is the **cell**, where you write code or text.

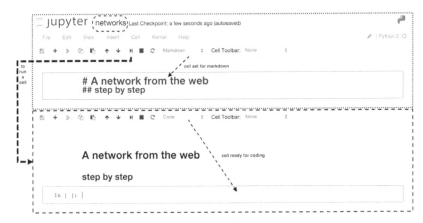

Figure 7.43 The first step in running notebooks. The upper figure shows the moment when you write some markdown; the lower figure shows the result when the cell was run.

My first cell of code will be exactly the same as in subsection 7.2.2 starting on page 259, but without the code for plotting (page 260). So, you simply go to Spyder, copy that code, and paste it without the last section on plotting. Now let me show you what I wrote next.

First, I save the network created into a local file. This is a particular type of file for networks, the **graphml**. Remember that I created the network by scraping data from Wikipedia, so whatever you build will disappear if you do not save it. Because this notebook is running in the repo folder, that file will be saved there too. After saving it, I call the file and store it in the object warNetData. Then, I will simply copy the plotting commands I did not copy before, but I need to reference the plot to warNetData, the object currently holding the data. Before plotting, I need to add a particular command NOT present in Spyder before:

%matplotlib inline

If you do not write that command, the plot will still be produced but it will be outside the notebook. Writing this command will force the plot to appear below the code. The code is shown in Figure 7.44.

The second piece of code, shown in Figure 7.45, might be a little advanced but it is interesting. This example shows on how to use a base map for your network. The network used the coordinates from Wikipedia, but now I am going to recompute those positions based on a particular map projection. I do that by

2) Saving the Network in a local file:

```
In [2]: net.write_graphml(warNet, "warNet.graphml",encoding='utf-8')
```

3) Calling the file just created:

```
In [3]: warNetData=net.read_graphml("warNet.graphml")
```

4) Plot the Network   ---- For plotting inside notebook!

```
In [5]: %matplotlib inline
        X=net.get_node_attributes(warNetData,'longitude')
        Y=net.get_node_attributes(warNetData,'latitude')
        countryNames=warNetData.nodes()
        posNet=dict((C,(X[C],Y[C])) for C in countryNames)
        net.draw(warNetData,pos=posNet,with_labels=True)
```

Figure 7.44 Coding in notebooks (I). Notice the **%matplotlib inline** code line. You need it so the plot will appear in the notebook.

calling the module `Basemap`, which helps me recompute the positions for the Robinson map projection. The code and the output can be seen in Figure 7.45.

This finishes the coding/ Save your work and, from the upper menu, press on `File` and choose `close and halt`. All the files are now in the repo folder,

5) Nicer plot, using robinson projection:

```
In [6]: import matplotlib.pyplot as plt
        from mpl_toolkits.basemap import Basemap as Basemap

        plt.figure(figsize=(20,10))

        r = Basemap(projection='robin',lon_0=0,resolution='l')
        posRobin=dict((country,( r(X[country],Y[country]))) for country in countryNames)
        net.draw_networkx_nodes(warNetData, posRobin,with_labels=True,node_size=50)
        net.draw_networkx_edges(warNetData, posRobin,with_labels=False,width=3,edge_color='yellow')

        r.drawlsmask() # background layer land-sea map

        plt.title('Historical border conflicts (Robinson projection)')
        plt.show()
```

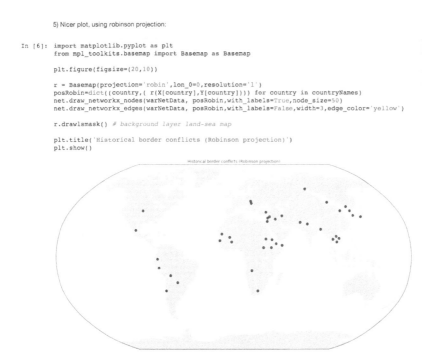

Figure 7.45 Coding in notebooks (II). Re-plotting the map with a layer below in another projection (Robinson).

so simply go to the GitHub desktop application, where you will commit and sync. I will name this commit "python code done" and write the same in the description.

Now that your files are on GitHub, you might think that you only have a repository like Dropbox for these files and that it is not possible to see the notebook online, as you could with the HTML file in R. But that is not so. GitHub can render an Jupyter notebook. Just go to the repo online, click on the notebook name, and you will see all the contents and output. Another option is to copy the URL of the notebook in GitHub; visit the link http://nbviewer.jupyter .org/ and paste that URL there. The output will look a little better (without the GitHub bars or menus).

References

Allison, Paul David. 2002. *Missing data*. Sage university papers. Quantitative applications in the social sciences, nos. 07–136. Thousand Oaks, CA: SAGE.

Allison, Paul David. 2014. *Event history and survival analysis*. Second edition. Quantitative applications in the social sciences, nos. 07–46. Los Angeles: SAGE.

ANES. 2014. *Users guide and codebook for the ANES 2012 Time Series Study*. Ann Arbor, MI and Palo Alto, CA: University of Michigan and Stanford University.

Arel-Bundock, Vincent. 2013 (Aug.). *WDI: World Development Indicators*. Washington, DC: World Bank.

Arnold, Tim. 2014 (Nov.). *Manipulating PDFs with Python | Python*.

Bivand, Roger, Pebesma, Edzer J., and Gámez-Rubio, Virgilio. 2013. *Applied Spatial data analysis with R*. Second edition. New York: Springer. OCLC: ocn857289562.

Box-Steffensmeier, Janet M., and Jones, Bradford S. 2004. *Event history modeling: A guide for social scientists*. New York: Cambridge University Press.

Brunsdon, Chris, and Comber, Lex. 2015. *An introduction to R for spatial analysis & mapping*. Los Angeles: SAGE. OCLC: ocn904424364.

Chrisman, Nicholas R. 1998. Rethinking Levels of Measurement for Cartography. *Cartography and geographic information science*, **25**(4), 231–242.

Danneman, Nathan, and Heimann, Richard. 2014. *Social media mining with R*. Birmingham, UK: Packt Publishing.

Davidson-Pilon, Cameron. 2015. *Lifelines: Survival analysis in Python*.

DeBell, Matthew. 2010. *How to analyze ANES survey data*. Tech. rept. nes012492. Palo Alto, CA, and Ann Arbor, MI: Stanford University and the University of Michigan.

Duck, Matt. 2013 (Oct.). *wbpy*. wbpy - Python interface to the World Bank Indicators and Climate APIs. https://github.com/mattduck/wbpy

Elff, Martin. 2015 (Mar.). *Tools for management of survey data, graphics, programming, statistics, and simulation*. Package 'memisc'. https://cran.r-project.org/web/packages/memisc/index.html.

European Commission, Organisation for Economic Co-operation and Development, and SourceOECD (Online service) (eds). 2008. *Handbook on constructing composite indicators: Methodology and user guide*. Paris: OECD.

Feinerer, Ingo, Hornik, Kurt, and Software, Artifex, and GPL Ghostscript, Inc (pdf_info ps taken from. 2015 (July). *tm: Text Mining Package*.

Figueroa, Adolfo. 2008. Competition and circulation of economic elites: Theory and application to the case of Peru. *Quarterly Review of Economics and Finance*, **48**(2), 263–273.

Forta, Ben. 2000. *Sams teach yourself regular expressions in 10 minutes*. Indianapolis, Ind: Sams.

Garrard, Chris. 2016. *Geoprocessing with Python*. Shelter Island, NY: Manning Publications. OCLC: ocn915498655.

Goyvaerts, Jan, and Levithan, Steven. 2012. *Regular expressions cookbook*. Second edition. Beijing: O'Reilly.

Grolemund, Garrett, Spinu, Vitalie, and Wickham, Hadley. 2016 (Sept.). *Make dealing with dates a little easier [R package lubridate version 1.6.0]*.

Lawhead, Joel. 2015. *Learning geospatial analysis with Python: An effective guide to geographic information system and remote sensing analysis using Python 3*. Birmingham, UK: Packt Publishing. OCLC: 934039792.

Lawson, Richard. 2015. *Web scraping with Python*. Birmingham, UK: Packt Publishing.

Levenshtein, V. I. 1966. Binary Codes Capable of Correcting Deletions, Insertions and Reversals. *Soviet physics doklady*, **10**(Feb.), 707.

Mitchell, Ryan. 2015. *Web scraping with Python: Collecting data from the modern web*. Beijing: O'Reilly.

Mosteller, Frederick, and Tukey, John Wilder. 1977. *Data analysis and regression: A second course in statistics*. Addison-Wesley Series in Behavioral Science. Reading, MA: Addison-Wesley.

Munzert, Simon. 2014. *Automated data collection with R: A practical guide to Web scraping and text mining*. Chichester, UK: John Wiley & Sons.

R Core Team. 2015 (Aug.). *Read data stored by Minitab, S, SAS, SPSS, Stata, Systat, Weka, dBase, ...*

Raghunathan, Trivellore. 2015. *Missing data analysis in practice*. Boca Raton, FL: CRC Press.

Ram, Karthik. 2015 (July). *rdrop2: Programmatic interface to the 'Dropbox' API*.

Richardson, Leonard. 2015 (Nov.). *Beautiful Soup*.

Rubba, Christian. 2016 (May). *htmltab: Assemble data frames from HTML tables*.

Ryan, Jeffrey A., and Ulrich, Joshua M. 2014 (Jan.). *xts: eXtensible time series*.

Sherouse, Oliver. 2014 (May). *wbdata*.

Simon, Herbert A. 1996. *The sciences of the artificial*. Cambridge, MA: MIT Press.

Solon, Gary, Haider, Steven, and Wooldridge, Jeffrey. 2013 (Feb.). *What are we weighting for?*. Tech. Rept. #18859. Bureau of Economic Research, Cambridge, MA.

Stevens, S. S. 1946. On the theory of scales of measurement. *Science*, **103**(2684), 677–680.

Temple Lang, Duncan, and CRAN team. 2015a (June). *RCurl: General network (HTTP/FTP/...) client interface for R*.

Temple Lang, Duncan, and CRAN Team. 2015b (June). *XML: Tools for parsing and generating XML within R and S-Plus*.

Velleman, Paul F., and Wilkinson, Leland. 1993. Nominal, Ordinal, Interval, and Ratio Typologies Are Misleading. *American statistician*, **47**(1), 65.

Index of R and Python Commands Used